Making Contact

Making Contact

The Therapist's Guide to Conducting a Successful First Interview

Leah M. DeSole, Ph.D.

with

Alyson Nelson, Ph.D
Laura L. Young, LMSW

PEARSON

Boston • New York • San Francisco
Mexico City • Montreal • Toronto • London • Madrid • Munich • Paris
Hong Kong • Singapore • Tokyo • Cape Town • Sydney

Executive Editor: Virginia Lanigan
Series Editorial Assistant: Scott Blaszak
Marketing Manager: Kris Ellis-Levy
Composition and Prepress Buyer: Andrew Turso
Manufacturing Buyer: Andrew Turso
Cover Coordinator: Rebecca Krzyzaniak
Editorial-Production Coordinator: Mary Beth Finch
Editorial-Production Service: Stratford Publishing Services
Electronic Composition: Stratford Publishing Services

For related titles and support materials, visit our online catalog at www.ablongman.com.

Between the time web site information is gathered and then published, it is not unusual for some sites to have closed. Also, the transcription of URLs can result in unintended typographical errors. The publisher would appreciate notification where these errors occur so that they may be corrected in subsequent editions.

Library of Congress Cataloging-in-Publication Data
DeSole, Leah M.
    Making contact: the therapist's guide to conducting a successful first
    interview/ Leah M. DeSole.
        p. ; cm.
    Includes bibliographical references and index.
    ISBN 0-205-41935-6 (alk. paper)
    1. Interviewing in mental health—Technique. 2. Interviewing in psychiatry—
Technique. 3. Mental health personnel—Training of. 4. Mental health personnel and
patient. I. Title.
    [DNLM: 1. Interview, Psychological—methods. 2. Professional-Patient Relations.
    3. Psychology, Clinical—methods. WM 141 D467m 2005]
RC480.7.D47 2005
616.089′075—dc22   2005048728

Printed in the United States of America.

10 9 8 7 6 5 4 3 2 1   10 09 08 07 06 05

To my mother,
For asking how you could help and giving generously of your time.

To my sons,
For your patience.

To my sister,
For making me laugh and giving me perspective.

To Dr. Robert T. Carter,
For the mentorship that made it possible for me to write and publish this book.

To the universe,
For teaching me to be grateful on a daily basis.

I am blessed.

CONTENTS

Preface

Making Contact: The Therapist's Guide to Conducting a Successful First Interview is targeted toward two groups: students who do not quite see themselves as professionals yet and the professionals who train them. What these students—and their trainers—have in common is that the clients with whom they are about to work *will* view them as full-fledged professionals.

The main goal of this text is to assist students in the transition from training to practice. It is meant to serve as a conversational primer for trainees in the various helping fields. Those trainees include counseling and clinical psychologists, psychiatrists, and social workers. It is also appropriate for psychiatric nurses, pastoral counselors, licensed mental health professionals, and a number of other paraprofessionals in the field of mental health. Essentially, it is intended to prepare students for the workplace.

Much of what *Making Contact* presents spans theoretical orientations. As I have surveyed current texts, what I have found difficult is that much of the information provided is specific to a given theoretical orientation (e.g., psychoanalytic, cognitive-behavioral, or biological models). My contention is that this specificity is not only unnecessary but professionally problematic. It is unnecessary because the majority of the skills involved in preparing a clinical professional in training to meet, engage, and interview his or her client for the very first time are universal. It is professionally problematic because it forecloses learning: providing information that is theoretically specific to trainees who are just beginning their career limits their field of vision. It excludes ways of practice to which they might be temperamentally better suited or intellectually more inclined.

I believe that not only students but trainers, supervisors, and teachers of fledgling clinicians in the helping fields will benefit from this material. I have served as a fieldwork director, and I have placed students at fieldwork, internship, and externship sites. I am well aware of students' fears regarding their initial contact with clients. Their feelings, more often than not, are healthy and predictable. A primer detailing what to expect when you meet with your client for the very first time would go a long way toward helping professionals-in-training manage these feelings. In so doing, students will be more emotionally present for their training and therefore of better service to their clients.

Likewise, in my capacity as teacher I believe that this book will be a useful adjunct to courses in skills training, practicum, and internship supervision. There are numerous textbooks that address specific intake, evaluation, and assessment procedures. However, the abundance of information these books provide can be overwhelming to a professional-in-training. What gets lost are vital practical matters: how to set up one's office, prepare for the first session, open the session and introduce oneself to the client, develop rapport, manage the interview, and bring the session to a close. In this regard, *Making Contact* will serve as preparation for real-life situations. It will assist students to translate learning into action. In so doing, it will reinforce students' learning *before* they actually meet with their first client.

Finally, I should note that I have served on site as a supervisor at a psychological services agency. I believe this text would be appropriate for a variety of site supervisors who oversee several interns at once and are obliged to single-handedly guide their professional development. *Making Contact* will be indispensable to initiating professionally relevant conversations among supervisees who are engaging in sustained client contact for the first time. This text makes no assumptions about what may appear to be basic matters, such as how to introduce oneself to a client, keep track of time, or arrange the space in which one works. In addition, each chapter raises multicultural issues. Topics related to race, religion, ethnicity, gender, and other aspects of the self are woven throughout the material in order to provide critical clinical knowledge and stimulate professional self-awareness.

Reviewer Acknowledgment

I would like to thank the following reviewers for their comments and suggestions: Joshua M. Gold, University of South Carolina; Kathleen McElroy Head, University of South Carolina; Laura Hensley, Louisiana State University; Adam L. Hill, Sonoma State University; Beulah M Hirschlein, Oklahoma State University; David D. Hof, University of Nebraska at Kearney; Jennifer C. Lewis Jordan, Clemson University; Karl Knobler; James W. Lichtenberg, University of Kansas; Aimee H. Moles, Louisiana State University; Toni R. Tollerud, Northern Illinois University; and Jim Verhoye, Metropolitan State University.

Introduction

Therapy is an encounter between two people.

—Barbara Gerson

This book is about You, the beginning clinician. It is easy to forget that therapy involves at least two people, the client *and* the clinician. Textbooks about clinical interviewing, in particular, typically focus on the client's experience. As a result, it is easy to overlook *yourself* as mental health professional in training.

The purpose of this book is to focus on your clinical training. Its objective is twofold: (1) to facilitate your professional development in new and varied settings and (2) to nurture your commitment to the people with whom you will work as a professional in the field of mental health.

Moreover, this book addresses something so fundamental that it is often neglected: how to make contact with a new client. It is my contention that making the initial contact with a new client matters greatly, for it is the foundation of many clinical encounters yet to come.

In my experience, many mental health professionals are not adequately prepared to begin our professional training, let alone meet with our clients for the first time. I recall when I began my clinical training as a psychologist. I was one of four interns starting a placement at a hospital. The first intern was dressed in a suit and tie; the second intern wore a blouse, short skirt, and high heels; and the third intern wore a conservative dress. In contrast, the fourth was wearing sweatpants and a top. It was clear by our appearances that none of us knew what to expect that first day. We did not know with whom we would be interacting or what beginning work would entail. Were we there simply to get IDs, fill out tax exemption forms, and complete some paperwork? Might we meet with our supervisors and be assigned a caseload? Would they *actually* expect us to see clients on our first day?

We looked at each other and chuckled. It was clear, just by looking, that each of us had different expectations; each of us felt unprepared in our own way. Although we did not know one another, we were fortunate that we all had a sense of humor, the capacity to acknowledge our collective anxiety, and the willingness to support one another under conditions of uncertainty. I had friends who were not as lucky. They arrived at their placements alone or among more competitive peers. Their confidence suffered, as did their training.

You may not call yourself a professional yet, and you may not think of yourself as a professional yet, but the people with whom you are about work will see you as a professional. How you take up your role as a helping person matters, regardless of your role in the mental health field. You may be managing the telephone lines and fielding patient telephone inquiries or screening clients as they arrive for services. You may be a psychologist, social worker, counselor, nurse, pastor, or psychiatrist-in-training. If none of these titles fit, however, you can be sure that you will nonetheless be providing an invaluable service if you are working in a mental health profession. You have a vital role to play.

Making Contact is written for clinicians-in-training who are familiar with the principles of psychology and have studied basic counseling skills. It is intended to facilitate your transition from the classroom to the real world. Specifically, its purpose is to prepare you for training in real-life settings. Your experiences may vary. You may be on an internship or externship, at a fieldwork or field placement site, or assigned to a specific rotation and population. Nonetheless, you are at the point in your career where you are putting your principles into practice. You are being challenged to integrate your personal self and your professional knowledge in order to become an effective professional in the mental health field.

This book is intended as a guide to enable you to begin this process. And it is a process. It does not end with the initial contact; it is only beginning.

Organization

I find it helpful to know how a book is organized before I begin reading it. Ideally, such knowledge will allow you, the reader, to pick and choose the chapters that are appropriate to you given where you are in your training. That being said, I do not wish to dissuade readers, like myself, who tend to approach books in a more orderly (dare I say compulsive) manner, beginning with page 1 and ending with that final, concluding page. *Making Contact*, after all, is written with a logical internal consistency in mind.

Making Contact consists of thirteen comprehensive chapters. These chapters are organized into four distinct parts: Part One (Preparing to Make Contact with Your Client), Part Two (Meeting Your Client for the First Time), Part Three (When Special Circumstances Arise), and Part Four (After Making Contact with Your Client). In conclusion, there are appendices containing samples of professional forms.

Part One describes the work that goes into getting ready for your initial client contact. This section identifies several logistical matters of which you should be aware before your first interview, such as how to settle into your agency or institution, prepare in practical ways for your first client interview, and get ready emotionally to see your client. It also concerns orienting yourself successfully as a new professional in your chosen career. Overall, this section focuses on finding a manner of integrating your cultural and personal style with your professional style.

Part Two defines "the arc" of the initial contact. It explains how every session has a beginning, a middle, and an end. This section also examines how a professional's objectives change over the arc of the initial session. In so doing, it provides behavioral suggestions; namely, how to make the introductions and start the session, how to make an assessment and discover why the client is really there in your office, and how to end the session. Last, but not least, this section addresses such practical concerns as saying goodbye, collecting payment, and scheduling the next session with your client.

Part Three identifies some of the unique situations that may arise over the course of the initial contact. This section highlights knowing your site's protocols and your supervisor's procedural expectations. It also makes two points: first, expect the unexpected; and second, realize that the unexpected need not be unmanageable. In addition, this section makes some useful suggestions regarding awkward situations that may arise in the initial contact. One is how to deal with difficult clients—for example, clients who talk too much or too little. Another concerns ways to approach sensitive subjects. And finally, this section reviews what to do in cases of emergency—for instance, when a client talks about committing suicide or threatens violence.

Part Four will help you understand and organize the experience you have just had with your client. From a personal standpoint, this section addresses how to productively reflect on your experiences with clients. From a professional standpoint, it describes how to develop your professional skills and utilize supervision effectively. It emphasizes the all-too-important nitty-gritty that often gets lost when you are first learning to deal with clients, such as fulfilling your site's requirements for paperwork, knowing your site's expectations regarding documentation, and facing the challenge of report preparation.

Terminology

Before I begin, I want to make a few notes about terminology. Terminology frequently varies depending on one's professional training, the setting in which one works, and one's theoretical orientation. As a professional in the mental health field, I believe that the language we use to express our ideas about our clinical work is important. On the service provider side, I use various terms in this text to identify members of the helping professions: counselor, practitioner, helper, clinician, social worker, psychologist, and psychiatrist.

Terminology becomes more complicated when it comes to identifying or labeling the recipients of the services we provide. The use of the term *patient* reflects the medical model that once dominated the mental health field. Some professionals consider it familiar and comfortable; others consider it pathologizing and even patronizing. In reaction, some professionals in particular mental health specialties, such as social work, use the term *client* rather than patient. My understanding is that this term is used in order to convey respect and to emphasize the strengths of those whom we serve. Of late, I have even heard professionals use the terms *consumers* and *customers*. Presumably in an even greater effort to empower the people to whom we provide services.

Given my training, orientation, and experience, I will use the words *clients* and *patients* interchangeably throughout this text. Let me say up front, sometimes I consider it helpful for clients to see themselves as patients. In my experience, it can be profoundly therapeutic to allow them to take up "the sick role," whereas clinicians assume the role of "healer" or "caregiver." In contrast, there also are times when I view it necessary or helpful to identify those whom I serve as clients. I believe the term *client* is inherently more authorizing and implies a more active role than the term *patient*. In certain circumstances this sense of authorization is necessary insofar as it is empowering and facilitates the attainment of counseling goals.

Another important terminology issue regards gender. I will make an effort to vary my use of *he* and *she* for *both* the clinician's and the client's gender. Although this creates more complexity for the reader, I believe it is important to remind ourselves that contrary to what the history of psychology would lead us to believe many clinicians are female and many clients are male.

Similarly, I will also vary the racial/cultural references I make to clients *and* clinicians in examples throughout the text. Again, I do this to alert the reader of his or her assumptions regarding race and culture in the provision of mental health services. I want to actively swim against the tide of what Robert V. Guthrie (1998) refers to as the "myopic view" in the historical reporting of the mental health field, where as he puts it "even the rat was White." In addition, please note that I will capitalize words referring to racial/ethnic groups, such as "Whites" or "Puerto Ricans," whenever the word refers to a specific people.

Overall, insofar as questions of terminology are concerned, let this be a part of the learning as well! I do not wish to offend or upset some of my readers, but I realize that some may not like the words I use to refer to various sociocultural groups. My intention in my choice of terms and selection of words is to stimulate productive conversation and debate among the students, professionals, and professionals-in-training who read this book.

Some Questions to Consider

1. What anecdotes have you heard about first client contacts?

2. If you have been a patient yourself, what was it like to meet with your therapist for the first time?

3. Take a moment and imagine your first client. What assumptions do you make about your client's culture (e.g., gender, race, ethnicity, socioeconomic status, and so on)?

4. What steps have you taken to prepare yourself for your initial meeting with your client?

5. Is there a patient with whom you dread working? If so, why?

Part I

Preparing to Make Contact with Your Client

I was once told that love is the only experience at which one fails until one succeeds. The premise of this saying is twofold: success requires failure (*so be prepared for failure*) and one day you will succeed (*if you keep trying*). Preparing to see your client for the first time is a little bit like looking for love—you are bound to have some painful failures before you get it right. And when you get it right, meaning the client has arrived and is seated in your office, memories of your prior failures will fade. Note: they will *not* disappear. Ideally, they will hover sufficiently in your consciousness so that you can learn from their memory and not be crippled by them. It is then that the learning begins.

It typically takes time to prepare to see clients. Rare is the intern or trainee who arrives at an agency to find a ready, willing, and complete caseload. Even if you are so lucky, work remains to be done. For example, you will need to familiarize yourself with your institution's policies and procedures *before* you meet with your clients for the first time. You also will need to prepare for the emotional issues that may arise, both for yourself and the client, during that initial contact. The following four chapters detail how to prepare to see your client. The first chapter concerns how to settle into your new environment as a professional-in-training. The second chapter addresses how to prepare yourself practically for client work; for example, how to arrange for the initial interview with the client. The third chapter discusses how to prepare yourself emotionally for the initial contact. Last, but not least, the fourth chapter focuses on your professional development. It addresses what you need to do to see and present yourself as a professional in the agency in which you are working. Overall, the following chapters in the first part of *Making Contact* will help you orient yourself successfully as a new professional in your chosen career.

1

Settling into Your Site

> *There are many simple ways to transform your workplace into a sanctuary that enlivens your soul.*
>
> —Pat McHenry Sullivan

Chapter Goals

This chapter will help you to:

1. Orient yourself to your site.
2. Identify your site's protocol: mission and philosophy.
3. Clarify the population your site serves.
4. Elucidate your supervisor's expectations of you.
5. Familiarize yourself with the physical setting of your site.

Orienting Yourself

You may be at your site now or you may be preparing to go to your site for the first time. Perhaps you have been there for a little while and you are asking yourself, "How did I get here?" and "What do I do now?" The answers to these questions vary a great deal depending upon your field, your program, and your level of study. Rest assured, however, that you are asking the right questions—questions that are appropriate in this stage of your professional development. These questions merit your thoughtful consideration. That you are asking these questions *now* is healthy and bodes well for your professional development. You may not be able, as the Sullivan quote at the beginning this chapter suggests, to literally transform your workplace into a sanctuary. However, you may be able to meet it head-on in ways that will make the most of your training experience. The purpose of this chapter is to help you consider questions such as "What do I do now?" and to help you orient yourself as a professional at your new site.

Straightaway, be aware that you and your clients have much in common. Some of you are mandated: you have been placed or assigned to your site. Some of you are voluntary: you are there by choice and you have been able to select your placement or rotation. And some of you are between these two: it was your choice to do this work and you may have had some input in the process, but in the end you had to let go of the results. You are like your clients in another important regard. Some of you are happy to be where you are, some are clearly disappointed or displeased, and still others have mixed feelings. I encourage you to be aware of the full range of the thoughts and feelings you are having at this moment about your site and how you got there. It may help to stop and jot them down in the margins of this book right now. You need not act on them, but knowing them may help you in the future to establish empathy with your clients—who will likely arrive at your site in much the same way that you did, feeling somewhat as you feel now.

Protocol

If I had a commandment for professionals-in-training to prepare them for this critical stage in their professional development it would be "Know thy agency in which ye work." There are many types of agencies that provide mental health services. There are hospitals, community centers, college mental health clinics, schools, and state agencies, just to name a few. There are several ways to find out about your agency before you arrive there. First, you can start with your program coordinator or the person who assigned you to this placement. He or she may have "inside" knowledge of your site that would be helpful to you. Unfortunately, there are likely to be many professionals-in-training like yourself and only one program coordinator. This therefore may not be the most available source of information. Second, read your agency's literature and look at their web site, if they have one. This represents their public face, and it is likely to give you an idea of how your clients will view the agency's services. Third, and finally, ask your peers. In particular, seek out people who have worked at your agency and ask them what their experience was like as a professional-in-training.

Every agency in which you work will have its own culture or protocol for working with clients. An agency's protocol includes its mission as well as its philosophy toward working with clients. An agency's protocol also involves knowing the people, or population, to whom you will be providing services. Although you may not be aware of it, you convey your agency's mission and philosophy when you meet with your clients. Indeed, these aspects are implicit in the initial contact you have with clients. Thus, you need to be clear about the agency's mission and philosophy from the outset.

Mission

Although some organizations do not have a stated mission, most organizations do. Often a "mission statement" is literally written in their literature or charter. Examples of mission statements are such as "to provide high-quality mental health services at a low cost to children and adolescents" or "to provide the high-est-quality vocational rehabilitation services to adults with disabilities in order to enable them to lead independent, self-directed lives." Ideally, the mission statement describes the purpose of the agency. Knowing this purpose will help you understand and define your role in the organization.

Philosophy

Some organizations also have philosophies underpinning or guiding their mission. A philosophy may be thought of as the orientation or approach to working with patients. Examples are such as an adherence to a 12-step program, a cognitive-behavioral orientation, or a particular religious perspective. Some agencies have an eclectic orientation, allowing professionals in different departments, programs, or areas to function according to the philosophy they choose. What is important for you to know as a professional-in-training is that your training will be influenced by your agency and/or supervisor's philosophy. As a consequence, it is your job to be aware of this philosophy before you begin your work. You need to recognize that you will be trained from your agency's perspective, of which there are likely alternatives. As the saying goes, there are many ways to skin a cat. You are about to learn one way. Do not take it at face value; realize that alternatives exist regardless of whether you decide to pursue them in the future.

The Population: Whom Will You Be Seeing?

Where the agency's mission and philosophy come together centers on the population served. In other words, who are the people to whom you will provide counseling? *You need to know the population with whom you will be working in order to be prepared and effective.* This is an apparently simple statement that contains much complexity. Let me offer an example. You are assigned to the methadone maintenance wing of a hospital or agency. It is likely that your population will consist of adults who have been diagnosed as heroin dependent. However, even in an apparently straightforward assignment like this one numerous questions remain. How did the clients get referred to the program? Are they voluntary, mandated, or somewhere between? Are there requirements or criteria for remaining in the program?

Now take a moment to consider other clinical factors such as treatment frequency, mode and method of treatment, diagnosis, and length of stay. How many times will you be expected to meet with the client per week? Will you be meeting with the client individually and/or in a group? Do treatment goals include reducing harm and weaning clients off methadone? Are the clients dually diagnosed or solely chemically dependent? For example, some people are primarily mentally ill with chemical addiction as a secondary diagnosis (e.g., MICA patients), whereas others are primarily chemically addicted with mental illness as a secondary diagnosis (e.g., CAMI patients). It would be important in this case to clarify the diagnoses of the clients your program serves. As you can see, there can be ambiguity even in an apparently obvious setting, such as this example of a methadone maintenance program.

There are several basic questions you may wish to ask your supervisor before you start seeing clients. You may want to start with a general question, such as one of the following:

- "Dr. Kim, can you help me prepare by telling me what to expect? For example, tell me how a typical client may present."
- "Tom, I think it would help if I knew more about the patients I will be seeing. What could you tell me you think I really need to know before I schedule my first client?"
- "Carol, you may have told me this before, but I was wondering what kinds of concerns the people I see here most likely will have."

These are prompts, or examples, of how you could communicate with your supervisor about issues that may arise at work. Feel free to use them as a starting point for developing your own means of self-expression. Each supervisor or trainee will have a different style.

There are also more specific questions you may want to ask your supervisor before you start seeing clients at your site. For example:

- "Dr. Jimenez, will the patients I see be seeking services here voluntarily or will they be mandated by the courts or their employers?"
- "Mr. Peterson, how often do you expect me to see someone once they have been assigned to me—once a week or more? And how long is the course of treatment?"
- "Ms. Cataldo, how long is a session typically here?"
- "Hakeem, will the patients I see typically have a psychiatric diagnosis? Which are most common?"

In addition to the aforementioned information, there is another vital piece of the puzzle that needs to be in place before you see your first client. Namely, you need to familiarize yourself with the sociocultural aspect of your agency's clients. These factors may vary widely depending on the region in which you live and the community your agency serves. Significant sociocultural aspects include age, gender, race, ethnicity, religion, socioeconomic status, ability/disability, and sexual orientation. In turn, each of these has several components that encompass the individual, family, and community levels.

Now I want you to stop once more. Close your eyes, and imagine the client who sits before you. What are your assumptions about the clients to whom you will provide counseling? Again, you may want to jot down a list of your assumptions in the margins of this book in order to become conscious of your expectations—and even your fears. I think that an excellent way of conceptualizing this information is the RESPECTFUL Cube by Allen Ivey (2002), where the word RESPECTFUL is an acronym for "religion, economic class, sexual identity, psychological maturity, ethnic/racial identity, chronological challenges, trauma, family history, unique physical characteristics, and language/location of origin." I encourage you to explore the RESPECTFUL Cube framework as well as other paradigms for understanding cultural aspects of our clients' (as well as our own!) lives.

Be aware that supervisors differ in their level of comfort with discussing the sociocultural aspects of their clients' lives. Some supervisors are quite forthcoming about this information; some are not. Nonetheless, I encourage you specifically to ask your supervisor about the backgrounds of the agency's clients. For example, you might begin by asking:

- "Chris, in your experience, with whom will I be working as an intern? For instance, what is likely to be someone's racial and ethnic background?"
- "What is the age range of the clients I will be seeing?"
- "Dr. Umali, you can help me prepare for my patients by telling me a little more about what to expect. What are some of the norms of the clients here? For example, what religion do they tend to be?"
- "Mr. Wood, do your clients tend to be married, single, or involved with significant others? Do many clients have children?"
- "Ms. Weinstein, do we mainly see lower-income people or is there a range in socioeconomic status?"
- "How do you approach the family in the individual's treatment here? I am used to constructing a genogram, but I wonder how you gather someone's family history."
- "Mr. Vasquez, tell me what your sense is. Will the clients likely be of my racial-cultural background or a different background?"
- "Mariko, how do you ask consumers about their sexual orientation? Are most of the people here gay or lesbian? Do you ever work with a transsexual or transgender population?"

As you can see, the list of questions you might ask your supervisor about the clients you will see may be long and varied. Many trainees feel uncomfortable asking these questions, for a variety of reasons. Possibly you are concerned about what these questions might reveal about you vis-à-vis your strengths and weaknesses. You may prefer to appear all-knowing and fear that making inquiries reveals your professional inadequacies. For example, I have had trainees say to me:

- "Will my supervisor think I am snobby if I ask about the socioeconomic status of the clients I will be seeing?"
- "Will my supervisor think I am gay if I ask if they see gay clients?"
- "Will my supervisor think I am racist if I ask about the race or ethnicity of population the agency serves?"

The list of reasons for *not asking* potentially meaningful questions is endless. (Please note: subsequent chapters will directly address your own emotional preparation as a professional in training in the mental health field.)

For the time being, I encourage you to put your clients' needs above your own fears as you discover them through your self-evaluation, and ask your supervisors what you need to know. Be sure to make your inquiries in a productive and polite fashion. You are not merely being curious, you are asking for information you need to know in order to work responsibly and effectively. In my experience, most supervisors are pleased and flattered to have the opportunity to be acknowledged as experts at the site in which they work! If you are hesitant to ask the aforementioned questions, there is at least one question I encourage all trainees to ask:

- "Tell me, is there anything of which I should be aware regarding my clients' sociocultural backgrounds and how it might influence my work with them?"

This question may seem like a mouthful, but basically it gets to the heart of the matter. You need to know what you need to know about your clients' sociocultural contexts in order to be of service to them.

Some Questions to Consider

1. What was your first response when you learned of your placement?
2. How have your feelings changed since you learned of your placement?
3. What populations do you expect to serve? Describe their cultural attributes?
4. What specific concerns do you have about working with these populations?
5. How will you find ways of meeting these concerns?

Your Site, Your Supervisor, and Your Role

I have made two major assumptions in what I have written thus far: you have only one role in your agency and you have just one supervisor to whom you report. However, both of these assumptions may be false. You very well may serve in more than one department and hold more than one role. You may have one supervisor or several. Nonetheless, the aforementioned still applies, but it applies exponentially if you have more than one supervisor and must juggle more than one placement. It will require additional work on your part. Regardless, it is important that you seek clarification concerning each agency's and each supervisor's expectations for you as a professional-in-training. These expectations may be varied. They are likely to include time expectations and paperwork expectations, as well as the fulfillment of general role obligations. Each of these is addressed in the following sections.

Time Expectations

Probably the most basic aspect of a job's role and responsibilities concerns time expectations. From the outset, you need to establish with your supervisor the days you will work and the hours you will work each day. This may vary enormously from site to site. At some agencies, you are expected to work daily for a set period of time each day. At other agencies, you work two or three established days a week from 8:00 A.M. to 4:00 P.M. And yet other agencies may expect you to work at the convenience of your clients. If your clients work during the day, you will need to be available every night at the agency. These arrangements may be out of your control (e.g., dictated by your program), or you may have some flexibility in making arrangements with your supervisor. Notwithstanding, you need to be clear with your supervisor what hours and days you will work.

If you work in more than one department, you will need to clarify your schedule with each department. For example:

- "Dr. O'Conner, I work in pediatrics on Tuesdays and Thursdays. I want to work in this rotation but how might I fit it into my schedule?"
- "Ms. Murray. I understand that you expect me to be here all day on Wednesdays but there is a regularly scheduled staff meeting in the outpatient department on Wednesday afternoons. How could you help me handle this time conflict?"
- "Dr. Rosario, I just want you to know that I was assigned to the substance abuse unit in the mornings. How will it be for me to come here daily in the afternoon?"

Another issue concerning your training pertains to knowing the modality in which you will be working. Will you be providing individual treatment? Will you work with couples or families? Will you lead or co-lead groups? For the first interview, you will need to know the specific purpose of your initial contact with the client. If this is not clear prior to your engagement at your site, I encourage you to ask your supervisor about her expectations regarding treatment modality. You might ask:

- "Claire, I just want to be clear on this point. Will I only be working with clients individually?"
- "I expect to see patients individually. Will there be instances where this is not the case?"
- "Marisa, I was under the assumption that I'd only be working with families. Is this the case?"

Craig (1989) details several types of interviews that may be conducted with clients. For example, there are interviews with clients who have specific diagnoses or psychopathologies (e.g., affective disorders, diagnoses of substance abuse, and/or eating disorders). There also are interviews with a specific focus, such as intake interviews, forensic interviews, vocational assessments, and an assessment of suicidal potential. For example, you may be responsible for making a referral to other services, providing a daily living assessment, or doing a preliminary psychopharmacological evaluation. You need to explicitly clarify the objective/s of the first interview with your supervisor prior to meeting your patient for the first time. Essentially, I recommend that you ask your supervisor his expectation regarding the purpose of your meeting with the client. There is a basic question that I find helpful. Simply stated, it is: "When I leave my first session with the client, what information would you like me to have gathered?" In my experience, this simply inquiry can serve as a valuable touchstone for further dialogue with your supervisor around expectations and goals in working with clients. Both you and the supervisor at your site need to be in agreement regarding the purpose of your role.

We have just reviewed the types of interviews you may be expected to conduct, such as intake interviews or vocational assessments. Superceding the type of interview conducted, however, is your orientation toward interviewing. For example: Is it behavioral? Is it psychoanalytic? Is it humanistic? It will be helpful if you enter into the first session with some sense of how you view your orientation or way of working with clients. Moreover, you need to understand both your supervisor's orientation and how your supervisor envisions your orientation. It is likely that your orientation will reflect your job role, that is, whether you are a social worker, psychologist, psychiatrist, licensed mental health counselor, pastoral counselor, or other professional in the mental health field. Each type of professional may engage in the initial interview with a somewhat different purpose.

In addition, before the first interview you need to know whether the relationship you are establishing with the client is intended to be long or short term. Will you be expected to meet with the client only once, or twelve times, or will your relationship with the client be ongoing? Talk about this issue up front with your supervisor because it is likely that you will need to address it in the first session with your client.

Paperwork Expectations

Paperwork: it is the bane of professionals in the field of mental health. Be aware that all clients have files or charts to which you will contribute. In theory, they are needed to maintain a client's history and coordinate treatment. In reality, the maintenance of files and charts can feel like a burden. It often leads to burnout among mental health professionals. As Kottler (2003) acerbically notes: "Paperwork is just one example of a product that pleases funding and accreditation agencies but drives clinical personnel up the wall." As a professional-in-training, you are not exempt from the responsibility of filling out paperwork—far from it. Indeed, you are most likely in the unique position of finding yourself given paperwork others ought to be handling! That said, there have been some strides in recent years to minimize paperwork. Most notable among them is the notion of the paperless office, in which all client charts are computerized and no paper medical charts exist. This is not the reality in most agencies. Even if it were, computerization offers no panacea for paperwork ills. It tends to be the same character disguised in different clothes, albeit you can change them more easily. Computerized or not, there are often forms that have to be filled out before you see your client for the first time, forms you fill out to acknowledge your client's arrival, forms to detail the nature of your visit, and (not least) billing forms to complete.

Sometimes your supervisor will tell you all you need to know about the paperwork involved in seeing clients. Other times, you may need to prompt your supervisor for the information. You may want to ask your supervisor if you could peruse some closed charts in order to familiarize yourself with the paperwork protocol of the agency. It may be appropriate to ask:

- "Dr. Meyer, I assume there are individual charts kept on patients. How can I access them or add to them as needed?"
- "Jocelyn, could you tell me a little about the paperwork kept on each client?"
- "Misha, I know that some of this information goes on the computer and some is kept on paper. Can we review what is involved for each patient with whom I will be meeting."

Be aware that some supervisors are more organized than others. And, as Lukas aptly notes, "Supervisors are busy people. They have their own case loads and frequently have other administrative responsibilities . . ." (including other supervisory responsibilities). Your supervisor may be ready to show you all of the forms you will need, and where to get them. More likely, your supervisor will be eager to direct you to a receptionist or other colleague to assist you in your practical preparation to see your client. If you have a peer at the organization, I recommend that you seek him or her out and ask what directions he or she has been given. Peers may be quite helpful, depending on the culture from which you come and the agency's culture into which you are entering. The bottom line is that you want to know what forms, computerized or otherwise, you are supposed to have filled out before and after your first client contact.

Your Work Environment: The Physical Setting

The work environment matters. For some people it matters more; for some people it matters less. It may be a good idea for you to take a moment and consider where you fall along this continuum. Do you like a clean desk? Do you prefer to have a private space or share an office with others? How does a rundown environment affect your mood? Does lighting matter to you? There are an infinite number of variables that influence one's work environment and one's perception of one's work environment. Consider what matters to you and how you can approximate that reality at work. Although it may be difficult, I encourage you to transform your workplace and create, in the words of Pat McHenry Sullivan, (2003), "A place where you feel inspired to do your best."

When you arrive at your site, most likely you will be assigned an area in which to work. However, this is not always the case. There is a well-known hospital in New York City in which the psychology interns literally carry their offices on their backs: they are not assigned work spaces, and they are expected to carry all they need with them in a backpack, including their coat. However, this is one extreme. Typically, you will be assigned a space. Sometimes you will have to share this area with others; sometimes it will be your area alone—your designated area. Also, find out where you will be seeing clients. You may see clients in your designated area, if it affords sufficient privacy and safety, or you may see clients elsewhere. This is an important point to clarify with your supervisor before you make your first client contact.

In addition, you want to familiarize yourself with your entire site and not just your work space. You may feel like a tiny cog in a big machine, but each cog is vital to the next. To do your best work, you need to understand the layout of the big machine. For example, knowing where the outpatient area is may not matter to you if you work in the inpatient area, but when you discharge your clients from the inpatient to the outpatient area you better know where it is! Most likely, if you don't take them there yourself, or tell them where it is, they will never make it there—and so much for all the good work you did for them as an inpatient.

Some supervisors are great at orienting new trainees to the work environment; others are not. If your supervisor does not give you a tour or walk you through the site, find someone who will. You want to know not only where you will be working but the location of amenities. Where is the telephone and/or fax machine? Where are supplies kept? Where can you get coffee, and where can you have lunch or grab something to eat on the run? Is there a refrigerator to which you have access? As you walk through the site, be mindful of any distinctions made between client areas and employee areas. There will come a time that you will need to direct a client to a telephone, bathroom, or place to sit and you need to know where these designated client areas are.

Summary

In this chapter, I have described how to settle into your site. This may have read like common sense to some of you. For others of you, perhaps a great deal was new. There are five points I want to emphasize. First, it is invaluable to orient yourself to your workplace, even if you only see yourself as there for a short time. Second, you need to be aware at the outset of your agency's mission and protocol. Third, it is important to be familiar with the specific population with whom you will be working. Fourth, you need to understand your role in order to be an effective clinician. Clear communication with your supervisor regarding your role and responsibilities is vital. Finally, take time to familiarize yourself with your work environment—literally and figuratively to "settle in." In the end, your site is the foundation for your work: it is the space where your work becomes real. How to settle into this foundation is what this chapter has been all about.

Some Questions to Consider

1. What are your apprehensions about questioning your new supervisor closely about her expectations of you? What can you do to surmount these apprehensions?

2. What personal habits must you reform or hone to handle the paperwork requirements at your placement?

3. What can you do to make your designated work area the best environment for you?

2

Practical Issues in Preparing to See Your Client

Before you meet with your first client, there are practical issues to consider and settle so that you can begin the session feeling prepared and professional.

—Rita and John Sommers-Flanagan

Chapter Goals

This chapter will help you to:

1. Feel comfortable with your role in the first interview.
2. Arrange the space in which you will initially meet with patients.
3. Clarify the paperwork the first interview entails.
4. Understand what you communicate when you make a first appointment.
5. Direct your patient to the agency where you will meet for the initial contact.

The First Interview: Your Role

Your role in the first interview will vary depending on several factors, such as the agency in which you are working, your supervisor's expectations, your expectations, your specialty area (e.g., psychologist, psychiatrist, psychiatric nursing, licensed mental health counselor, pastoral counselor, social worker), and the requirements of the program or school where you will receive your credentials. Primary among these factors is the site where you are trained. Sites typically have specific positions, placements, or rotations to fill, and they are accustomed to filling them routinely on a monthly, semester, or year-long basis. *Sites have work to do, and they take on trainees to get the work done.* I emphasize this point in order to help you keep your role in perspective. Indeed, sites vary a great deal in their commitment to the quality of training they provide.

Sites take on trainees not only to get work done but to enhance their prestige. They enhance their prestige by establishing their reputation as a teaching site. Their status rises via affiliation with your school or program. To outsiders, it appears that your school or program has given them the rubber stamp of approval by entrusting them with the training of their students. There is some truth to this statement among strong, reputable programs. These programs require your site to meet certain requirements, and they monitor the provision of these requirements (e.g., that a minimum number of supervised patient hours are provided or formal training presentations are held). In so doing, the requirements of your program or school influence your role as a professional-in-training. From an agency's point of view, you are there to be productive; from your program's point of view, you are there get the training you need to become a competent professional. It is, at heart, a bartering system in which programs or schools provide the labor and sites provide the training. Who gets the better end of this exchange is debatable. In effect, your training is in the middle. You may be wondering who manages bartering system. The answer is supervisors. Supervisors tend to be those accountable to your school or program, and ultimately they are accountable to the demands of their own bosses. From your supervisor's perspective, trainees like you routinely move through the agency. Supervisors train you as they have trained your predecessors.

Essentially, it should be clear how the agency in which you are working, your school or program, and your supervisor's expectations set the tone for your work with patients. You may be wondering at this point, "What about my expectations?" Your expectations *do* matter. However, as a trainee, it is rare that you will be asked what you would like to learn and with whom you would like to work. This does happen on occasion. Feel fortunate if it happens to you! Indeed, I encourage you to be prepared, just in case, to identify a few realistic training goals that could be met on your behalf. However, more likely than not your role has been defined before your arrival and you simply need to step into it. This may be a source of disappointment and frustration for some, particularly those of you who have specific goals in mind and for whom a hands-on experience marks a cornerstone in training. This may be a source of relief for others, such as those of you who have outside commitments or already feel relatively skilled and eager to work independently.

Regardless of your expectations, I recommend that you clarify your supervisor's expectations regarding the first interview before you even contemplate meeting with patients (see Chapter 1). In particular, I encourage you to distinguish between *the how* and *the why* of the initial interview when you talk to your supervisor. In practice, this distinction is somewhat artificial, but theoretically it is clear. *The how* is tangible. For example, it includes how to contact the patient, schedule the first appointment, direct the patient to the agency, arrange your meeting space, and prepare the necessary first-visit paperwork. In contrast, *the why* of the initial interview is relatively intangible. It includes the structure of the interview, the way in which ideas are expressed by patients and clinicians alike, and the goals of the initial interview.

Part One of this book essentially concerns the "how" of the initial interview; subsequent parts describe the "why," as well as the challenges that arise when the "hows" and "whys" begin to overlap. Such is the excitement of the work upon which you are about to embark! Let me begin by discussing the physical setting—literally the place where you will sit down and talk with your first client. Succeeding sections of this chapter will address critical minutiae of paperwork, as well as contacting patients and directing them to your site.

Holding the Initial Interview: The Physical Setting

I attended a conference where an internationally renowned lecturer was giving a workshop. In the midst of his video presentation, he flashed a slide on the screen. It simply said: "FURNITURE." It drew a laugh from participants at the workshop, in that it seemingly came out of the blue. However, he contended that the topic was relevant to the work of counseling. He returned to this slide at the presentation's end and asked us all to consider several questions. Do we use a couch? Do we use chairs? Are the chairs high or low? Is there a table in the room; and if so, where is it, how high is it, and what is its proportions? Is there a desk in the room? If you have a desk, do you sit behind it? Where is the clock—or is there a clock present at all? Do we keep tissues in the patient's reach? Do we keep a pen and paper handy? Do we take notes? The questions were many and varied.

As he went through these questions, I thought of the first time I read Dr. Nancy McWilliams' (1999) description of her office during an initial patient interview in the book *Psychoanalytic Case Formulation*. I remember being surprised by it. Indeed, she goes into great detail about her own style of interviewing. She writes: "At the time of the appointment, I shake hands, show the person in, and invite him or her to sit wherever would be comfortable, explaining that I will sit at my desk because it is easier for me to take notes there" (p. 31). What surprised me most was that she actually *sat behind a desk* during her first session with a new patient. According to my training in the field of mental health at that time, such an arrangement was verboten.

The renowned lecturer subsequently revealed his office arrangement at the presentations' end: a tall upright chair for the therapist, a tall upright chair for the patient, and a tall round table. He and his patient sit next to each other at the table at an angle. Paper and pencils are on the table for both to use. Tissues are always within the client's reach. The clock is in plain view for both patient and therapist. I heard his description of his office and my jaw dropped. I immediately compared my own work space to his. First, I thought of the differences: I had no table and no tall chairs, and there was nothing between me and the patient. My office contained a low chair with an ottoman for me, and a low couch with pillows for the patient. I held the paper and pencil. Second, I thought of the similarities: we both kept tissues in reach of the patient and clocks in plain view for patient and therapist alike.

You could infer much about the way he works and the way I work with patients given this description of our office arrangements. You could also make an educated guess about our respective disciplines. What this example elucidates is the importance of the physical setting. Each choice you make sends a message to your patient about you, your orientation, and your expectations of the patient. Think about what you want to communicate. Indeed, I encourage you now to take a moment and consider each of the aforementioned questions. What would your ideal office look like? In other words, how would you furnish and decorate your office? Perhaps more importantly, what do you believe it would communicate about you and your expectations of counseling to patients?

You cannot control how this communication is interpreted, but you ought to be aware of the communication you are sending. Think of your office as a modern painting you have created. What you see and what you *intended* your patient to see in the painting may vary. Depending your orientation, the disparity between your viewpoints may be meaningful. For example, I once had a patient come into my office and sit in my chair—leaving the couch free for me. Could this patient have been communicating to me her concerns about control or narcissistic tendencies? Or, might she simply have been naive and sat in the seat that first caught her eye? Regardless, she was potentially providing me with information about herself. To the extent that this information was relevant to our work together, it was noteworthy. I recommend that you attend to this type of information in your first session with your patient.

As I noted in Chapter 1, when you arrive at your site most likely you will be assigned an area in which to work. This may or may not be the space in which you meet your patient for the first time. Clearly, it is an important point to clarify with your supervisor before you make your first client contact. Ask your supervisor where you will see patients. If you have your own office in which to do work and see patients, you may have some latitude in terms of how to arrange your space— bringing in tissues, clocks, pen, and paper. I recommend that you get your supervisor's permission if you are going to change furniture or substantially rearrange a room before you meet with your patients for the first time. Indeed, seeking your supervisor's permission may serve as a valuable springboard for the discussion of clinical concerns.

Remember to think in terms of safety as well. You want to have easy access to the door in order to be able to leave your office easily in case of an emergency. You will also want a telephone nearby if a crisis arises, such as your patient fainting or threatening you. Some sites have buzzers or intercom systems instead of telephones for this purpose. You will want to know where these are if this is what your site provides. In an ideal situation, your office will have a small window that allows others visibility in case of emergency. It may be that you will work at a site where safety is not a general concern or you will have a supervisor who is inattentive to either your safety or that of the clients. You will need to take the initiative under these circumstances and do some planning on your own behalf. And these situations will arise. For instance, when I was in a masters program I worked at a site as a counseling extern where I initially met with clients in a small office in the back of a large, old building. I thought nothing of it at the time. Subsequently, at a staff meeting I naively reported a new patient's description of a dream he had about hurting me and the people with whom he was living. Staff members immediately expressed concern not only about his violent fantasies but about the fact that I was meeting with new patients in a relatively secluded office. Afterward, I was assigned a less isolated, safer space in which to meet with new patients. Neither my supervisor nor I were attentive to safety issues in this circumstance. Learn from my experience: it is imperative that *you* are attentive to both your client's safety and your own in the initial interview.

Trainees often share whatever office is available. The available office may vary by the hour, day, or week. You will need to check with your site and your peers how multiple bookings are managed. Sometimes people sign a scheduling sheet and book the room ahead of time for appointments; other times people work through a secretary or receptionist to reserve a space. Make some inquiries and find out how any communal space is managed. Take a look at the space, and plan in advance how you might want to arrange it in advance for the times you see patients there. I once worked at a center where I routinely arrived fifteen minutes early to reorganize the office space. My coworker liked to sit behind a desk during the initial interview, and I did not. If I did not get there early and he had used the office before me, I found myself without time to rearrange things comfortably for my work. I literally had to forage around the center and find an extra chair and clock from other offices before doing an intake interview.

In still other instances, you may be asked to meet with a patient for the first time in his or her own room. It may be a hospital room, community residence of some sort, or a home visit. In each of these examples, issues regarding privacy and safety arise. I have already addressed safety issues in a private office setting; planning for safety does not vary greatly in other settings. Privacy, however, does become a different issue. Privacy is diminished in a hospital room where there are only curtains separating patients, a cubical in which there is no solid wall, or on a home visit when family members may be walking in and out. Why does privacy matter? Basically, you are less likely to get accurate information if patients are aware that what they are saying will be heard by others. Without accurate information, it is unlikely that you will learn what the patient really needs—and thus simply will not be of best service to the patient. In instances where privacy is limited in the initial interview, I recommend acknowledging it directly; for example:

- "Mr. Thompson, I know we don't have privacy here because there are other patients in the room, but tell me as best you can how I may be of assistance to you."
- "Delia, this is where we will be meeting. I realize privacy is limited, so I will keep my voice down. Please tell me when you feel like privacy is an issue."
- "Mrs. Woods, I know we don't have a lot of privacy here with your family members walking through. Rather than giving me part of the story or saying something untrue, tell me when you are uncomfortable and you do not want to answer a question."

In each of these examples, you are acknowledging the limitations of the situation and conveying respect for any discomfort the lack of privacy may create for your patient. You also are increasing the chance that you will obtain accurate information and your patient will return for another session.

Paperwork

As I noted in the previous chapter, paperwork is the bane of most professionals in the field of mental health. Nothing has changed since you last read those words! Again, be aware that all clients have files or charts to which you will contribute. At some sites these are computerized; at other sites these are kept on paper. For the sake of simplicity, when I refer to paperwork I am speaking generically in terms of the record that is kept on a client, albeit literally on paper or on a computer. There are almost always forms that have to be filled out before you see your patient for the first time. It may as simple as filling out a form to schedule the appointment itself or a form to acknowledge your client's arrival. These basic forms are needed to not only document that the visit occurred but to ensure that the client is properly billed.

Sometimes your supervisor will tell you all you need to know about the paperwork involved in seeing patients prior to the first interview. Other times, you may need to prompt your supervisor for the information. It becomes so second nature to many supervisors that they simply do not think to mention it. Nonetheless, it is appropriate for you make such inquires as:

- "Dr. O'Brien, is there paperwork I am supposed to complete before I meet with the patient for the first time?"
- "Gary, are there forms to be filled out or is there something I should enter into the computer before I meet my patient for the first time?"
- "Mr. Smith, I want to get this right. What is the procedure for new patients? Tell me what documents I need to fill out before the first visit."

As with all previous examples, please feel free to use your own words. Each supervisor or trainee will have a different style. The aforementioned are simply prompts, or starting points, to orient you toward practically preparing to see your patient. And by all means, if you do not get an answer you understand (or you forget what you were told!) I encourage you to either return to your supervisor or a staff member for clarification. The bottom line remains unchanged: you want to know what forms, computerized and alike, you are required to complete for the initial interview (see Chapter 13 for more detail).

Contacting Patients

In most instances, you will schedule your first appointment with your patient yourself. You may contact the patient by telephone or letter. There will be times, however, when an appointment will be made for you, or a colleague asks you to meet with someone on an impromptu basis. Notwithstanding how the appointment is made, it is important to bear in mind what is communicated when it is made.

Communication

The actions and attitudes you adopt when you schedule the first interview matter. The patient is likely to follow your lead: the more at ease you seem the more at ease your patient is likely to feel. Be mindful, your actions and attitudes set the ball rolling for subsequent communication in the session. Careful consideration of patient greetings and how a patient cares to be addressed helps create a relationship grounded in mutual respect (see Chapter 5 for more on this topic). It lays the foundation for the initial interview.

You will likely develop your own unique "introductory ritual" as you gain experience (Sommers-Flanagan & Sommers-Flanagan, 1999). In other words, you will acquire a standardized way of greeting new patients. It is invaluable to contemplate your own "ritual" before the initial contact. It is also invaluable to remember that the purpose of this greeting, however you choose to structure it, is to convey a warm, professional image. Talk to your supervisor about how she greets patients (e.g., does she use sir names or first names?) and find out what are your site's expectations. Role-play with your peers, family, and friends. All of this will enable you to be at ease. As I have said before, being at ease matters: it is the foundation for establishing rapport.

Telephone

Prepare what you are going to say in advance before you even pick up the telephone to make the first appointment. There are four possibilities: no answer, the patient answers, an answering machine picks up, or someone other than the patient answers. I recommend writing a script or a checklist for yourself detailing what you will do or say for each alternative. It sounds silly, but writing a script facilitates the entire process. At best, you won't use it. At worst, whoever answers the telephone will not be aware that you are consulting a script as you speak to them.

Now let's move on to the possibilities. You telephone your patient for the first time. The first possibility, no answer, is easiest: plan to call back maybe two more times before writing a letter. The second possibility is usually the best: the patient answers. In this case, I recommend keeping it simple. For example, asking directly for the person with whom you whish to speak *without* identifying who you are, why you are calling, or the agency with which you work:

- "I am calling for Pam Nelson. Is she available?"

In this instance, you get lucky and the patient answers the call. All you have to do is identify yourself and your agency. Then you can suggest a day and time for an appointment. Again, I recommend that you role-play this with a friend or peer.

Dare I suggest a supervisor? After all, some patients are more polite, flexible, and easier about scheduling than others.

A third possibility is that someone other than your patient answers the telephone. If your patient is home, hopefully whoever answered the telephone will simply put her on the line. Sometimes it is not this easy. Someone else may answer and be evasive, or the patient may not be home. In either of these cases, you need to have a response ready.

- "It is fine if Pam isn't available right now. I'll call back?"
- "So Pam isn't home? Could you tell me when would be a good time to call back?"

Essentially, you want to say what you can to get your patient on the telephone without revealing the purpose of the call. You must respect patient confidentiality. In this instance, I encourage you to ask your supervisor what type of identifying information you can or cannot leave with a person who is taking a message. For example, I once worked at a mental health center. We were instructed to leave a message such as:

- "This is Tina Robinson. I am calling for Carol Smith. Please return my call at your earliest convenience. I may be reached at (telephone number)."

What is noteworthy about this message is that it did not reveal that it was a mental health practitioner who was trying to reach the patient. In so doing, patient confidentiality was preserved.

Essentially, the same advice that holds true for leaving a message with a person also holds true for leaving messages on answering machines—the fourth and final possibility. Again, you need to consult with your supervisor about what type of message you may leave on a machine. Be mindful of the need to respect confidentiality. Consider: Who might hear that message? How would your patient feel if his wife heard that he was in therapy? How might your patient feel if her mother knew she was seeking counseling? These are the types of questions you need to ask yourself before you leave a message on a prospective patient's answering machine.

Letter

Some agencies use form letters to contact patients. Ask your supervisor if there is one they use, or create one yourself. Essentially, a form letter is the easiest way for you to contact your patient. If there is a form, usually all you will have to do is fill it out and mail it to the patient.

In Person

There are several ways to initiate a session when a patient has been referred to you on an impromptu or emergency basis. Be aware that in these instances the patient is usually sensitive to the fact that she has been referred for psychological help.

You want to normalize the patient's experience to the best of your ability and explain your role.

- "Hello, I am Dr. Nelson. Ms. Talton and I work together. I'm a psychology intern and sometimes she asks me to meet with her patients. She says that you've had trouble sleeping lately and you've been feeling kind of down for the past few weeks. If you tell me a little more about what's been going on for you, maybe I can help. How does that sound?"
- "I am Mrs. McNeil, a counseling intern at the hospital. I know you weren't expecting to see me, but Dr. Uzarek often asks me to meet with his patients when he thinks I can be helpful. I see a lot of people here with issues like yours. How would you feel about taking a moment to talk with me?"
- "Hi, I am Terry. I understand that you came here because of some injuries you sustained and you are not feeling well. I am a psychiatric resident here and Mark Consuelos, your social worker, thought that maybe we should meet. What do you think?"

Once the in-person contact has been established, you may proceed as you would with any other first interview.

How to Get to Your Site: Giving Directions

It may seem obvious to you, but often a patient will need directions getting to your site. Be ready to give directions. Your goal is to maximize the probability that your patient will make it to the first appointment. It is important to be aware that many patients do not ask for directions *even though they need them*. Patients may be embarrassed to ask or they just may not think of it in the moment. Consider as well the larger clinical picture. A patient's difficulty asking for directions may also be a manifestation of his psychological issues. For example, depressed people often feel helpless. This sense of helplessness may lead them to be poor planners and not think clearly. Thus, they may be unlikely to ask for directions. Similarly, manic or hypomanic people are not planners, albeit for different reasons than those who suffer from depression. Again, they probably would not ask for directions even though they may need them. Whatever the reason or cause, it is clear that you need to ask your patients if they need directions to get to your site. The premise is basic: a patient who knows where you are and how to get there is more likely to show up for the appointment!

Indeed, I routinely ask all patients whether they are new to the agency and if they would like directions. These directions include the location of my agency, where and with whom to check in, and where to wait to see me. When you give directions, you want to be simple and concrete. For example, ask how they plan to get to your office. I am a firm believer in "cheat sheets." I recommend that you literally write out the directions to your clinic or office and be ready to read them aloud as needed. You may want to create respective directions to describe how to get to your location by public transportation, by foot, or by car.

Some agencies are bigger than others; you may also want to be prepared to give your patients clear and concise directions for reaching your office once they are in the agency building itself. Keep in mind agency building protocol as well. Some sites require an identification card and ask all visitors to sign in at the front desk. Tell your patients if this is the case. In addition, note if there are any items that are not allowed in your agency. For example, facilities routinely ban any liquor or guns.

As you can tell, I advocate providing more, rather than less, when it comes to directions. For example:

- "It may seem like I am going overboard here, Mr. Philips, but I want to give you some directions. I work in a big building. Do you have a paper and pen handy to write them down?"
- "I understand it will be your first time coming here. Let me give you some directions. You may want to write them down."
- "I think you may have been here before, but would you like me to give you directions?"

Last, but not least, make sure they have your name, office number, and telephone number written down. Even knowing just one of these three bits of information will help them arrive at your office if they get lost. They can ask a receptionist for help if they know your name. Armed with your office number, they can always ask a security guard for directions. And finally, with a telephone number they can always give you a call.

In conclusion, I always ask: "Do you have any questions about how to get here?" You may be thinking, "What more could they possibly need to know?" But you will be surprised and they may have a lot to ask. In some cases, a patient will have a follow-up question you cannot answer. If this occurs, you need to say to the patient something like:

- "I recommend that you call the bus station and ask them which bus will drop you off at this street."
- "I don't know the answer to that. Let me find out and call you back."
- "Can you hold for a minute? I will find out the answer to that question."

In asking these questions, remember: your goal is to maximize the probability that your patient will make it to your office.

Summary

This chapter describes how to prepare in specific practical ways for the first interview. For some of you, this material may have been obvious. For others, it may have been overwhelming. A lot of work goes into preparing for your initial contact with your patient. You need to be aware at the outset of your agency's protocol and mission, as well as the population with whom you will be working. Moreover, much of the preparation that goes into the first interview involves communicating with your supervisor. Your supervisor can help you address paperwork concerns and practical concerns regarding how to arrange your office and manage safety issues. Your supervisor can also instruct you about how to make the first appointment itself—whether by telephone, by letter, or in person. Overall, it is my intention that this chapter will act a touchstone for you to think about what you communicate regarding how and when you make the first appointment with a patient.

Some Questions to Consider

1. Describe the ideal physical setting for your first patient interview. What does this setting communicate regarding your expectations of the patient?

2. What adjustments can you make to bring your actual work site closer to your ideal work site?

3. What safety concerns do you have at your work site? How might you remedy them?

4. What privacy concerns do you have at your work site? How might you ameliorate them?

5. If you were to prepare a script for your first telephone contact with a new client, what would you say?

3

Preparing Emotionally to See Your Client

Be a lamp unto yourself.

—Buddha

Chapter Goals

This chapter will help you to:

1. Explore your feelings about being in training.
2. Examine your feelings about engaging in clinical work.
3. Acknowledge the fears you have about meeting a client for the first time.
4. Identify your expectations in relation to the first interview.
5. Develop techniques and strategies to prepare emotionally to see your client.

Your Feelings

Why begin with feelings? Well, as students most of us are accustomed to staying in the realm of thoughts. You have probably completed a lot of coursework, read a great deal of theory, and absorbed a wide range of information. In other words, you have *thought* at length about the work ahead. But herein lies the paradox: you may not have *thought about your feelings* lately. During our clinical education many of us have either ignored our feelings or pushed them to the background.

I encourage you now to bring your feelings to the foreground. The goal of this chapter is to shift your focus and facilitate your awareness of your emotional life as it specifically relates to your professional life. Let me make this clear at the outset: I do not believe in functioning or acting from feelings alone. Rather, the

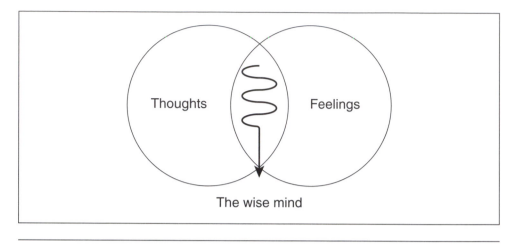

FIGURE 3.1   *The Wise Mind Model.*

goal is to be fully intellectually and emotionally attuned and attentive to your environment—to develop what in the Buddhist philosophy is referred to as the "wise mind (Clemmens, 2004)." Each of us, as is true of our clients, has "a wise mind" we can access. Visualize the wise mind as the overlapping area between our thoughts and feelings (see Figure 3.1).

The premise of this concept is that neither thoughts nor feelings alone confer complete knowledge, understanding, or insight. To be more precise, wisdom results from the integration of both thoughts and feelings. As is true in many experiences in life, it is a case of the whole being greater than the sum of the parts. Our feelings about an experience exponentially inform our thoughts, and our thoughts exponentially inform our feelings.

In the past decade, Daniel Goleman (1997) has emphasized the importance of feelings in his work on "emotional intelligence." His work popularized the notion of recognizing and utilizing one's knowledge of one's feelings in everyday life. In so doing, he demonstrated how it is invaluable for clients and clinicians alike to know what they are feeling, to understand why they are having their feelings, and to have the freedom to manage their emotions in ways that benefit themselves and others.

This chapter began with a quote from the Buddha. Over 2,500 years ago, he said to his students: "Be a lamp unto yourself." He asked them to look inward. The Buddha's words highlight how self-knowledge and awareness of one's feelings impart wisdom. Likewise, I encourage you to look inward in order to prepare emotionally for your initial contact with clients: develop your ability to become attuned to what you are experiencing at a given moment. I distinguish between two levels of emotional preparation. The first level concerns preparing for training—getting ready to be a beginner or a novice in the workplace. The second level concerns preparing to work specifically as a clinician in the field of mental health. This involves becoming aware of how *you* feel as you anticipate sitting with a client for the first time.

Preparing Emotionally to Be a Trainee

Each of you is approaching your training for the initial contact with clients from a particular level of experience. For some, this may be your first work as a professional; for others, it may be the most recent in a series of professional experiences. Regardless, it is a significant change. Stop for a moment and consider how you feel, in general, about change. People vary in their level of comfort with change. Some people love it, and some people hate it. These are the extremes. The reality for the rest of us is complex; change stirs up mixed feelings. Take a moment and complete the following sentence.

- When I think about change, the first thing I feel is _____.

Does the answer come easily to you? If you are one of those people who gravitate toward extremes (e.g., "It's great" or "I dread it"), your answer may immediately be apparent. The chances are it is not.

Indeed, it is not easy for the majority of clients (and counselors alike) to answer the question "How do you feel . . ." about most things. People are often at a loss for words when it comes to describing how they feel. I know that I am. I also know I am a visual person. Literally seeing the feeling word sometimes helps me to recognize and label my experience. To help you tap into your feelings about change, consider the list shown in Figure 3.2. It was adapted from Hill and O'Brien (1999), who categorized emotions and sorted them into an "emotion word checklist."

Look over this list and think about what it will be like for you to experience the change you are about to undergo—the transition from student to trainee. How will it alter your life? On the most basic level, your education will no longer be about a test or paper grade. You will be forming relationships with clients as well as co-workers; you will be actively involved in the lives of others. You will be accountable to a supervisor to whom you will report. Most likely you also will be accountable to someone from your program who is monitoring your training. People have mixed feelings about reporting to, let alone working with, others. A myriad of issues may crop up concerning authority, control, evaluation, failure, and even success.

I recommend that you try to anticipate your feelings about these issues before they arise. To this end, you may want to review and complete the sentences shown in Figure 3.3. Each relates to the experience of being a trainee. When possible, write down your first reaction. Refer to Figure 3.2, the emotion checklist, if you have difficulty finding the right word or words to fill in the blanks. As you may imagine, there is no limit to the list of possible sentences to complete! This list only represents a beginning.

Emotion Word Checklist

Calm-Relaxed

• at ease	• peaceful	• safe	• serene	• cool

Happy-Joyful

• glad	• optimistic	• lucky	• pleased	• excited

Vigorous-Active

• adventurous	• daring	• enthusiastic	• spirited	• alive

Competent-Powerful

• bold	• effective	• courageous	• fearless	• strong

Concerned-Caring

• interested	• helpful	• comfortable	• unselfish	• giving

Respectful-Loving

• admired	• lovable	• respected	• respectable	• loved

Tense-Anxious

• alarmed	• impatient	• nervous	• worried	• uneasy

Sad-Depressed

• down	• sullen	• tearful	• miserable	• upset

Angry-Hostile

• agitated	• perturbed	• resentful	• disgusted	• enraged

Tired-Apathetic

• exhausted	• sluggish	• sleepy	• run down	• weary

Confused-Bewildered

• baffled	• hesitant	• lost	• shaken	• unsure

Criticized-Shamed

• embarrassed	• humiliated	• ridiculed	• ostracized	• abused

Inadequate-Weak

• cowardly	• helpless	• incompetent	• vulnerable	• meek

FIGURE 3.2   *The Emotion Word Checklist.*

You may experience a range of feelings as you complete the sentences of Figure 3.3. For those of you who have been a trainee before—perhaps for whom clinical work is a second career—I encourage you to consider how it feels to be a trainee again. Some people find it difficult to be in training anew; others are more comfortable with it the second or third time around. If the experience of being in training is novel for you, consider how you approach new experiences. Some people are intimidated by new experiences; others are excited by them. Overall, I encourage you to do some emotional soul searching and become attuned to how you feel about being a trainee.

Fill in the Blank: Feelings About Being a Trainee

- When I think about meeting my supervisor/s, I feel _____
- When I anticipate being accountable to my supervisor/s, I feel _____
- When I think about meeting my co-workers or peers, I feel _____
- When I think about being told how to conduct myself as a counselor by my supervisor/s, I feel _____
- When I contemplate my supervisor leaving me alone and providing me with little direction, I feel _____
- When I think about being unsure of my clinical skills, I feel _____
- When I contemplate writing a process recording, I feel _____
- When I imagine my supervisor providing me with feedback about my process recording, I feel _____
- When I imagine giving my supervisor my first written report, I feel _____
- When I imagine my supervisor returning my first written report and providing me with feedback about it, I feel _____
- When I consider audiotaping my session with a client, I feel _____
- When I consider playing an audiotape of myself in session with a client in front of my supervisor, I feel _____
- When I consider playing an audiotape of myself in front of my peers, I feel _____
- When I consider videotaping my session with a client, I feel _____
- When I consider watching a videotape of myself with my supervisor, I feel _____
- When I consider watching a videotape of myself with my peers, I feel _____
- When I think about my supervisor providing feedback to me about my clinical skills, I feel _____
- When I think about my peer/s providing feedback to me about my clinical skills, I feel _____
- When I think about my supervisor criticizing my work, I feel _____
- When I think about my supervisor praising my work, I feel _____
- When I think about my supervisor writing my evaluation, I feel _____

FIGURE 3.3 *Fill in the Blank: Feelings about Being a Trainee.*

Preparing Emotionally to Do Clinical Work

The first level of emotional preparation concerns preparing to be a trainee; the second level concerns preparing to do clinical work itself. Shea (1998) describes this as the vantage point at which "the clinician attempts to look *within himself or herself*" to inform diagnostic interviewing (p. 516). He encourages clinicians to be aware of how they feel during the initial interview. Indeed, Shea asserts that "vivid feelings" may emerge over the course of a diagnostic interview. It is invaluable for a clinician to be aware of these feelings in order to provide effective treatment.

A friend of mine recently told me about his experience as a patient the first time he saw a therapist. It was a therapist whom he really liked and found helpful. As treatment neared its close, the therapist told him that he had been the therapist's first client. The therapist also told him how he literally threw up after their first session together! Now each of us could infer how this therapist felt from this behavior; indeed, my friend has his own theory. What do you anticipate *feeling* the first time you see a client?

You will not be able to envision every possible clinical scenario. Each client will be unique, and each time you meet a new client your experience will be unique. Nonetheless, my guess is that the *next* time my friend's therapist saw a client he did not throw up. There is something about the novelty of a new situation that brings with it its own attendant range of emotional responses—especially anxiety. McWilliams (1998), an experienced psychologist, readily acknowledges the difficulty that comes with interviewing someone for the first time. She admits: "I generally take copious notes, for purposes of both recording important information and *giving myself a task that distracts me from my own anxiety about a new situation*" (p. 31, emphasis added).

Lukas (1993), an experienced social worker, also contends that the most common response when you start an interview is *anxiety*. In a nutshell, she describes this as ". . . worrying about what you are supposed to do or say next, at the same time as you are trying to listen, look, think, pay attention to what you are feeling, and make some sense out of all of it." In other words, as a new trainee you will "have to learn to tolerate the feeling of *not knowing*" (p. xiii). It is difficult for most people to "not know." It engenders feelings of helplessness, frustration, and powerlessness. It is particularly challenging for new trainees who want to apply their skills and assist their clients—clients who come to counseling in a great deal of pain and wanting their problems solved.

Consider, now, how you feel about doing clinical work. Once again, I encourage you to do some emotional soul searching and become attuned your feelings. Now I ask you to review the list of feeling words and to fill in the following sentence.

- When I think about meeting a client for the first time, I feel _____.

What were the feelings that emerged when you completed this sentence? Some of you may not have been able to answer this question. Some of you may have been thinking, "How absurd, I cannot imagine every possible clinical scenario." Indeed, this is true. And you cannot imagine every possible client who may sit before you and to whom you will have an emotional reaction.

Nonetheless, I encourage you to be mindful of the emotions you will experience on a gut level when you sit with a new client. Be open to "feeling your feelings." In so doing, you can learn to identify and label them as they arise. You can use your feelings to inform your knowledge of your client. When you sit with a new client, consider:

- What is it like to sit with this client?
- How do I feel with this client?
- What do I imagine the client feels toward me?

Now that you have considered these questions, *do not* act on your emotions immediately. *Do* take a moment to consider what they may convey about the client and your relationship to the client.

For example, your feelings may seem unnatural or unusual to you. You may think, "Wow, I feel right at home sitting with this client, and I don't usually establish rapport this easily." Likewise, you may feel uncomfortable with the client. These emotions may communicate on a deeper level (e.g., that the client is dangerous, naive, untrustworthy, or seductive). Your feelings may communicate something about the client's general psychopathology or way of being. Perhaps more importantly, you want to consider how your experience with the client contributes to her reason for seeking treatment now. It is in the context of assisting your client that you need to be aware of your emotions. In this way, your feelings are a potential source of data about the client and the nature of the clinical work to be done.

Acknowledging Fears

Chances are you will experience a myriad of emotions as you begin your clinical training. Among all the feelings you will experience, fear may be the most difficult emotion to acknowledge. It also may be the most difficult topic to discuss with your supervisor. For this reason, I discuss it first and separate from other feelings.

Fear is a complex, and usually intense, emotion. It may range from trepidation to terror. Essentially, it is a biological response to a perceived threat in the environment. It connects to a primitive "fight-or-flight" mechanism in the human brain. On a behavioral level, the fight-or-flight mechanism may lead to conflict avoidance or conflict engagement. This may translate into a variety of clinical responses. For example, you may sit with a client and think:

- "There is no way I can work with him—he scares me."
- "I feel uncomfortable being alone with her. Maybe my supervisor should evaluate this client instead of me."
- "Someone with more experience needs to see this client. I don't think I can help."
- "This client is fine. I can understand her anger. I don't think she needs therapy."

Regardless of your reaction, the basic premise remains the same: it is based on fear. This is both the good *and* the bad news.

The Good News

The good news is that being aware of your fear can provide you with important information about the client—information that will facilitate your work together. You need to know when you feel afraid. Your fear, to the extent it is based in reality, provides you with data about the client. For example, you may sit with a client and experience a sense of caution or dread you don't typically feel with other clients. Your emotional response in this instance may reflect how the client is feeling during the interview. The client may or may not be aware of these feelings. Your awareness of them, however, may enable you to help the client feel more at ease and facilitate your initial interview.

Your emotional response in the initial interview is also a source of information regarding how your client relates to other people. It provides you with a mirror of how the client is perceived by, and interacts with, others. After all, a client who evokes fear in you is likely to evoke fear in others. You can use this experience as a clinician to gain insight into your client's issues or psychopathology. Your fear may signal the presence of mild psychotic symptoms or paranoia. In addition, it may contribute to the client's presenting problem—whether the problem is getting along with co-workers or maintaining family ties. Likewise, you want to explore the client's awareness of the fear he evokes in others. Is it the client's intention to evoke fear? Is the client cognizant of his effect on others? These are significant questions to explore. They are but a few of the issues to address with your supervisor *after* you meet with a client for the first time. Please note, I do not recommend sharing your emotional response with the client during the first interview. Take time to discuss it first with your supervisor (see Chapter 11).

I once met with a client individually who was causing a disturbance on the unit of a hospital in which I was working. The client was an older gentleman. He was soft spoken, made little eye contact, and appeared kindly. Nonetheless, I felt uncomfortable in our brief session. I did not feel threatened, but I did feel vaguely unsafe. I remember thinking to myself, "What am I worried about? He is harmless." I experienced other emotions as well, such as caring and concern, but the presence of these other feelings only led to my confusion. I experienced a wave of shame as I thought about wrestling this old man to the ground if I needed to during the session. I shared my reactions later with my supervisor, and I added somewhat sheepishly, "The session just felt creepy." She nodded, knowingly, and said that he was a convicted pedophile. Unbeknownst to me, he was serving time in a mental institution. He was only on the unit temporarily while he was awaiting surgery for prostate cancer. Suddenly all my feelings made sense, and I was glad I had been attuned to them.

It is clear that you need to know when you feel afraid *for the client's sake*, but what about for your own sake? Remember, the basic function of fear is to keep you alert and protect you from a perceived threat. You may meet with a client for the first time and feel very wary, even physically threatened. Ask yourself, "What do I fear about this client?" Consider whether your fear is on an emotional or physical level. You will need to understand and manage your fear on an emotional level in order to be of service to your client. As noted earlier, your fear is an issue to be worked out in supervision and, perhaps, your own personal therapy. Fear on a physical level, however, is an entirely different matter. It is a danger signal. It represents a potential safety issue you need to discuss immediately with your supervisor. It may be addressed in a variety of ways, whether your supervisor assigns the client to another clinician or you agree to change the conditions under which you meet with the client. The good news in this case is that being readily and appropriately in touch with your fear could save your life.

The Bad News

Bad news often accompanies good news, and there is no exception with fear. The fear that can help you in one instance can hurt you in another. For example, it can distort your view of the client and, in so doing, hinder your work together. Indeed, it can reveal information about *yourself* that you are not eager to face. One example is fear related to racism. Given the level of racism embedded in our society, White trainees may be particularly fearful of African American clients or clients who come from racial/ethnic backgrounds that differ from their own. Another example is the fear associated with gender. Female trainees may harbor the thought that all men are dangerous and therefore feel afraid of being alone with male clients in general. These are important fears for all trainees to work through in supervision and in personal therapy. Otherwise, they threaten to compromise the patient's treatment and the trainee's ethical responsibility to "do no harm."

Shea (1998) identifies seven core fears that may drive an individual. Trainees, as individuals, are not immune from these emotions. Consider Shea's list following.

1. Fear of being alone
2. Fear of worthlessness
3. Fear of impending rejection
4. Fear of failure
5. Fear of loss of external control
6. Fear of loss of internal control
7. Fear of the unknown

Each of these fears may arise in the initial interview, in one form or another. Take a moment and look over this list. Try to put them in order from those you fear the most to those you fear the least in your clinical work. What is at the top of your list? What is at the bottom? Think about yourself, your strengths and weaknesses, and your personal dynamics. How do you make sense of your fears?

The majority of clinicians experience some trepidation at the thought of being alone with a client, any client, for the first time. For most people, a strange situation and a strange person evokes apprehension—not unlike the fear of the unknown. It is the clichéd "strange situation" in which anything is possible. As a trainee, the fear of being alone and the fear of the unknown may be particularly strong. You have less experience and more circumstances are new to you. You are still learning and struggling to develop your own skills in an unsupervised situation. Coupled with these fears is what I think of as performance anxiety issues; namely, fears of worthlessness, rejection, and failure. As trainees, you are subject to evaluation by both clients and supervisors. Your performance is monitored. Your clients may actively reject you by refusing to work with you, or passively reject you by not showing up for their appointments. Alternatively, they simply may not appear to make progress. Each of these circumstances invites feelings of worthlessness and failure. They also suggest a loss of control. You may be frightened of your client's impulses (e.g., "What if he threatens suicide"), as well as your own, such as "What if I blush?" or "What if I laugh inappropriately?" Given your personal dynamics, some of these fears may be stronger than others; all of them may be scary. Here, you need to do some soul searching and consider what is true for you. It is your responsibility to address these fears as they arise in order to be of service to your clients.

A handful of you may be thinking, "I feel confident. I don't have any of these fears." If this is indeed what you are thinking, your absence of fear is cause for concern. Remember: the basic function of fear is to keep you alert and protect you from potential danger. At the very least, you need to be open to experiencing a range of fear-related emotions in order to attend to your own safety. Minimally, I encourage you to engage in self-exploration if you have difficulty identifying your fears. Acknowledge what may impede you from recognizing them and accept that there may be many impediments. For example, clients and clinicians alike concede that it is frightening to feel fear. Your impulse, as a consequence, may be to deny fear rather than experience it. Similarly, as a trainee you may not want to admit your feelings because you view fear as a weakness. Perhaps you connect weakness with incompetence, and you worry that others will think you are an incompetent clinician if you admit to being fearful. The possibilities are endless. Essentially, these are but a few of the reasons you may not be aware of *or want to acknowledge* your fears as a trainee. The bottom line is that being aware of all of the feelings you have when you sit with a client is healthy, including fear.

Identifying Your Expectations

The expectations you have about your clients matter. They are often complex; they include what you anticipate your experience will be like when you sit with a client as well as your fantasies about what the outcome of treatment will be. And they are important insofar as they have the potential to influence what actually transpires between you and your clients. The psychological literature is rife with examples of how teachers' expectations of their students' achievements predict their students' real achievements. Likewise, your expectations of your clients' capabilities can affect the outcome of counseling. As a consequence, it is invaluable for you to thoughtfully explore the expectations you hold as a clinician in training *before* you begin working with clients.

For example, when I began my education in the field of mental health I thought I was going to help people who were victims. I expected to work with people who were suffering in order to ease their pain and enable them to empower themselves. Subconsciously, I made a distinction in my mind between victim and victimizer: some people were the injured parties and others were the perpetrators. It is important to understand that I was *unaware* of holding this expectation as a novice counselor. Indeed, the very idea that I held this expectation took me by surprise when I first began seeing clients. At that time, I worked with families at a community services agency. I did intakes and managed a small caseload of families to whom I provided counseling services. On one occasion, I did an intake with a mother and child. The child's father had recently been released from prison. The father had been imprisoned for several charges, one of which was hitting his son in the head with such force that a metal plate had to be inserted in his son's skull. The counseling goal, ostensibly, was family preservation: to reunite the father with his wife and son in order to enable the family to remain "intact." At the time, I remember feeling distraught. I instinctually hated this man whom I'd never met. I was puzzled by his wife's excitement about her husband's release and wondered what could lead her to expose her son to further abuse. I was also perplexed by the little boy, who looked forward to his father's homecoming and professed love for his "papa." Most importantly, I agonized over the potential outcome of counseling. Would my help to reunite this family put the son and wife back in danger? It was a moment when my expectations came to the surface. If I had not identified and explored them in supervision, I could not have proceeded with this case. Processing my expectations was invaluable to providing optimal services to the client.

In another instance, I remember working with a Vietnam War veteran who was suffering from post-traumatic stress disorder. He had lost one leg and a testicle in the war. Nonetheless, he returned home to marry and have several children. He was a successful man who ran his own independent insurance company. In addition, he worked as a volunteer teaching children handgun safety. After several sessions, he acknowledged his early experience of childhood sexual abuse. While we worked through the impact this trauma had upon his life, I had the sense that he not only had been abused but had become an abuser himself. I immediately became confused. After all, in my mind clients were victims. My role was straightforward—helping survivors. What did it mean if a client was not only a survivor but an abuser? How would it influence our work together? My expectations about the nature of counseling quickly surfaced, and their importance became real to me.

I cite these examples to help you highlight your own expectations regarding your role as a clinician. In my experience as a supervisor, I have observed how expectations matter. I have heard everything from "I cannot believe that this sweet man is manipulating me" to trainees who think "every client is working some angle." I have seen trainees who appear to have a variety of complexes, ranging from the savior (e.g., "I know he'll stop drinking this time") and the sadist (e.g., "there was no way I would see her since she did not show up on time") to the narcissist (e.g., "she did not succeed with thirteen other counselors but I think I can help her"). These may seem like extremes, but you will be surprised by how easily you and your peers can fall into them. They can, and will, limit your effectiveness as a clinician. Like the teachers whose expectations set the level of achievement for their students, your expectations will limit what your clients can attain in counseling.

Often, there is no complex involved. Exploring your expectations may be as simple as discovering that you do not want to believe bad things about your clients. Take a moment and consider what specifically would be a bad thing to you—what characteristics or circumstances you would find intolerable in a clinical situation. For some trainees it is learning that their clients use recreational drugs; for others, it is sitting with a client who has poor hygiene, is grossly overweight, or is seriously mentally disturbed. On a more general level, it is easy as a trainee to slip into dichotomous thinking. You may believe either "the clients are honest and decent and struggling in an unjust system" or "the clients are lazy and don't really want to change." It is likely that your client's reality is far more complex and holding either view firmly will limit your effectiveness. I encourage you to be aware when this sort of dichotomous thinking arises in your mind. Anticipate complexity in the counseling process. Continually strive to be conscious of your expectations and the extent to which they influence your work with clients.

Techniques and Strategies for Emotional Preparation

There are many techniques and strategies that will help you prepare emotionally to meet with a client for the first time. Essentially, they are the same techniques you would recommend to a client who came to you and said, "How can I prepare for a new, potentially stressful, situation?" Take a moment and consider this question. How would you respond to this client? Think about how you might work, what you could say, and what you could do. Now envision yourself as this client. To what extent might you abide by your own counsel? What has helped you prepare for a new, potentially stressful, situation in the past? Here is where a little self-knowledge can go a long way in helping you to prepare emotionally to see a client for the first time.

Many of you know that there is an armament of empirically validated, cognitive-behavioral therapies to help people manage stress. These include deep breathing exercises, mental imagery, meditation, progressive relaxation, and self-talk, to name a few. Avail yourself of these techniques. Do not forget the time-honored practice of talking openly to a trusted friend or peer; indeed, sometimes talking to a good supervisor is enough. I am also an advocate of maintaining a well-rounded life. Have hobbies, engage in regular physical activity, and be attuned to your physical, mental, and spiritual selves.

As a supervisor and teacher, I use in-vivo exercises to help trainees prepare emotionally for clinical work. Role playing, videotaping, the use of two-way mirrors, and "fishbowl" techniques all help trainees practice their skills. I am also a proponent of script writing—literally writing lists of counseling prompts, routine clinical questions, feeling words, or whatever else will help you feel at ease. I encourage you to not only create your own cheat sheets but to use them when you first begin to work with clients. The use of these sheets can enable you to feel at ease on your first interview. Likewise, practicing with peers, although it may be awkward at first, is a wonderful way of developing confidence in your ability to work with clients and learn about yourself. If your supervisor does not provide these opportunities for you, find a friend whom you trust and create these learning opportunities for yourself. For example, form your own practice group among your peers. Each of you can take turns role-playing clients and counselors, sharing experiences, and pooling resources. Together, you can provide constructive feedback to one another. Alternatively, you may decide to pay a professional in your field to provide you with additional training. Trainees often take this approach when the orientation or style in which they would like to work differs from that of their supervisor or peers. I encourage you to be creative: do what it takes to get the training you need.

An underlying assumption here is that you will be dealing with discomfort in the first interview. Indeed, this is my expectation: trainees need to be prepared to deal with uncomfortable feelings as they arise. However, this is not my sole expectation. You will experience a myriad of emotions when you sit with clients, and you need to be attuned to them. The purpose of emotional preparation is to facilitate your ability to be in the present with your client and fully aware of your thoughts and feelings. There is a supervisor whom I know who has all of his supervisees engage in five minutes of meditation before they participate in supervision. Likewise, he encourages them to silence themselves and sit still for five minutes before they see a client for the first time. One purpose of this exercise is to focus the counselor on the here-and-now. This allows counselors to become aware of their thoughts and feelings when they work with clients. Although it may be impractical for your training environment, what do you think of this suggestion? How might you prepare on an emotional level as you prepare yourself to work with clients at your training site?

It is important to realize that there is a limit to self-knowledge. When this limit is reached, people seek assistance outside themselves—from other mental health professionals and other resources. Here is where engaging in personal counseling may be a good idea. "Physician, heal thyself" may be a truism, but it is also well known that a doctor who has himself as patient has an ass for a client. The majority of trainees and skilled professionals alike benefit from outside assistance at a number of points in their careers. And if these words do not convince you of the benefits to being in counseling yourself, bear in mind that there was a time in which training programs routinely required their trainees to be in some form of personal counseling. Indeed, countless clinicians believe that the experience of being a client is a prerequisite to being an effective professional in the field of mental health.

Summary

This chapter described how to prepare emotionally to see your client. Emotional preparation occurs on two levels. First, there is the experience of preparing emotionally for being in training itself. Second, there is the experience of preparing emotionally for working specifically in the field of mental health. All trainees bring their own set of expectations into the experience of conducting the first interview. I believe it is important to make these expectations, *and the feelings accompanying them*, conscious. Some of these feelings involve fear—fear about your competence as well as fear regarding the client's emotional stability. Acknowledging and managing your fears is vital to your training. Also expect to experience feelings other than fear. If you are open to them, a wide range of emotions will emerge when you begin working on site with new clients. Consequently, I propose several specific techniques and strategies to help you cope with these emerging feelings. You can become an effective clinician! Preparation on both a practical and an emotional level is invaluable to conducting a successful initial interview.

Some Questions to Consider

1. You are about to meet your client for the initial interview. What five feelings do you anticipate experiencing?

2. You are about to transition from student to trainee. What emotions do you think you will experience?

3. When were the last three times you felt afraid? Each time, how did you handle your fear?

4. How have racial–cultural factors influenced your expectations of clients?

5. What specific techniques and strategies will you use to prepare emotionally to meet your clients for the first time?

4

Seeing Yourself as a Professional

Talent counts thirty percent; appearance counts seventy.

—Chinese proverb

Chapter Goals

This chapter will help you to:

1. See yourself as a professional.
2. Define and identify the levels of professional communication.
3. Understand your site's expectations.
4. Integrate yourself with your professional style.

The First Interview: Seeing Yourself as a Professional

There are many twists and turns on the road map of adult life, particularly in the vocational area: rare is the person who holds only one job or works in only one organization for a lifetime. If you are reading this book, no doubt you are experiencing one of life's twists and turns. You are in the midst of the process of becoming a professional in the field of mental health. One of my favorite metaphors for this experience is that of the lobster shedding its shell. A lobster grows by forming and sloughing off a series of hard protective shells. It expands from within as it matures. With each expansion, it must discard its old protective shell. In so doing, the lobster lies open and exposed until the new protective shell hardens.

You are not unlike this resilient crustacean while you orient yourself successfully as a new professional in your chosen career. In your education you have grown. You may have gone to class in jeans and a T-shirt, chewing gum, working on assignments when and where you want, coming and going to lectures as you please—but now things will be different. You are getting ready to expand and acclimate to a new environment. Expect to feel somewhat vulnerable and exposed while you grow. Like the lobster, you will have to shed your comfortable shell. For some of you, this may entail only a change of clothes. For others, it is very likely that you will have to adapt your personal attitudes, work habits, and daily schedule. These transitions inevitably will occur, and reoccur, over the course of your career as you are exposed to different training environments and work in new settings. Professional self-development in the field of mental health is a lifelong process.

It is important to note that each of you is coming to the mental health field from your own perspective. You already have a set of life experiences. Thus, you are not all beginning this process as lobsters of the same size! Take a moment and consider your vocational experience to date. What careers have you had in the past? What job or role did you hold prior to moving into this field? Your ability to see yourself as a professional may depend on your vocational experience or inexperience.

For some of you, this may be your first experience working full-time in the labor force. You are transitioning from being a student to becoming a professional. You have not held a full-time, year-round job or had the experience of settling into the workplace and expecting to stay. In this instance, seeing yourself as a professional may represent a significant transition, both personally and professionally. You might have just completed your undergraduate degree, and you are going directly to work as a counselor. You might be a graduate student who is on the verge of becoming a licensed psychologist, social worker, or mental health counselor. Or, you could be a medical student who is about to start working at a hospital as a psychiatric resident. If you do not identify with any of these roles, you can be sure that you will be working with someone, somewhere, who functions in one of them. There are many possibilities in the field of mental health.

For others of you, this may not be your first experience working full-time in the labor force. Indeed, you may have been in the labor force for quite awhile, even while you were a student. Transitioning into the mental health field will be a different type of adjustment for you than it is for someone who is coming directly from school into the workplace. You are probably older than most students. You are more likely to have made a careful, conscious decision to enter the field and become a clinician. Basically, you may be more amenable to change because you have decided to change. For you, moving into the field of mental health may involve a shift from a "day job" mind-set to a professional mind-set. Alternatively, it may involve experiencing what it is like to be in one profession as opposed to another, such as the law versus social work. For still others, it may represent a different change altogether: moving from unpaid to paid work. For instance, you may be a parent returning to the public labor force. Regardless of where you are coming from in the labor force, becoming a clinician is a significant life transition. And with this transition will come some adjustments.

As you read this chapter, think about the adjustments ahead of you given your experience as a student or worker (or both) to date. I encourage you to consider how these experiences influence the expectations you hold about becoming a clinician. I believe this exploration will provide a firm foundation from which you can grow into your new shell—that of a professional.

Becoming a Professional

What does it mean to become a professional, let alone a professional in the field of mental health? *Merriam Webster's Dictionary* (2005) defines professionals as people who exhibit "a courteous, conscientious, and generally businesslike manner in the workplace." Professionals are considered learned and skilled by others in their area of expertise. In addition, it is assumed that they conform to the ethics and standards of their given specialty. For example, to be a professional psychologist you would need to demonstrate that you are skilled and knowledgeable in the area of psychology. You would tangibly demonstrate your competence by obtaining a license from the state in which you practice. Moreover, your practice would have to conform to the ethics and standards of the profession of psychology in order for you to be considered a professional. In the United States, these ethics and standards are clearly outlined by the American Psychological Association, the official national association for psychologists.

It is more difficult to characterize the rest of Merriam Webster's definition; namely, to specify what constitutes a "courteous, conscientious, and generally businesslike manner" for a psychologist. It highlights the complexity of becoming a professional in the field of mental health. After all, once you are on the job rare is the patient or co-worker who will ask you about your licensure status or inquire about your knowledge of the ethics and standards of your profession. They will, however, immediately be able to observe your manner, bearing, behavior, and style. It will be apparent from the first interview; your manner is a signal of your competence with patients, co-workers, and supervisors.

Professional Communication

Communication, in general, occurs on two levels: verbal and nonverbal. Professional communication occurs on both of these levels as well. Significant nonverbal cues include your general appearance, facial expression, eye contact, body language, and proxemics. Significant verbal cues include your vocal tone, rate of speech, fluency, and use of silence. Moreover, verbal and nonverbal cues interact to form what is arguably a third level of communication. For example, a clinician who is articulate and polite yet comes to the first session appearing unkempt and disheveled is communicating something to the patient. In this case, the clinician is sending a mixed message: there is a discrepancy between the clinician's verbal and nonverbal cues. The patient may wonder whether to pay attention to what the clinician says ("Gee, he sounds competent.") or how the clinician looks ("How can he help me when he looks like such a mess?"). At best, this discrepancy will only confuse the patient. At worst, it will undermine their work together. Indeed, the patient may not return for a second session.

Seeing yourself as a professional involves paying attention to the verbal and nonverbal cues you are sending. It also includes being attuned to how your verbal and nonverbal cues interact. I encourage you to develop your awareness of the impact you make upon those around you as you read the following sections.

The Nonverbal Level of Professional Communication

Your general appearance provides the basic foundation of nonverbal communication to the client. It is immediate and visible. Nonetheless, some trainees scoff at having to attend to their general appearance. I have heard more than one trainee resist dressing appropriately for work, stating, "I did not go into this profession to wear a suit." I find this a curious stance to take. Sometimes it reflects innocence or even ignorance. Many trainees, absorbed in their learning and focusing on their patients, simply forget that their patients are looking at them. They are not sensitive to the impression they make on their patients when they first meet them. Other times, it reflects real resistance. It is a reluctance to engage in self-exploration. Some trainees fear what they will learn about themselves and what they might have to change. Still other trainees resist looking at themselves out of narcissism. Privately they believe that coworkers and clients should trust them implicitly because of their title and education.

As difficult as it may be to accept, appearances do matter. Indeed, the responsible clinician takes into account the appearance of the patient. For example, you would be remiss in your duties if you did not notice that a patient came to the first interview on a hot day in August wearing a fur coat. Might this signify that the patient is eccentric or perhaps that the patient is seriously disturbed? It is unclear how to interpret this patient's appearance from this data alone. Nonetheless, it is clear that the patient's appearance matters: it communicates information regarding the patient's health and well-being on a nonverbal level.

Observation is an essential therapeutic skill; it is one means of understanding your patient. Your thoughtful observations provide data about patients for supervision, case conferences, and even managed care. In turn, others use this data to form clinical hypotheses, make diagnoses, and establish treatment goals. When your observations are accurate, they are helpful. But when your observations are inaccurate, they may be a major source of error. The practice of making clinical observations in a systematic way is referred to as the mental status exam. Clinicians from different disciplines in mental health may vary regarding the categories they use on the mental status exam. How they present this information may vary as well. For example, it may be written in a paragraph format or as a checklist (see Figure 4.1). Whatever the format, the mental status exam typically begins with a section on the patient's appearance. This is followed by a description of the patient's nonverbal communication style (e.g., facial expression, eye contact, motor activity, and body language).

Apparent Identifying Information: Nonverbal Cues

Age: _____   Race/ethnicity: _____

Gender: _____   Socioeconomic status: _____

Body Type
Underweight, overweight, normal, healthy, sickly, other: _____
Note physical abnormalities/scars: _____

Clothing
Formally dressed, casually dressed, disheveled, age inappropriate, sexually revealing, other: _____

Grooming
Well groomed, poorly groomed, normal, unusual, other: _____

Hygiene
Normal, body odor, bad breath, perspiration, other: _____

Hair
Color: _____ *Length:* long, short, medium, balding, bald, other: _____

Facial Expression
Relaxed, tense, happy, sad, alert, angry, smiling, distrustful, tearful, other: _____

Eye Contact
Constant, intermittent, infrequent, other: _____

Motor Activity
Normal, relaxed, restless, agitated, psychomotor retardation, catatonia, other: _____
Gait: normal, awkward, shuffling, staggering, rigid, other: _____
Mannerisms: tics, twitches, gestures, hand wringing, tremors, other:_____

Body Language
Leaning away, leaning forward, physically distant, physically close, appropriate smiling, inappropriate smiling, other: _____
Changes in skin color: flushing, blushing, hives, other: _____
Posture: poised, slouched, rigid, relaxed, ill at ease, other: _____

FIGURE 4.1 *The Mental Status Exam: Nonverbal Cues.*

Just as you observe your patients, your patients will observe you—although chances are they will not write their observations down! Moreover, there will probably form their own hypotheses about you. For example, a patient's hypothesis may be as simple as: "Wow, she looks like she knows what she is doing." What matters most is how the patient's observations (and subsequent hypothesis) will influence whether or not the patient returns after the first interview.

Take a moment and evaluate your own professional appearance. What type of hypothesis do you think a patient would form about you? Ask yourself this question: If you were doing a mental status exam on yourself, how would you fill it out? Look at Figure 4.1. Identify your nonverbal cues. Think about what comments you have heard about how you look. I encourage you to share your answers with someone you trust—someone who will give you honest feedback and whose perspective you value. You could even ask a friend to walk through Figure 4.1. with you and describe your nonverbal cues. This process will help you identify the quality of your nonverbal communication. By so doing, it will deepen your awareness regarding a key aspect of your professional communication. Fortified with this information and self-awareness, you are in a position to become the professional you wish to be.

The Verbal Level of Professional Communication

Typically when people talk about communication, they are referring to verbal expression. In the field of mental health, the verbal level of communication refers not to what is spoken but to how it is spoken. According to the psychologist Jeanne Heaton, (1998), "the way someone speaks often tells us more than what is actually said." For example, imagine seeing a patient for the first time and asking "What brought you here today?" In response, the patient states "I don't know." Said softly in a slow, halting manner, "I don't know" may suggest shyness, fear of ridicule, or discomfort. It may be interpreted as a symptom of depression. Spoken loudly in a rapid, staccato manner, these same words may communicate anger, confusion, or frustration. They may be a sign of an underlying manic state. Essentially, what this example reveals is that a patient's verbal cues matter. Indeed, it may be an indicator of a patient's emotional state and overall mental health.

The mental status exam uses several categories to distinguish verbal cues (see Figure 4.2). There are four general categories: quantity, rate, quality, and volume. Quantity refers to the amount of speech or how much a patient talks. Rate is speech tempo. It is the pace of a patient's speech. Volume describes how loudly or softly one speaks. Speech quality, in contrast, takes into account quantity, rate, and volume; it refers to a patient's general manner of speaking. In addition to these four general categories of quantity, there are other ways to characterize verbal cues. For instance, it is important to note the presence of speech impediments, as well as the client's or your own language fluency. Both will influence the patient's ability to understand and/or be understood in the first interview.

Just as you will learn a lot about patients from the manner in which they speak to you, your patients will learn a lot about you by attending to your verbal

Apparent Identifying Information: Verbal Cues

Interpersonal

Cooperative, friendly, forthcoming with information, submissive, defensive, evasive, guarded, apathetic, oppositional, resistant, seductive, other: _____

Speech

Quantity: responsive, talkative, taciturn, unspontaneous, unresponsive, other: _____

Rate: normal, pressured, rapid, slow, hesitant, other: _____

Quality: emotional, monotonous, whispered, mumbling, other: _____

Volume: normal, loud, soft, other: _____

Expressive language: normal, circumstantial, anomia, paraphasia, clanging, echolalia, incoherent, blocking, neologisms, perseveration, flight of ideas, mutism, other: _____

Speech impediment?

Language fluency: fluent in English, not fluent in English, accented English.

Mood

Euthymic, euphoric, elevated, depressed, dysthymic, angry, irritable, anxious, scared, overwhelmed, restless, empty, guilty, other: _____

Affect

Mood congruence: congruent, incongruent, other: _____

Variability: normal range, broad, restricted, blunted, flat, labile, other: _____

Appropriate to content: appropriate, inappropriate, other: _____

FIGURE 4.2 *The Mental Status Exam: Verbal Cues.*

cues. I encourage you to take a moment, as you did before, and evaluate your own verbal cues. What type of hypothesis do you think a patient would form about you based on your verbal cues? Again, ask yourself this question: If you were doing a mental status exam on yourself, how would you fill it out? Look at Figure 4.2 and complete the checklist pertaining to speech. In addition, I encourage you to answer the following questions.

- What is the quality of my speech like?
- Am I a garrulous person? Do I tend to speak only when spoken to?
- How do I make use of silence? Am I comfortable with silence?
- Do I speak unusually rapidly or slowly?
- Do I typically speak loudly or softly?
- Do I have an unusual voice in pitch or tone of which others have made note?

- What impression do I believe I make on others given my vocal quality?
- What concerns do I have about the way I speak?
- Has anyone ever commented on my speech? What comments have they made?
- What impression do I believe I make on clients based on my speech?
- Do I have an accent? How do I imagine this will influence my work with clients?

As in the section regarding verbal communication, I encourage you to share your answers with someone you trust—someone who will give you honest feedback. Consider whether the verbal messages you are sending are consistent with the verbal messages you intend to send.

A unique area of concern exists for clinicians for whom English is a second language. Of course, this is only an area of concern if your patients do not speak your native language. An analogous situation exists for clinicians who work with patients for whom English is a second language. In both situations, patients may wonder whether you can understand them if you do not speak their native language. The unspoken and vital corollary to this concern is: "Can you help me if you do not speak my language?" I encourage clinicians to address this issue in a straightforward manner, as in the following:

- "Mrs. Smith, I know I have an accent. Please tell me if you are having trouble understanding me or you think that I may be misunderstanding you."
- "Mr. Babinski, as you may be able to tell, English is my second language. If you think that I'm not grasping what you are saying, please tell me. I cannot help you unless you feel understood."
- "Sometimes my accent confuses patients. If I am unclear, feel free to tell me and ask me to clarify myself. I want to be helpful."
- "Mrs. Alvarez, Spanish is not my native language and I know that it is yours. I will have to speak to you in English. How will that be for you?"
- "Unfortunately, Mr. Koori, I only speak English. I know this is not your native language. If you ever wonder whether or not I understand you, please tell me. I want to work together to make therapy a success."

In my experience, what matters most regarding fluency concerns is that clinicians set a tone of openness and willingness. Effective clinicians are not only open with their own linguistic strengths and weaknesses but willing to work with patients about their real concerns.

The Interaction of Verbal and Nonverbal Communication Cues

It is important to acknowledge that there is an interaction between verbal and non-verbal communication cues: patients listen to your words while they observe what you actually do. Consider the extent to which your words reinforce your actions. Likewise, consider the extent to which your actions support what you are saying to the patient. Is there a discrepancy between what you say and what you do? Discrepancies matter. You need to be aware of them in the first interview because they may discourage your patients from returning for further treatment.

Consider the clinician who says in a lively, loud tone of voice at the end of the first interview "I think we can help" while simultaneously avoiding eye contact and leaning away from the patient. The clinician is sending a mixed message: the verbal cues convey a sense of hope, whereas the nonverbal cues convey a sense of hopelessness. What should the client believe? The patient is likely to feel confused, and this confusion will decrease the likelihood that the patient will return for services. This example highlights the importance of attending to the interaction of your verbal and nonverbal cues, particularly in the first interview.

Your verbal and nonverbal cues form the basis for interpersonal communication. They convey your overall attitude toward the patient. In addition, they relay your emotions: your mood and affect. Your mood is the persistent emotion that shapes your perception of the world. It describes how you feel nearly all of the time. In contrast, affect refers to the way you express your feelings. It is your emotional state at a point in time. In common parlance the terms *mood* and *affect* are often used interchangeably, but clinicians are careful to distinguish between them. Affect, in particular, carries a distinct meaning in the mental health field. Clinicians typically describe affect according to three key characteristics: congruence, variability, and appropriateness. Mood congruence refers to whether or not a patient's mood reflects a patient's expressed feeling. For instance, a patient who smiles while saying "I am really angry" displays mood incongruence; a patient who appears stern while making the same statement displays mood congruence. In contrast, affect variability refers to the range of a patient's expressed feeling. It may be normal and in full range, or it may be problematic: labile (cycling rapidly from one feeling to another), broad (expansive), flat (reveals no emotion at all), or blunted (within a limited emotional range). Last, affect can be distinguished by its appropriateness to content. In other words: "Does what the patient is saying correspond to how the patient is saying it?" For example, a patient who smiles while talking about his father's death has an inappropriate affect; a patient who appears sad while talking about his father's death has an appropriate affect.

Now return to Figure 4.2. Consider the interaction of your communications: how you typically interact on both a verbal and nonverbal level. Try to evaluate your interpersonal style, mood, and affect using this checklist. With regard to interpersonal style, ask yourself: What is my general attitude toward clients? There is a big difference between being condescending and confident, shy and disinterested, or friendly and subservient. Consider these differences and think about the attitude you would like to convey toward your patients. Concerning mood, ask yourself: "How do I feel most of the time when I am at work?" For instance, are you dissatisfied and disgruntled? An angry clinician is unlikely to be a helpful clinician. Likewise, you want to be aware of your affect when working with clients. Ask yourself: "Does my affect tend to be congruent with my mood, in normal range, and appropriate to content?" Being aware of your affect, the way you express your feelings, will enable you to communicate effectively with clients.

Once again, I encourage you to share your answers with someone you trust—someone who will give you honest feedback and whose perspective you value. Obtaining feedback from others will help you identify how your verbal and nonverbal cues interact. It will alert you to the quality of your communication. In so doing, it will deepen your awareness regarding a key aspect of your professional self: how you communicate with patients. Fortified with this information and self-awareness, you are in a position to become the professional you wish to be.

Understanding Your Site's Expectations

Communication occurs in a context. In this instance, professional communication occurs in the context of the site in which you are working. Just as you have your own expectations about what it means to communicate in a professional manner, your site does as well. Hopefully, at this point, you have some sense of what your own expectations are. What may be less clear to you are the expectations of your site. Your site's expectations include the views of your patients, as well as those of your supervisor, peers, and co-workers.

Site Expectations: The Perspective of Your Patient

Your patient's perspective involves viewing yourself through the eyes of your patient. Specifically, consider how you communicate: the interaction of your verbal and nonverbal cues. What type of first impression will you make when you meet a patient? Shea (1998) refers to this type of self-reflection as the development of a "watching attitude": a process of self-awareness in which a clinician develops a baseline understanding of his or her behavior and appearance. To facilitate this process, he encourages clinicians to ask themselves in the midst of an actual interview: "How do I appear to the patient at this moment?" (p. 542). He also recommends a clever exercise to help you answer this question: imagine a mirror dropping down in front of you as you speak to a patient. Examine your reflection. What do you see? Perhaps more importantly, ask yourself if you are content with your reflection. Do you see a professional in the mirror?

Over time you will develop the ability to imagine your reflection clearly and envision what the patient sees. However, this does not mean that you can control it; you do not have power over what the patient sees. You do have some influence, however, particularly if you have self-awareness. Being self-aware will allow you to adapt your behavior and appearance to the patient's needs as you deem necessary. For example, imagine that you are about to meet with a depressed patient for the first time. You are a naturally charismatic and friendly clinician. You typically talk a lot, speak fairly rapidly, and use gestures to communicate. In this situation, you may choose to tone down the level of your verbal and nonverbal communication because you are aware that the depressed attitude of the patient may predispose her to feel overwhelmed by your enthusiasm.

Effective clinicians are aware of their own behavior and appearance. They consider the patient's perspective, and when necessary they are able to make adjustments to enable the client to feel more at ease. It is common sense to adapt your manner from time to time based on your client's temperament and presenting problem. Nonetheless, I acknowledge that you cannot know for certain how a patient views you, despite all your efforts at self-awareness. What matters most is that you are mindful of the patient's perspective and develop a responsive, flexible manner. Indeed, your ability to be responsive and flexible to a patient's needs will increase the likelihood that a patient will feel comfortable with you. In so doing, it will also increase the likelihood that the patient will return for a second interview.

Site Expectations: The Perspective of Your Supervisors, Peers, and Coworkers

The patient's perspective involves viewing yourself through the eyes of your patient. That was simple: there was one person involved. However, expectations in the workplace are more complex: there are many people involved. They include, but are not limited to, your supervisors, peers, and coworkers. The specialty area in which you work also influences expectations. For example, social work, psychology, community mental health, psychiatry, and nursing each has its own set of professional standards. These standards dictate what is considered professional behavior and appearance.

Every site has its own culture or way of doing things. I encourage you to look for a site in which you feel comfortable and the culture seems natural to you. Unfortunately, for many trainees this is not possible. You will have no choice: you are placed at a site and assigned a supervisor. Whether you chose the site or it was chosen for you, rest assured that your behavior and appearance will not be accepted unconditionally by your supervisors, peers, and coworkers. For the most part, you will be expected to adapt and meet your site's expectations. There will be norms to which you will be expected to adhere. For instance, at some sites it may be improper to come to work unshaven and wearing jeans. At other sites, it may be fine—particularly on the days you are not seeing patients.

The best way to gauge what is acceptable behavior and appearance is to look around your site and observe your peers and superiors. Generally, these are the people who will be evaluating you and whom you will want to emulate. Observe and identify their verbal and nonverbal cues using some of the exercises in this chapter. To assist you in this process, I encourage you to check in with your peers. Trusted peers, not competitive ones, are a good resource for feedback. They are in your profession and therefore familiar with its standards. They are also not in a position to evaluate you. As a result, you may feel less defensive about any criticism you receive and more able to hear what they have to say. In so doing, you create the opportunity for dialogue about a range of professional issues, such as your field's standards, your site's standards, and how others view you. This dialogue may be invaluable in determining what type of professional you would like to be.

Supervisors are another resource for information regarding your verbal and nonverbal cues. Sorry to say, they are not always the best resource. Nonetheless, they will make judgments about your performance as a clinician based in part on your professional appearance and behavior. The end result is often disappointment for both supervisors and trainees. Supervisors feel dissatisfied, and trainees wonder why they did not get the feedback they needed *when they actually needed it*.

There are many reasons this situation exists, and I believe three of them are worth emphasizing here. First, some supervisors find it embarrassing or uncomfortable to tell you what they think about your style of communication if what they have to say may be perceived as unflattering. It may be their responsibility to give you this feedback, whether or not it is flattering, but they avoid it. They are especially loath to speak to you directly while they are still working with you on a daily basis. I have seen more than one supervisor avoid having a direct conversation with a trainee about her blushing, minimal eye contact, soft speech, or other signs of anxiety because it makes *the supervisor anxious* to give the trainee this feedback—especially if it is unsolicited. Likewise, they are loath to have a conversation with you about the length of your skirt, how you smell, or the size of your nose ring. Why? It simply makes the supervisor uncomfortable, and they want to avoid feeling discomfort.

A second reason trainees do not get the feedback they need regarding their verbal and nonverbal communication skills is that some supervisors do not pay sufficient attention their trainees. They are busy people and frequently do not have the time to give you the feedback from which you would benefit. Remember: from your perspective, you have only one supervisor. From your supervisor's perspective, you are likely to be one among many trainees. This is regrettable; it prevents you from getting the guidance you need.

Finally, a third reason supervisors do not talk to trainees about how they communicate is that supervisors take it for granted that you should know how to dress or how to behave when working with patients; they assume you are aware of the verbal and nonverbal messages you send. They prefer to allow the consequences of your appearance to speak for themselves. These consequences may be patients who don't return for treatment or other supervisors or peers who don't want to work with you. Essentially, it is often easier for them to give you feedback on your evaluation when you leave rather than while you are working with them on site. Although this is understandable, it is unfortunate. It prevents you from getting valuable feedback at a time when you would benefit as a developing professional.

Sometimes trainees make the mistake of only considering their effectiveness with patients when evaluating their own communication skills. Undoubtedly, it is vital to consider how your verbal and nonverbal cues influence your work with patients. The difficulty here is that good, lasting work with patients is often achieved in collaboration with others at your site. It is difficult to be a renegade as a trainee and achieve positive results. For example, your work with patients may entail connecting them to other services or obtaining consultations. It may be difficult to make these arrangements if your peers do not respect you. Your relationship with support staff is important as well. For instance, patients typically interact with receptionists who make their appointments and take their messages. Consciously or subconsciously, a receptionist with whom you are communicating poorly may not give your clients the attention they deserve. The bottom line is that you never know when you are going to need the assistance of others at your site.

I remember one instance when a new patient who was obese came to my office. I quickly realized that she could not sit on any of the chairs in my office; she needed a chair without arms. As I stepped outside my office to look for a chair, I saw the maintenance man and asked for his help. I had already established a rapport with him—he came to my office daily to take out the garbage, and we engaged in small talk from time to time. As a result, he was willing to drop what he was doing and lend me a hand. On a practical level, this experience immediately reinforced my sense of how important it was to work in coordination with others at my site: I needed a chair, and I got one quickly. However, this experience was significant on another level as well. When I returned to my office with the chair, I realized that the patient had observed my communication with the maintenance man. Our exchange had made an impression on her. I believe it would have adversely affected our first session had she witnessed me being rude or impolite. In fact, I surmised that she was pleased to see our friendly relationship. This experience taught me that it is invaluable to establish good communication with others at your site and that providing good services to patients requires teamwork.

Integrating Yourself with Your Professional Style

Some of you may be thinking at this point, "I don't need to worry about any of this. I would not have made it this far if my communication skills were poor." This may, in fact, be true. Nonetheless, there still may be room for improvement. Others of you may be wondering: "What about my expectations? What about my individuality?" Rest assured, your expectations and individuality *do* matter. Indeed, it is because they matter that I encourage you to be aware of how they are expressed in your daily communication. The challenge is learning how to integrate your expectations and your individuality with your professional style.

Every trainee has his or her own professional style. Likewise, every site has its own set of expectations for trainees, regardless of your specialty in the mental health field. Some sites are flexible and serve a heterogeneous patient population; others are rigid and serve a homogenous patient population. The degree to which you can express your individuality is usually limited by how flexible or rigid your site's expectations are, as well as by the patient population your site serves. If your style suits your site, you may not even be conscious of your site's expectations. This is the "fish in water" syndrome: you are so accustomed to your environment that you are unaware of it. To be sure, trainees become aware of their styles when they encounter a patient or coworker who differs from them. Sometimes these differences are minor, such as working with a group of peers who dress more casually than you do. Other times, these differences are significant, such as working with patients who talk more loudly and rapidly than you do. In these instances, the question of whether or not you want (or need) to conform to your surroundings arises.

The issue of conformity, undoubtedly, will crop up for you somewhere in your training. Some obvious areas where it arises are visible ones: piercings, tattoos, distinctive body marks, and dyed hair, to name a few. If there is something distinctive about your appearance, consider what it communicates to your patients and co-workers. You may not choose to change, but you do need to be aware of how your choices can influence others in your professional setting. For example, ask yourself, "What message might my dyed hair send about me to my supervisor?" or "How will my patients react to my pierced tongue?" In fact, a trainee in my program had a streak of pink in her hair and wore a tongue stud. When she first visited her site, she thought about these questions and decided to change her appearance. Only later did she realize that she would rather not work at a site that did not allow clinicians literally and figuratively to be "colorful." Likewise, she discovered that she felt ill at ease with patients who were uncomfortable with her distinctive appearance. This was important information for her to learn about herself and her professional needs.

I once worked for a supervisor who emphasized the importance of dressing professionally when working with patients. To him, this meant dressing formally (e.g., for men, wearing a tie). He particularly admonished trainees who dressed casually when they worked in rotations serving primarily low-income clients. He felt it was disrespectful and sent the message "I don't need to dress up for you." Not every supervisor for whom you work will share this point of view. There is no simple formula for what to wear to work in the mental health field. In general, however, I believe you need to think about the message your appearance communicates to your patients. Consider: "Does my appearance convey trustworthiness, respect, and competence?" Among a teenage population, the pink hair and tongue stud may convey this message; among a group of World War II veterans, it will not. I also believe that it is better to be overdressed than underdressed. You can usually take a jacket off or loosen up when you are overdressed, but it is difficult to compensate for being underdressed. This is primarily a concern when you go to a new site. After you have been at a site awhile, I recommend that you follow "the three bears rule": do not overdress, do not underdress, and wear what feels just right for you.

Other issues that arise at sites pertain to cultural differences such as race, religion, and ethnicity. For example, a trainee once described how difficulties arose at his site when he changed his hairstyle. He was African American; his supervisors and the vast majority of his coworkers were White. He attributed their discomfort to racial differences, noting that his clients (who were predominantly also Black) appeared to feel comfortable with him regardless of how he wore his hair. Similarly, issues may arise around ethnicity and religion. For example, an Orthodox Jewish male may debate whether to wear a yarmulke to work, a Christian may think about wearing a cross on her necklace, a Muslim woman may wonder whether to cover her head, and a Sikh doctor may ask himself whether he should wear his turban at work. These issues and others require the trainee to make choices. What choice is right depends on you and the site where you are training. It involves learning how to integrate your cultural and personal style with your professional style. It may take time to figure out what feels comfortable for you, and how you feel may change over your career.

Cultural issues in clinical practice are addressed in greater detail in subsequent chapters. Cultural issues, like personal ones, entail choices. Regardless of the choices you make, one point is clear: to be an effective clinician you need to be aware of your choices *and* the reactions they elicit from the people around you. Each choice you make sends a message about you. Think about what you want to communicate on an individual and cultural level. Of course, you cannot control how this communication is interpreted, but you ought to be aware of the communication you are sending. Indeed, by observing your clients reactions they provide you with information about themselves: Are they uncomfortable with cultural differences? Is their mode of adjustment flexible and adaptive? Successful clinicians are able to use this information in their work with patients from the very first session.

Summary

This chapter began with a Chinese proverb: "Talent counts thirty percent; appearance counts seventy." According to this proverb, a person's exterior matters much more than a person's interior. I cannot say that I agree with it, but it does make a valuable point: appearances matter. This is a point that some trainees, as well as professionals in the field, tend to overlook. To be a professional, you need to see yourself as one. For some of you this will be an easy task, but for others it will not. Much depends on your background and experience. This chapter described how to make this transition from trainee to professional. First, it clarified the importance of defining what it means to be a professional in the field of mental health. Second, it reviewed the levels of professional communication: verbal, nonverbal, and the interaction between the two. Third, it emphasized understanding the context in which your communication occurs; namely, your site. Your site includes the expectations of your patients, coworkers, and supervisors alike. Fourth, and finally, the issue of how to integrate yourself with your professional style was discussed. All trainees have their own professional style and way of communicating to others. In order to be an effective professional, you will need to be aware of your style and the messages you send to your patients—beginning from the first interview.

Some Questions to Consider

1. What are three significant changes you envision for yourself as you become a professional in mental health?

2. What do you anticipate your client will see as he or she looks at you?

3. What do you anticipate your client will think when as he or she listens to you?

4. Describe your personal style. How is it related to your cultural identity?

5. Have you asked your supervisor directly for feedback on your self-presentation? If you have not, how will you prepare to do so?

Part II

Meeting Your Client for the First Time

The very first session can be crucial, setting both the tone and the expectations for counseling.

—William R. Miller and Stephen Rollnick

The stage has been set, and you have arranged the initial client contact. It is time to meet the patient for the first time. At this point, you have gone about the process of preparing yourself for your first client interview. Namely, you are familiar with your supervisor's expectations; you are aware of the logistical concerns of the organization, hospital, or agency in which you work; and you are aware of the emotional issues that may arise, both for yourself and the client. Now it is time to move from fantasy into reality—and you are ready.

The following three chapters focus on the beginning, middle, and end phases of the first session. They detail what I refer to as "the arc" of the initial contact: it starts, reaches a central point, and comes to closure. Of course, the arc does not occur by itself. You are in the driver's seat as the professional in charge, and you will engage in activities to move the session along its natural arc. To this end, you will employ an array of facilitative strategies and techniques to smoothly shift the session from the beginning phase, through the middle phase, and to the end phase. Just as your professional behavior will change at each phase, so too will your professional objectives. The following chapters provide behavioral suggestions regarding how to begin, what to ask, and how to end the initial contact.

5

The Beginning Phase

You never have a second chance to make a first impression.

—Common wisdom

Chapter Goals

This chapter will help you to:

1. Establish rapport in your first client session.
2. Learn how to introduce yourself, manage time boundaries, and greet clients.
3. Clarify expectations: confidentiality, consent, role distinctions, and final questions.

Establishing Rapport

It is a truism that you never have a second chance to make a first impression. Perhaps a poor first impression is why many clients never return after the initial contact for their second session. In these instances, what went wrong? What *can* go wrong in the initial contact?

Many contend that what *can* go wrong (and right) pertains to the nature of the working alliance between the client and the counselor. Greenson (1967) first used the term *working alliance* to describe the relationship between clinicians and their patients. Depending on one's theoretical orientation, some believe that the working alliance itself is central to change (e.g., person-centered therapists). Others see it as an important component of change, but only as a means to an end (e.g., cognitive and behavioral therapists). Nonetheless, theoreticians, researchers, and practitioners agree—not to mention clients—the relationship between the client and the patient matters (Egan, 2002, p. 42).

I believe that it is appropriate to neither overvalue nor undervalue the importance of the relationship between the client and the counselor. In the end, the relationship is but one variable affecting the outcome of the counseling process. That said, *I maintain that establishing a working alliance, or therapeutic relationship, between the client and clinician is particularly vital in the initial contact*. Fundamentally, the initial contact involves establishing initial trust and rapport. It is unlikely that a client will return for subsequent sessions if he does not feel that he can connect and trust his clinician in the very first session.

How can you develop rapport with your clients? Othmer and Othmer (1994) present several strategies for novice psychiatrists who want to establish rapport with their patients. First among them is putting yourself, as well as the patient, at ease.

Feeling at Ease

Most clinicians feel nervous about their first client contact. After all, it is a new situation, and new situations are by and large anxiety producing. Take a moment and consider how you cope with anxiety in general. You may even want to write the answers to these questions down and discuss them in supervision. What thoughts run through your mind when you are anxious? How do you typically behave? What feelings come up for you when you become anxious (e.g., fear, worry or impatience)? What are your autonomic responses (e.g., sweating, blushing, quickened breathing).

I ask you to consider these questions because your first client contact will be anxiety producing. And you are likely to react to your first client contact in much the same way you would react to any other anxiety-producing situation. In this case, I want you to prepare for it in order to help you experience it in a constructive manner. You need to contemplate not only the nature of your anxiety but how you will cope with it. It may be as simple as taking care of yourself before you step in to take care of a client. How to take care of yourself can easily be summarized by the acronym HALT: you do not want to feel particularly *hungry*, *angry*, *lonely*, or *tired* before your first client contact. In other words, get a good night's sleep, make sure you have had something to eat that day, be aware of the available support staff on hand at your site, and be mindful of your mood.

Another effective means of coping is planning and preparation. Educate yourself about your site and the population with whom you will be working. Get ready for as many client questions and scenarios as you can contemplate. Review Part One Practice or role-play with your peers and/or supervisor. And then, after all that planning and preparation, realize that the unexpected may happen! If the unexpected happens, and you make a mistake, it is okay. Mistakes are an opportunity to implement change and to learn more. Just as few people win their first race, few clinicians walk away from their first client contact feeling as if they did everything well. Remember: learning to be an effective clinician is a marathon, not a sprint. In the long run you will win; you will learn how to become a competent professional.

Some clinicians put themselves at ease before their initial client contact by using relaxation techniques. It may help you to take a deep breath or two before you meet with your patient for the first time. Alternatively, you may benefit from implementing a more formal technique such as five minutes of meditation or progressive muscle relaxation. Many people find imagery helpful. Imagine yourself as an effective clinician. Do you have a professional role model? Is there a clinician whom you would like to emulate? Think about the positive action you want to take in order to be the clinician you wish to be.

Taken together, the preceding describes ways of putting yourself at ease before your initial contact. All of this is implied in Othmer and Othmer's (1994) contention that psychiatrists who want to establish rapport with their patients must first feel at ease with themselves. Yet even they acknowledge that this is merely a precondition. More must be done to establish rapport.

Creating an Empathic Presence

Effective helpers establish rapport by communicating an empathic presence with their clients (Egan, 2002). They establish this empathic presence by verbally and visibly "tuning in" to their patients. In so doing, they demonstrate that they are listening to and care about their patient's concerns.

However, here is the surprising fact: to develop rapport with your patient you must first take a look at *yourself*. Most of us, when possible, eagerly learn as much as we can about the patient. What we overlook is ourselves and the importance of our own presence. Consider your nonverbal behaviors: posture, gestures, eye contact, physical proximity, facial expressions, physiological responses (e.g., sweating, blushing, quickened breathing, and so on), and general appearance. You communicate to your patient first through your nonverbal behaviors.

Think for a moment: How might you *nonverbally* create an attentive presence—one that will encourage the client to open up and trust you? Will you look at the ground, gesticulate wildly, blush and appear disheveled? Most of us, if we have reached this stage, do not intend to. However, it is surprising how many new clinicians will come to work underdressed, have difficulty making eye contact, and move awkwardly the first time they meet with a client. Needless to say, none of these behaviors will inspire rapport in the initial contact. Most of you are probably saying to yourselves, "Oh no, that is not how *I* will behave." Yet many of you will, under different guises. A good example of what many clinicians fail to consider is the "resting face." Everyone has a resting face: the way our facial expression looks when we are at rest or in a contemplative mode. Is your resting face serious, relentlessly cheerful, or neutral? Some of you may have a resting face that even looks angry. Those who know you well disregard it, and it is no matter of concern. Indeed, they may not even notice it anymore. Yet for a patient meeting you for the first time an angry "resting face" may be quite off-putting.

Consider another example. What do you do when you hear a sad story? Do you become anxious, sweat, or blush? Do you feel like crying or smiling? Do you reflexively lean toward or move away from someone? Whatever you do, you want to be conscious of it. When patients come in for their initial interview, they may have a sad story to tell or a story that elicits some other strong emotion in you such as revulsion or helplessness. You need to be prepared to experience the variety of emotions your patients may express while remaining constructively engaged with them and managing your facial expressions.

That said, I encourage you to be mindful of your presence. An exercise that may be helpful involves closing your eyes and taking a moment to experience how you currently feel. Are you muscles relaxed or tense? Is your posture straight or slouched? Are you feeling tense or relaxed? Now envision sitting with a client for the first time. If you know your setting, picture the room, where you will sit, and how you will be dressed. Think about the feeling tone you would like to convey in the initial contact. If none of this comes to you easily, put some more thought into it. Talk about it with your supervisor. Talk about how you would like "to be" with your patient—your vision of what is a therapeutic environment and the steps you can take to create it where you will be working.

Noting that nonverbal communication skills are sensitive to cultural differences, Egan (2002) uses the acronym SOLER to summarize the stance a clinician can adopt in order to visibly "tune in" to clients. The model is as follows. S stands for *sit squarely*, orienting your body toward the patient to indicate involvement; O stands for *sit openly*, without your arms and legs crossed; L stands for *lean* toward the patient as they speak to you; E stands for maintain enough *eye* contact to reveal your interest in the patient; and R stands for be as *relaxed* as possible so as to put the patient at ease. Keeping in mind the SOLER acronym may make you mindful of your nonverbal communication with patients.

Becoming mindful of the signals your body sends is the first step toward developing a working alliance with your patient. In addition, the preparatory work you have done in Part One will help you to become aware. Once you are aware, you can learn to use your body as means of communicating the messages you would like to convey to your patient. You can be an intentional, empathic helper. In this way, you can establish rapport with your patient the very first time you meet with her.

The Introduction: Time Management and Greetings

Thus far, I have described what are essentially nonverbal skills: putting yourself at ease and developing self-awareness. However, nonverbal skills are not the only means of facilitating rapport with your client. Counseling, after all, is essentially a verbal endeavor. It involves what you say as well as what you do. In most instances, the introduction is your first contact with your client.

The introduction serves several purposes. Primarily, it establishes you in your role as clinician. The introduction also invokes your authority and identifies your expertise as a helping person. These conditions are necessary to facilitate rapport with patients—in addition to putting yourself and the patient at ease (Othmer and Othmer, 1994).

The setting in which the introduction takes place may vary a great deal for your initial contact. In some settings, a secretary or clerk alerts you to the client's arrival. It is then your responsibility as the clinician to go into a waiting area and usher the client into your office. In other settings, where there is no secretary or clerk, you may need to periodically check the waiting area yourself, announce your client's name, and see whether he has arrived. In yet other hospitals or agencies, another worker situates your client in an office for you; you simply walk in to greet him. Alternatively, the client may have been given your office number, and you merely wait for the knock on the door to greet him. A final possibility is some type of residential, inpatient, detention, or hospital site where you go to the room of the client for the session. If a client is bedridden, I encourage you to sit down at the client's bedside. As indicated in Part One, this is information of which you should be well aware before the initial interview. If the initial contact is occurring in your office, you want to be sure it is arranged to your liking before the session gets underway.

Regardless of the circumstance, the introduction begins before the first word has been uttered. Just as the client will be attuned to your nonverbal communication, you may need to be attuned to the client's nonverbal communication. You can learn a great deal simply by observing how the client responds to the social ritual of meeting someone for the first time. Do not forget: you have at your disposal each of your senses. How does the client appear? Does she have an odor—what is her personal hygiene like? What does she communicate by her tone of voice or manner of speaking? What is conveyed by her gestures—does she limply shake your hand or appear to shy away from you? Be mindful and alert to the client's communication before the session gets underway. Many observations may be taken at face value, but many may be meaningful as well. Time will tell.

Time Management

Generally, it is up to the clinician to begin the session. And it is important to begin the session on time. Your expectation of timeliness reinforces your authority and expertise as a helping person. Remember: the patient is paying for your time and attention; you are essentially providing him with a service (albeit a complex one). It is your responsibility as the clinician to attend to and maintain the time boundaries. It conveys respect to be punctual, and good clinicians are respectful of their patients. Conversely, it communicates disrespect to be late. Depending on the patient's culture or expectations, it may send the patient the message that he does not particularly matter to you. You cannot control your client's response to your behavior, but you can control your own response—and if you are late your response should be apologetic.

There are instances in which you will be late for the initial contact. It may reflect your thoughts and feelings about your new role as a clinician. It is also possible that you may be late for reasons beyond your control. Whatever the reason, it is a matter to be acknowledged to and discussed with supervision. There is no need to be defensive if you are late for the initial contact. There is a need, however, to briefly and directly acknowledge your lateness. It is also common courtesy to apologize for your lateness. For example, you may say:

- "I am sorry I am late; I ran into an emergency."
- "I am running a bit late today. I apologize."
- I'm sorry to have kept you waiting. I am running behind today.
- "I apologize for my lateness; I had an earlier appointment that took longer than I'd expected."

Subsequently, if you are late you will need to clarify whether or not you will extend the time of your appointment. You explicitly may want to state:

- "Because of our late start, could we extend this session? How are you doing for time?"
- "I'm sorry we are getting off to a late start. Unfortunately, I cannot extend this session. Let's plan to make it up next time."
- "Since we are getting off to a late start, let's make up the time next session. I'm afraid I cannot make up for it this session."

There are also occasions when the patient is late for the initial contact. Again, it is your responsibility as the clinician to attend to and maintain the time boundaries. How you will interpret it is another matter. Your patient's behavior is grist for the therapy mill; it may reflect his thoughts and feelings about therapy. Conversely, sometimes a patient is late for reasons that are unrelated to his therapy experience. The patient's lateness, insofar as the initial contact is concerned, certainly is a topic of conversation for supervision. On a more practical level, you may or may not be able to extend the length of the session to accommodate your patient's lateness. Many would argue that it would be unwise to extend the initial contact even if it were possible, on the grounds that a patient should feel the natural consequences of his behavior. The reality is usually more complex. For example, you may have to write a report for your supervisor and need to hold a complete session. Regardless of the circumstances, plan in advance what your response will be if your patient is late. Discuss possible responses with your supervisor. It may be appropriate to state:

- "Since you were late getting here, Mr. Jones, the session will have to be shortened. Hopefully next time we can have a full session. We have so few; it's important to keep to our scheduled sessions."
- "I know life happens, Ms. Lucas. There are times that everyone is late. However, we really need to stick with our scheduled time. Let's have a full session next week."
- "We all run late sometimes. Fortunately, I can extend today's session. In the future, it is important to stick with our scheduled time."

Be aware that like your patient you probably will have a reaction to your patient's lateness. Depending on your culture, your site's atmosphere, or your workload, you may not mind your patient's tardiness to the initial contact. However, there may be times when you will mind. You may find it irritating and annoying. You want to be aware of these feelings, but you do not want to communicate or act on them. Later in the session you will clearly state your policy regarding lateness. In the initial contact, mentally make note of your reactions and plan to address them in supervision.

Greetings

There are many ways to begin the initial interview. Essentially, in the greeting you want to confirm the client's name, present your credentials, and introduce yourself. At this point, the issue is: How will you address your clients and how they will address you? Most institutions or agencies have a standard regarding how people address one another. They will have a level of formality or informality to which they will want you to adhere. For example, at many hospitals it is the protocol for both client and clinician to refer to one another by last name, with the clinician going by Ms., Mr., or Dr., as applicable. In some less formal organizations, it may be agreed that both client and clinician use first names. In other instances, how you refer to the client and how the client refers to you may be a matter for your discretion. What matters is that you know your site's protocol and adhere to it if there is one. If you are unsure, ask your supervisor.

It is often good to begin the initial contact by checking the client's name and introducing yourself *in the manner in which you would like to be addressed*. Be clear on your opening statement. I recommend that you practice aloud before you meet with your client for the first time. Over time it will become automatic and feel natural. In the beginning it can seem quite awkward. Some possibilities include:

- "You must be Thomas Carlson. I am Gregory James, your social worker. You may call me Greg. Would you like me to call you Thomas, Tom, or Mr. Carlson?"
- "I am Mr. Nelson, your counselor. I am pleased to meet you Mr. Smith."
- "Are you Thomas Imbuye? Have I pronounced your name correctly? I am Miss Clarion. May I call you Mr. Imbuye?"
- "I am Dr. Thompson. It is good to see you Mrs. Yuhan. Have I pronounced your name correctly?"

Sometimes a client will want to deviate from what you prefer to be called. If they wish to be more formal (e.g., call you by your last name rather than first), that is usually deemed acceptable. However, if they wish to call you by your first name and you prefer to be called (or it is the protocol) by your last name, it is appropriate to say in a kind, direct manner:

- "I know you may feel comfortable being more informal, but in this agency the clinicians go by last names, Mr. Jordan."
- "I don't know if you realize it Ms. Romirowsky, but it is customary here for the clients to call the counselors by their last names."

- "I know you like to call me by my first name, Mrs. Lambruso, but I would feel more at ease if we used last names."
- "On this unit, we like to call people by their last names and have them refer to us by last names. I hope you are comfortable with that."
- "It is our agency's standard to use last names. I would like to call you Mr. Rosenbaum and you can call me Ms. Hanley."

As noted earlier, there are instances in which how you refer to the client and how the client refers to you are a matter for your discretion. Your site may not have a protocol. Indeed, your supervisor may recommend that you leave it up to the client to determine how she would like to refer to you for diagnostic reasons. Some contend that there is meaning in how your client chooses to refer to you, and you want to be able to uncover this meaning by being open in your introduction. For example, if you say something open ended to the client such as "Welcome, you must be Mark Carter. I am Jane Deckenhoff," your supervisor may want you to interpret how your client responds. Does he immediately refer to you as Jane? As Ms. Deckenhoff? Or does he ask what you would prefer?

In general, it is important to acknowledge that students often have a difficult time greeting clients. It can be awkward to engage in a behavior that is new, and students have never before greeted a client. In addition, some students feel awkward with greeting a client owing to their embarrassment over their student status. They may fear the client's reaction to their student status. Will the client view them as unskilled? Will the client detect their inexperience and be irritated? Will they get angry that they were not assigned a "real" clinician? One thing is clear: you cannot control how your client reacts to your student status. You can control how you present yourself as a student. In my experience, this issue is often the pink elephant in the room. The best way to address it is to address it directly—while expressing confidence in yourself and being straightforward about your training. For example:

- "I am Wendy Chen. I'm in the graduate program in counseling psychology. I will be working with you today Ms. Carleton."
- "Good morning, Ms. James. I'm Ms. Gellar, a psychology intern."
- "I am Louis Agarro, and I am working on my master's degree. It is nice to meet you, Ms. Hilton. Please call me Louis. May I call you Jenna?"
- "I am Dr. Santierro, and I am a resident on your unit today. Good to meet you, Mr. Dunley."

The actions and attitudes you adopt as a student matter in the initial contact. They set the ball rolling for subsequent communication in the session. Careful consideration of client greetings and how a client cares to be addressed helps create a relationship grounded in mutual respect. It lays the foundation for the interview to come.

Greetings: Nonverbal Cues and Cultural Norms

As important as the verbal aspect of a greeting is its nonverbal aspect. I discussed nonverbal cues in general when describing how to create rapport and establish an empathic presence in the initial contact. Now I want to address the specific pairing of the greeting with the nonverbal cues. This includes what is commonly referred to in psychological parlance as proxemics (personal space issues) and kinesics (body movements, facial expressions, gestures, and eye contact). Here it is invaluable to be aware of your style. For instance, I like to make direct eye contact, extend my arm, and give a firm handshake. If the patient is not seated, I will often gesture toward the seating and allow him to choose where he would like to sit.

Your style may differ significantly from my own in different ways. Some clinicians are quite directive; they point to where they want the patient to sit. Others clinicians do not believe in making physical contact with their patients. Indeed, they recommend waiting for the patient to reach forward before going to shake a patient's hand (Sommers-Flanagan & Sommers-Flanagan, 1999).

You will likely develop your own unique "introductory ritual" as you gain experience (Sommers-Flanagan & Sommers-Flanagan, 1999). In other words, you will acquire a standardized way of greeting new patients. It is invaluable to contemplate your own ritual before the initial contact. It is also invaluable to remember that the purpose of this greeting, however you choose to structure it, is to convey a warm, professional image. Talk to your supervisor about how she greets clients and elicit your site's expectations. Role-play with your peers. All of this will enable you to be at ease. As I have said before, being at ease matters: it is the foundation for establishing rapport.

Note as well that your patient will have a style too. Sometimes it is immediately apparent to the clinician that the clinician's style dovetails well with the patient's; sometimes it is not. There is a moment in time in which you will need to take the patient's "cultural temperature." In other words, quickly intuit how she would like to be greeted—with a particular handshake style or no physical contact at all.

There is considerable evidence that race, culture, ethnicity, and gender may affect communication styles (Sue & Sue, 2003). For example, shaking hands is a gesture that varies from culture to culture. Women of some racial/ethnic or religious backgrounds never shake hands with men. In yet other cultures, what hand is used for shaking may carry cultural implications. And then again, some cultures eschew the handshake altogether: to bow is traditional. A parallel may be drawn with eye contact. In American culture, diagnostic significance is often attributed to eye contact or lack of eye contact. Americans typically consider direct eye contact a sign of health. Poor eye contact is seen as negative, perhaps conveying uncooperativeness or depression. But in some cultures it is considered rude to look a person who is unfamiliar to you in the eye.

A culturally competent clinician is knowledgeable about how race, culture, and gender affect communication styles; she is aware of one's own communication styles; and recognizes that no one style or orientation is appropriate for all patients (Sue & Sue, 2003). In this regard, clinicians need to be open and flexible in their interpretation of social cues. Often it is helpful to ask your supervisor and your peers about the racial, cultural, and religious backgrounds of the agency's clients. Find out what the norms of are of the groups with whom you will be working. Above all, do your best to communicate respect and acceptance.

You may not know the cultural norms of your patients, but you ought to know what your own norms are. I have acknowledged that I like to make direct eye contact and shake hands in my initial client contact. Your norms may differ from my own. All of which leads to the recognition that it is important to be yourself when greeting the patient. In other words, if you greet a client and the client responds by asking "How are you," you simply reply, "I am fine, thank you." Do not ignore friendly overtures. As Basch (1980) describes:

> If you do not respond to a greeting or to some innocuous remark about the weather. . . you are telling something about yourself that may be quite inaccurate. A patient is going to start wondering whether you are always so mean, or whether there is something about him that you do not like, or whether you do not care about the people you see and just want to get it over with, and Lord knows what else. In any case, whatever conclusion the patient reaches is going to influence what he says subsequently and how he says it. (p. 7)

Small talk often puts clients at ease. In the initial contact, it is appropriate to respond directly and politely to a patient's brief remarks at the start of the session.

I do not mean to imply that basic social amenities do not have hidden significance. Much like patient punctuality or lateness, it all remains grist for the mill in supervision. Moreover, there are some topics you may want to avoid, such as the patient's appearance, clothing, or hairstyle. Patients may experience these comments as too personal or judgmental in nature. Counseling is not a social situation, and you do not want to encourage your patient to think of you as their friend. In this regard, egregious small talk with patients is off task and therefore inappropriate. All of which leads us back to the question, what will your patient expect in the initial contact?

Clarifying Client Expectations

Clients often come to counseling as a last resort: whatever they have been doing is no longer working for them. They are suffering some degree of pain or discontent. Sometimes there is a concrete symptom or behavior they want to rectify, such as compulsive hand washing or a fear of driving. Other times, someone they know and respect has told them they need therapy. Maybe they have been "ordered" to get help by their place of work or the legal system. Regardless of how or why they got there, it is important to educate clients. Demystify the counseling process straightaway. Even if the client has been in counseling before, it is crucial to clarify what it will be like with you *now*, in the setting in which you are working.

You want to be simple and direct with your client before she tells you her reason for coming to counseling. Counseling should not be mystery—a "black box" for your client (Egan, 2002). There are four general points to concisely cover before the body of the initial contact gets underway. First, you want to discuss confidentiality and its limits. Second, you want to obtain your client's consent if you are audiotaping or videotaping the session. Third, you want to provide the client with an explanation of the purpose of the interview—perhaps noting how you envision the client's role and your own as you go forward. Fourth, you will want to check in with your client to see if your client has any questions or concerns.

This all may sound like a lot. In truth, it happens very quickly—in the first five minutes of the session. The sections that follow expand on each of the four points noted here.

Confidentiality

The first step in orienting clients to the counseling process is informing them about the nature and limits of confidentiality. Of course, this requires that you are clear about the nature and limits of confidentiality at the site in which you are working. All U.S. health care providers are governed by The American Health Insurance Portability and Accountability Act of 1996 (HIPAA). HIPAA is a set of rules that took effect on April 14, 2003. These govern patient/clinician interaction. HIPAA provides discrete guidelines regarding informing patients of how their personal information will be used, the overall confidentiality of patient information, and the documentation of privacy procedures at the particular site in which you work. These are federal guidelines; please note that how they are applied may vary from state to state as well as from institution to institution.

Check with your supervisor prior to the initial contact and inquire about the site's modus operandi regarding confidentiality. Ask about their level of HIPAA compliance. Often, the agency or organization in which you are working will have a standard confidentiality form or statement. If there is a form, usually all you will have to do is present it to the client and review it with her. It may require the client's signature or it may not. The following is sample conversation you might have with your client.

- "Before we begin, I want to briefly review the idea of confidentiality. I do not know if you have heard of it before, but basically 'confidentiality' means that what you say here stays here; what we talk about here is private and I won't be sharing it with other people. Nonetheless, there are some limits to confidentiality—times when you tell me something that I will need to share with others. This is a form we give out to our clients. Please read it over and [either "tell me what you think" or "sign it at the bottom," depending on your site]. Do you have any questions about confidentiality?"

At some sites, it is customary to include the client in this process and say:

- "If I ever need to share with someone what has gone on in our session, I will tell you. It is possible that you may be a part of the process; for example, you may be there when I contact the proper authorities. If I have to break confidentiality, I still want to be here for you as your counselor."

If your site has no confidentiality form, it will still behoove you to educate your client about the nature of confidentiality. Your conversation with the client may go like this:

- "Before we begin, I want to briefly review the idea of confidentiality. I do not know if you have heard of it before, but basically confidentiality means that what you say here stays here; what we talk about here is private and I won't be sharing it with other people. Nonetheless, there are some limits to confidentiality—times when you tell me something that I will need to share with others. For example, if you tell me something revealing that you are a danger to yourself or others, or if you talk about child abuse, then I am obligated to break confidentiality and contact the proper authorities. Another example would be if you ask me to provide information about you to another person, usually another professional such as an attorney or a doctor. Then I can provide the information as long as you give me written permission. Basically, as I said before, what you say here stays here, within certain limits. Do you have any questions about confidentiality?"

In some cases, a client will have a follow-up question. He may ask, "What constitutes child abuse?" If this occurs, you need to be ready to describe your state's specific criteria for child abuse or neglect. Similarly, the client may ask other questions about what constitutes "harm to self or others." These questions may signal that the client has concerns regarding trust issues. Alternatively, these questions may indicate that the client struggles with suicidal or homicidal thoughts. Regardless, you will want to respond to his questions directly and in a compassionate manner. You want to encourage the conversation. Indeed, it is crucial to know whether or not the client struggles with suicidal or homicidal thoughts. (For more guidance regarding how to work with these concerns, see Part Three.)

Discussions of confidentiality may lead your client to ask about record keeping. It is not uncommon for a client to ask what type of records will be kept about his visits. Again, you need to respond to these questions in a straightforward fashion.

- "Yes, I will make a note of our session. My notes will be kept in your chart. My supervisor will have access to these files, and the secretary will too. However, they will keep your records confidential."
- "Yes, I will be keeping a record of our session. This record goes in your chart, but your chart is kept confidential."

Be aware that HIPAA guidelines distinguish between *progress notes* (observations given in medical or health care records) versus *psychotherapy notes* (records of communications during individual or family counseling that are maintained in addition to and *kept separate from* medical or health care records). There are legal issues attached to each type of note of which you should be aware. If you work in an organization that permits both types of notes, ask your supervisor for direction regarding their maintenance and how to explain this distinction to your clients.

Discussions of confidentiality and record keeping may also lead your client to ask about supervision. In most instances, you are under supervision. If this is the case, you need to tell the client something like:

- "I am in training, so I have a supervisor who will check my work. She will have access to your records—but it is in service of helping you. She also will respect your confidentiality."
- "As you know, I am in training. As a part of my training, I am in group supervision. My peers and my supervisor will have access to my work. Please know, they also work on your behalf. They will respect your confidentiality."
- "I work as a part of a team; what we say to one another is confidential. Sometimes the team will have discussions about a particular case. In these instances, if I share information the purpose is to help me provide you with the best treatment possible."

These statements may generate further questions, but more often than not they are sufficient to put a client at ease. Essentially, what you want to do is educate and reassure the client regarding confidentiality. Your goal is to be honest while putting the client at ease.

Obtaining Consent

At some sites, it is customary to audiotape or videotape sessions with patients. The patient must be made aware of any audiotaping or videotaping that occurs. Usually this is obvious because the equipment is in plain sight. Nonetheless, you must obtain your patient's consent if you are taping the session. Your site may not have a standard consent form, in which case obtaining verbal consent via the audiotape or videotape itself is considered sufficient. For example:

- "As a part of my training, I am required to audiotape our sessions. In this way, the agency is able to ensure that you get the best service possible. Is this okay with you?"
- "I am required to videotape our sessions. Consequently, you can rest assured that you will get the best help possible."

Ideally, the agency or organization in which you are working will have a standard consent form for audiotaping or videotaping sessions. If there is a form, usually all you will have to do is present it to the patient and review it with her *prior to taping*.

- "Here is the form explaining our site's video- or audiotaping procedures. Please take a moment to read it. I will need you to sign it in order to tape our sessions."
- "This form explains the video- or audiotaping procedures. Please take a moment to read it and sign it."

Be aware: both you and your patient are likely to feel initially uncomfortable with taping. (See Chapter 2 for further instruction regarding preparation for taping sessions.) However, the patient is likely to follow your lead: the more at ease you appear with taping the more at ease your patient is likely to feel. Sometimes patients are quite amenable to taping; sometimes they will want to ask you some questions about it, such as "Who will see this tape?" What will happen to it after the session?" "Can I keep it?" You will need to be prepared to answer these questions. The answers are likely to depend on the agency in which you work. Different agencies and institutions have different policies regarding the handling, storing, and destruction of student tapes.

Basically, the patient who makes such inquiries is expressing concern about confidentiality. Much like the issue of confidentiality, you will want to educate and reassure the patient regarding the privacy of the work in which you are both engaging. Once again, your goal is to be honest and straightforward while putting the patient at ease.

Aside from audiotaping or videotaping concerns, there are other situations in which you will need to obtain consent from your clients. Note: you may not release any information about your contact or treatment of a client without first obtaining informed, written consent. These situations include the release of protected health information to any outside authority, such as a physician or psychiatrist, regarding treatment concerns (e.g., treatment goals, HIV-related information, and alcohol or other substance-related information).

Differentiating Your Role from the Client's Role

Both the client and the counselor enter the initial contact with expectations. As the clinician, it is important that you orient the client toward the work in which you will be engaging together. Essentially, you clarify your role and the client's role. After you both have sat down, exchanged greetings, reviewed confidentiality and record keeping, it is time to explain the purpose of the initial contact. This may vary depending on the site in which you are working, your professional status, and your theoretical orientation.

You should be entering into the first session with some sense of what your role is. In Part One, you were encouraged to consider your level of training as well as how you define your role as a clinician—whether you are a social worker, psychologist, psychiatrist, licensed mental health counselor, or other psychology professional. Each type of professional may engage in an initial contact with a somewhat different purpose. Do you provide psychoeducation? Therapy? Referrals? Placements? Psychopharmacological evaluations? You may see yourself as fulfilling all or none of these purposes. Of equal importance, how does the setting in which you are practicing conceptualize your role? Both you and the supervisor at your site need to be in agreement regarding your role and responsibility. It may be that your site provides you with a specific function to fulfill, in which case you may say to the client:

- "I understand that you are feeling depressed and considering medication. My role is to ask you about how you are feeling and gather some information in order to make a decision about medication. I will usually begin by asking you what is going on for you and then we will get into some specifics."

- "At this center we provide short-term counseling. I will be able to see you for twelve visits. In that time, it will be important for us to work together on formulating a treatment plan that will offer you some relief. Today, I will begin by asking you a lot of questions since I don't know you, but next time I may want you to do more of the talking."
- "The purpose of this interview is for me to learn more about your relationship to your children in order to provide advice to the courts. I want to start by asking some questions, but then I will give you a chance to speak more freely."

Layered on top of all of these questions lies another important consideration. Do you have a specific orientation, or model, from which you work? For example, are you psychodynamically oriented, a cognitive-behaviorist, or do you espouse a medical model? Your theoretical orientation will influence how you conceptualize both your role and the client's role. As a result, theoretical orientation will influence what you communicate to the client in the initial contact. For example, do you envision yourself as an expert who assumes full responsibility for the direction and outcome of therapy? Alternatively, do you simply see yourself as providing a climate for change and decline to accept responsibility for formulating treatment plans for your clients? These are two extremes. Whatever your stance, it is critical that you make a statement or two about what your role as the clinician will be and what the client's role will be. It may go something like this:

- "I view my role as helping you to recognize your strengths and discover what is preventing you from using them. I view your role as being open with me about your experiences in life."
- "Counseling is a process that invites you to look honestly at your behavior and make decisions about how you would like to do things differently or maybe stay the same. I will ask you to talk openly about your thoughts, feelings, and behaviors. I will expect you to share them with me whenever possible—and when it is not, please tell me."
- "I want to tell you a little about how I work. I believe in working collaboratively while focusing on two areas. One, we will work with very specifically around the concern that brought you here. Two, we will work around feelings. In my experience, your concerns also have something to do with the way you feel about yourself."

It is often a good idea to end with a question in order to get a sense of the client's perception of your style. Essentially, you are checking in with your client to see if his expectations are in keeping with your own. For example, you may say:

- "At times, I may ask you to try on new behaviors or do new things. How does that sound to you?"

- "It may be uncomfortable at times, but I am going to encourage you to become aware of your part in your current problems. What do you think of that?"
- "On occasion I will encourage you to explore the ways in which you could live differently now. How will that be for you?"
- "I will encourage you to be active in this process; to explore alternatives. What would that be like for you?"

Sometimes the client will have a strong reaction to your style. She may enthusiastically concur and appear quite comfortable, in which case you may move ahead with the session. Perhaps you will want to add, "I'm glad it sounds good to you; please tell me if your thoughts or feelings start to change in work together." Alternatively, it is possible that your client may express some misgivings with your approach—or even vehemently disagrees with it. You may have some latitude regarding how you will work with the client, depending on your site and orientation. All of this leads into the next area of inquiry: e.g., eliciting client questions.

Any Questions?

It is appropriate to ask if the patient has any questions before delving into the substance of the session. Often, a simple direct question is sufficient.

- "Is there anything you would like to ask me before we begin?"
- "Before we begin, do you have any questions you'd like to ask me?"
- "Do you have any questions for me before we begin?"

Keep in mind that many patients have what I call "the magic wand" fantasy: they seek a solution to their problems outside themselves *that they believe the therapist possesses.* If you intuit that this is the case with a particular patient, it needs to be dispelled at the outset. In a kindly and hopeful manner, you might say:

- "I don't have any magic wand, Mr. Romero, but I believe that if we work together you will experience some relief."
- "Over time, counseling will enable you to feel better. Sometimes people feel worse before they feel better, but if you are committed to the process I think you will feel better in the long run."

Ultimately, you want to be sure that your expectations and your patient's expectations of are consistent. Sometimes it is simply enough to ask your patient whether or not he sees the purpose of the interview the same way you do. Other times, further exploration is required.

Summary

In this chapter, I have described how to begin the initial contact. I described the actions and attitudes I believe contribute to the successful commencement of the first session. These include establishing rapport, introducing yourself to the client, and clarifying counselor and client expectations. To some of you, this all may seem deceptively simple. To others, it may seem overwhelmingly detailed. You will find your natural style over time and with practice. Nonetheless, every time you meet with a new client and you find yourself in a new situation you are likely to feel some anxiety. It is good for you to be in touch with this feeling, for it is likely that your client will feel the same way—and a little empathy can go a long way.

Some Questions to Consider

1. Recall the last time you felt anxious. What did you do to make yourself feel more at ease? What can you do to make yourself feel more at ease with a new client?

2. What challenges do you face as you contemplate establishing rapport with a client?

3. What assets do you have when it comes to establishing rapport with a new client?

4. How may clients from various cultural backgrounds respond to yourself-presentation? How can you present yourself in order to be respectful of them?

5. What will be your introductory ritual?

6. How will you clarify confidentiality and gain consent at your site? Practice aloud.

6

The Middle Phase

If you don't crack the shell, you can't eat the nut.

—Persian proverb

Chapter Goals

This chapter will help you to:

1. Define the middle phase of the first interview.
2. Describe the foundation: taking a nondirective, biopsychosocial approach.
3. Identify content: opening questions, presenting problem, and symptoms.
4. Examine process: pacing, making transitions, and monitoring session depth.

What Is the Middle Phase?

According to a Persian proverb, "If you don't crack the shell, you can't eat the nut." The first phase of the initial contact is like the moment you crack the shell: you begin the session in a way that encourages your patient to open up. You don't want to push down too hard, all at once, sending pieces shattering all over the place. Rather, you want to proceed gently. You introduce yourself, establish rapport, and review confidentiality agreements. In addition, you may explain the purpose of your work together. As detailed in Chapter 5, your purpose will vary depending on the site in which you are working, your professional status, and your theoretical orientation. The beginning phase of the first contact with a new patient is vital. It provides the foundation for not only the middle phase of the initial session but your work together in the future.

The middle phase evolves from the first phase as you and your patient become comfortable with each other. It begins, in earnest, once the patient begins to share with you about his reasons for seeking treatment now. In order to reach the middle phase, you need to sustain the rapport developed in the first phase—the quality that Morrison (1995) defines as "the feeling of harmony and confidence" between patient and clinician (p. 23). Good rapport is essential because it yields practical results. It the short term, it enables your patients to talk freely and disclose personal information. In the long term, it facilitates your ability to enable patients to achieve their therapeutic goals.

Returning to the Persian proverb, the middle phase arises when you get to meat of the nut: the patient's stated reason for seeking treatment now. You may be wondering at this point whether my analogy is appropriate. After all, the word *nut* has another meaning: crazy. When you call someone a nut, or a nutcase, you are questioning their sanity. Many patients with whom you will meet for the first time will feel crazy. As a matter of fact, it is not unusual for a patient to say in the first session:

- "I feel like I am going crazy."
- "I've never done this before and I can't believe I'm here now. I feel like a nutcase."
- "This is crazy. I never thought that I would be here again with someone like you."

Even when patients do feel sane and recognize that it is healthy to seek assistance, they may be self-conscious. They may be concerned about what you and others think of them. Indeed, they may be eager to hear your perceptions as a professional in the mental health field. For example, don't be surprised if a patient asks you directly:

- "Just talking to you, I feel crazy. Am I going out of my mind?"
- "What do you think? Am I crazy or something? Do I really belong here?"
- "I don't understand how I ended up talking to you. Do you think I'm crazy?"

I cannot tell you the "correct" answer to questions such as these. I can tell you that a patient who fears being crazy is in a great deal of distress. The nature, intensity, and duration of every patient's distress will vary. Consequently, each patient's inquiry regarding his or her "craziness" may merit a different response.

Although I do not believe there is a correct response to questions such as these, I do believe that there is an insufficient response; namely, "Don't worry, you're fine." It is insufficient for several reasons, three of which are noteworthy. First, it negates patients' experiences to tell them that they are fine when they do not feel fine. By negating patients' experiences, albeit unpleasant ones, you may make them feel more unstable—wary of their own thoughts, feelings, and judgments. This is inherently countertherapeutic. Second, sometimes patients actually are disturbed. They have something genuine about which to be concerned. In this instance, telling a patient that he is fine may be more about assuaging your own fears of assisting a patient in distress than truly assessing her well-being. Such a response is in service of you rather than the client. Consequently, like the first response it is countertherapeutic. Third, and most importantly, by responding with a quick "don't worry, you're fine" you learn nothing about the nature of a patient's current distress. Your reply, essentially, forecloses further communication.

The middle phase is about communication and understanding. Indeed, it may be helpful to conceptualize your role in the middle phase as understanding how and why the patient feels crazy at this time. Your goal is to enable them to share with you what they view as the nature of their "craziness." This is "the meat of the nut" in the Persian proverb. Bear in mind that each clinician may approach the same patient differently. In this instance, when a patient asks you directly if you think they are crazy you might say:

- "A lot of people come here feeling crazy. I am here to learn more about what you consider crazy. Together we will try to figure it out."
- "I am not surprised that you feel crazy given all that you have gone through. To be of assistance, I need to know more about what is making you feel crazy."
- "You wonder whether you are going crazy. Well, a lot of people who come here do. I am here to try to understand so that the team I work with here can help you."

The preceding example of a patient who worries about being crazy illustrates how the middle phase of the initial contact may flow naturally out of a patient's spontaneous dialogue. Alternatively, the middle phase may begin once you ask the prototypical opening question: "Tell me what brought you to seek counseling (or therapy or help) at this time." (Sommers-Flanagan and Sommers-Flanagan, 1999). An opening question, such this one, encourages the patient to begin talking while the clinician observes and listens attentively. Essentially, the clinician is gathering information about why the patient is here now.

The nature of the information clinicians gather in the first interview is referred to in clinical jargon as "the signs or symptoms of the presenting problem." It is also referred to as the *content* of the session. Clinicians gather information in different ways. How they do this, or what transpires between the patient and the clinician, is referred to as the *process* of the session. A clinician's theoretical orientation tends to guide both the content and the process of the first interview. In so doing, it is the foundation of a clinician's work.

This chapter begins with a discussion of how different theoretical orientations may guide a clinician's attitude in the first interview. Although I eschew theory, I specifically advocate a nondirective, biopsychosocial approach in the middle phase. Succeeding sections of this chapter distinguish between the content and process of the clinician's work at this phase of the first interview. This chapter is deceptively complex. It may help to return to the notion of "the arc" of the first session: it starts from the beginning phase, reaches a central point, and comes to closure at the end phase. You embark on your ascent up the arc in the middle phase of the first session. To ascend successfully, you must start from a firm foundation.

The Foundation: Two Approaches to the Middle Phase

In the middle phase of the first session you explore the patient's current reasons for meeting with you. A clinician's theoretical orientation, in part, dictates how this exploration takes place. According to Murphy and Dillon (2003), one's theoretical orientation provides "a framework for understanding and interpreting the client's story" (p. 5).

To illustrate, let's reconsider the case of the patient who is concerned about being crazy. There are numerous ways you could conceptualize the patient's struggle, depending on your orientation. For example, you may consider it an expression of the patient's learned helplessness. Alternatively, you may view it as a representation of the patient's unresolved dependence issues. Then again, you may regard it as the patient's assumption of the "sick role" in his or her family of origin. Why does your conceptualization of the patient's problem matter? It matters insofar as it influences how you work with the patient. For instance, one clinician may choose to actively question and direct the patient throughout the session. Another clinician, operating from a different approach, may prefer to let the patient speak freely. Still other clinicians may focus on the system (e.g., family or school) of which the patient is a part. They would explore group functioning rather than focus on the individual sitting before them.

This example illustrates how there are many ways of working with patients—even when there is only one presenting problem. These different ways of working with patients are termed *theoretical orientations*. Indeed, according to Ivey and colleagues (2002), more than 250 theories of change exist. It is impossible to describe the full array of theoretical orientations that exist, let alone discuss their implications for the first interview. Rather than provide you with a superficial list of distinctions, I encourage you to take advantage of the many resources you have at hand to understand the differences among theories, particularly as they apply to the population with whom you will be working. Talk to your supervisors about their theoretical orientation toward counseling patients. Ask your supervisors to recommend a book or two that would help ground you not only in their way of working but in ways of working in general with the population at your site. I also encourage you to inquire among your peers about their site experiences and the theoretical orientations to which they are being exposed. For instance, if you are working in a nursing home with depressed older persons it would be helpful to compare notes with your peers training in similar situations. In addition, a good book about theories of psychology is indispensable. Have it on hand and use it as a reference when you need it. Last, but not least, the Internet is an invaluable resource. It may be readily used (via reputable site resources) to obtain information about different ways of working with different patient populations and diagnoses.

Adherence to a given theoretical orientation is helpful insofar as it expands your perspective; it allows you to "appreciate the patient as alive, real, dynamic, and unique" (Gruba-McCallister, 1989, p. 30). The theoretical orientation to which you adhere is invaluable for another reason: it enables you to establish your professional identity. For example, adhering to a single approach permits you to say with certainty "I am a psychoanalyst," "I am a cognitive-behavioralist," "I am a gestalt therapist," and so on. In so doing, it may also provide you with confidence, which is invaluable at this stage in your professional development.

Nonetheless, I encourage you to resist the pressure to adopt a given theoretical orientation in the middle phase of the first session. In this regard, I share Murphy and Dillon's (2003) concern that "a rigid adherence to theory may impede the flexibility necessary to work with clients and their stories and may limit the imagination out of which new theories may evolve" (p. 5). Strive to maintain your curiosity and imagination. Allow patients' stories of their struggles to emerge naturally as you solidify the clinician-patient relationship in the middle phase.

Likewise, I encourage you to be open to different ways of working at this point in your professional development. I say this because chances are you are about to become the proverbial "fish in water." You are about to be immersed in a way of working to which your supervisors and coworkers also adhere. If you are immersed in this water long enough, you will simply swim along and cease to notice that it is there. You run the risk of becoming unaware of your options; that is, you may forget that there are other ways of working in the service of your patients. At this point, you may be wondering, "So what if find a way of working that suits me?" Well, truth be told, it is fine to adopt a specific theoretical orientation. The problem is that your way of working may not suit all of your patients. What will happen at your site if your patients don't respond to your theoretical orientation? (And, trust me, there will be patients who will not respond in a discernible way to your way of working.) At best, these patients may be seen as hopeless or intractable cases. At worst, these patients will be labeled as resistant and uncooperative. You and your co-workers may blame them for not getting better. Regardless of the reason, if you recognize only one theoretical approach to treatment it is likely that some patients will remain untreated. This would be a grave mistake.

There is no silver bullet in the field of mental health. No one theoretical orientation is better than another; rather, a given theoretical orientation may be more appropriate for some patients, diagnoses, and stages of change than others. Exposure to different theories at this stage in your professional development will allow you to identify treatments that suit both you and your patients. Complicating matters further (or making them more interesting, depending on your point of view) is the fact that patients may have more than one presenting problem. As a consequence, patients may benefit from *more than one* theoretical approach. They may benefit from multiple modes of treatment as well, such as individual, group, and/or family therapy. For example, a combination of cognitive-behavioral individual therapy and dynamic couples' counseling may be advisable for a patient who is anxious about leaving the house alone and is experiencing marital discord.

In addition to its direct effect on patients, familiarity with multiple theoretical orientations can help you coordinate care with your peers. Often the patients with whom you will work at your training site will work with not only you but with other professionals in the mental health field. There may be a team composed of social workers, physicians, physical therapists, and vocational counselors assigned to your patient's case. It is not enough to simply maintain contact with the other professionals on your patient's team. It is also vital to understand how others on the team are approaching the needs of the patient who is sitting before you. For example, you may be a social worker with a behavioral orientation, but you need to understand the basic tenets of the medical model in order to synchronize care with your patients' psychiatrist. In this case, part of your work with patients may be to ensure that they are taking their medication as prescribed. Understanding the psychiatrist's theoretical orientation and being able to discuss it with the patient will facilitate the patient's treatment. Indeed, it may be crucial for success.

Nondirective Approach

Although I do not advocate adherence to a given theoretical orientation at this stage in your training, I do advocate a specific approach in the first session. The approach I support is *nondirective*. In the psychological literature, one way of distinguishing among theoretical orientations has been to categorize them as either directive or nondirective. Directive orientations (e.g., cognitive-behavioral) envisage an active, expert clinician who leads patients to examine specific thoughts, feelings, and behaviors. Directive clinicians typically ask precise questions, that require either a simple "yes" or "no" response or one that is brief. In contrast, nondirective orientations (e.g., psychodynamic and person-centered) envisage a clinician whose role is to listen empathetically as well as reflect thoughts and feelings. Nondirective clinicians typically allow patients to talk freely, in an uninterrupted fashion, about topics of their choice.

There are three straightforward reasons I advocate a nondirective approach in the initial session. First, and foremost, a nondirective approach complies with the "Do no harm" philosophy to which many mental health professionals adhere. In my experience, new clinicians often underestimate the influence they have on their patients. You will see many patients and hear many stories over the course of the day as a clinician-in-training. Patients will come to you in distress and share their vulnerabilities. It will become a part of your routine to hear the intimate experiences of strangers. It is easy to become inured to this experience. However, I encourage you to remember the patient's perspective: although you may see many patients throughout the day, a given patient will see only you. As Yalom says, "The therapist has many patients; the patient, one therapist" (2002a, p. 44). The initial contact between you and your patients, as a result, is likely to be of significance to your patients in a way that it is not to you. Consequently, I encourage you to approach the initial interview with particular care and sensitivity. You may not be able to help every patient you see, but you have a professional responsibility not to make matters worse. You are obliged to do no harm. And I believe it is difficult to harm your patient by practicing the active attending and empathic listening skills a nondirective approach entails.

The second reason I advocate a nondirective approach in the initial interview is that it facilitates rapport. The rapport between a patient and a clinician refers to the quality of the clinical relationship. A good relationship entails warmth, empathy, and respect. Why does rapport matter in the first interview? Fundamentally, it matters because with good rapport a clinician is likely to obtain good information; that is, meaningful detail about a patient's current concerns. Obtaining good information is especially important in the middle phase of the first interview, when your goal is to elicit patients' stories as well as their candid understanding of why they are meeting with you now.

Third, and finally, I am a proponent of a nondirective approach because it affords the clinician flexibility. Recall that a directive approach entails an active clinician who asks precise question that require a simple response such as *yes* or *no*. In contrast, a nondirective approach entails a clinician's whose role is to listen empathetically as well as reflect thoughts and feelings. Nondirective clinicians encourage patients to talk freely and openly. When you begin with a directive approach, you foreclose your options: it is difficult to become less directive in the future. After all, patients readily become used to answering direct questions. If you suddenly switch from a directive to a nondirective format, patients sometimes feel at a loss for words. You are suddenly asking them to engage in unguided, open disclosure. Such a sudden shift may cause anxiety, and patients may become self-conscious. Until then, covertly patients may have received the message that the spontaneous expression of their thoughts and feelings is not what the clinician wants or needs to hear. And nothing could be further from the truth. When you begin with a nondirective approach, however, you keep your options open. You can become more directive in the future. Think of it as shifting gears in a car. It is one thing to go from first gear to third and slow down; it is another to go from third to first and speed up unexpectedly.

In the middle phase of the first interview you want to explore the patient's current reasons for meeting with you now. It is my belief that adopting a nondirective approach facilitates this exploration. It hastens rapport, and it is flexible. Perhaps most importantly, it complies with the "Do no harm" philosophy to which many mental health professionals adhere. This not to say that a nondirective approach is universally applicable: indeed, I encourage you to modify this approach as you become more experienced as a clinician. Nonetheless, I believe it is a good place to begin.

Biopsychosocial Approach

The biopsychosocial approach examines the patient's concerns in context. In the middle phase of the first interview, I recommend adopting not only a nondirective but biopsychosocial approach to working with patients. The biopsychosocial approach grew out of the realization that people's struggles are multifaceted; they occur on several levels. Biological, psychological, and sociocultural factors all may play a vital role in the etiology, maintenance, and resolution of a patient's current concerns. As a consequence, it is incumbent upon clinicians to examine both the intrapersonal (within the person) and interpersonal (between people) forces that contribute to the patient's reason for coming to therapy.

In contrast to the biopsychosocial approach, traditional psychological approaches emphasize the individual. Exploration focuses on the patient's intrapersonal functioning. This emphasis reflects the cultural values in which these psychological approaches were developed; namely, Western cultural values in which individualism and self-reliance are held in high esteem. As a consequence, clinical trainees historically have been taught to assess patients on an individual level. They have learned to attend to either the biological (chemical imbalance, genetic influences) or psychological (use of defense mechanisms, cognitive style, and behavioral response set) aspects of a patient's functioning. Indeed, mental health care providers are rarely trained to focus on both aspects at once; that is, the biological *and* psychological. Typically, it has been an either or proposition, as exemplified by a growing division of labor between psychiatrists who provide medication management and counselors who provide therapeutic services. Likewise, with the exception of the social work tradition there has been a tendency to overlook the sociocultural aspects of a patient's functioning. This lies in stark contrast to those cultures outside the West where the mental health field in its current form does not exist. In these cultures, the contribution of spiritual and interpersonal forces to an individual's struggles has long been valued.

Consider the case of a patient who meets with you and says, "I don't know what is wrong with me, I just feel blah." You explore further and discover that he sleeps an excessive amount each day, his appetite is minimal, and he has difficulty concentrating. He also acknowledges that he generally "feels down" most of the day. A biopsychosocial approach dictates that you look at his experience on the biological level and take into account how his physical health may contribute to his symptoms. Could he be suffering from hypothyroidism? Does he consume alcohol daily? Did he suffer a heart attack recently? If, indeed, the answers to any or all of these questions were affirmative, it is likely that the patient's physical problems would need to be addressed in order for him to feel better psychologically. Psychological intervention alone may not be enough to alleviate his depressed mood.

Even in this example, where the patient's apparent psychological difficulties have clear biological correlates, a biopsychosocial approach suggests that it would be a mistake to evaluate this patient exclusively on a biological level. The psychological level also requires attention. For instance, does the patient demonstrate rigid thinking or inflexible behavior patterns? Does he primarily rely on denial as a defense mechanism? Answering "yes" to either of these questions suggests that the patient would benefit from psychological intervention. Such intervention might facilitate the patient's adherence to his medication regimen for his thyroid condition, support his sobriety goals, or enable him to implement a new dietary plan following his heart attack. Indeed, recognizing how the psychological and biological interact may be invaluable to his treatment.

And the exploration does not end here. The biopsychosocial approach also dictates that you look at the patient's experience on the sociocultural level. How does the patient's sociocultural world influence his symptoms? Is he enduring incidents of discrimination in the workplace? Has his youngest child just moved out of the family home? Is he in an unhappy relationship? Has he recently experienced a crisis in religious faith? All of these factors may be significant and contribute to his reason for seeking treatment now. Most likely, to focus on one factor in isolation would be a mistake. It would not alleviate his symptoms of depression.

Clinicians who are culturally conscious recognize that there are sociocultural influences beyond the individual that expand, as well as limit, their patients' abilities to cope. I contend that it would be a grave omission to overlook the effect of these influences upon patients. According to Sue and Sue (2003), notable sociocultural forces include:

- The family (history, current influence)
- Stress of modern society (unemployment, poverty, adapting to technological change)
- Experiences of oppression (prejudice, discrimination, stereotyping)
- Effects of natural disasters (earthquakes, floods, hurricanes)
- Human conflict (war)

Increasingly it is recognized that clinicians need to view each patient from a variety of perspectives and in a culturally responsive manner. Most professional codes of ethics in the mental health field now dictate such responsiveness. It is my belief that attending to social, cultural, and environmental influences (factors in patients' environments) facilitates cultural responsiveness. As a consequence, I advocate a biopsychosocial approach in the middle phase.

The Middle Phase Begins

How does the middle phase begin? There is no clear line of demarcation in a real counseling session between the beginning and middle phases of the first interview. The transition between them may happen gradually or it may occur suddenly. Regardless of how it occurs, *the middle phase begins in earnest when patients start to discuss why they are currently seeking assistance.*

Content

The *content* of a session refers to what is said or the information exchanged between a patient and a clinician. The primary content of the middle phase concerns the patient's understanding of the presenting problem and its symptoms. One way to usher in this phase is with the opening question or statement.

The Opening Question or Statement

The opening question or statement marks the official moment you find out why the client is in your office *now*. Sommers-Flanagan and Sommers-Flanagan (1999) suggest the following prototype for the opening statement:

- "Tell me what brought you to seek counseling (or therapy or help) at this time."

Sommers-Flanagan and Sommers-Flanagan identify several key elements in this opening statement; namely:

1. *Verifying* that patients are indeed there for counseling
2. Getting *patients* to do the talking
3. Obtaining *specific* information about the reason patients are seeking services
4. Directing patients to disclose the precipitating events that led them to see counseling *now*—rather than last week or last year

This prototypical opening statement may not feel quite right to you. Over time, you will develop your own way of inquiring into the patient's current concerns. In the interim, I encourage you to bear in mind these key elements. For example, the following are a few other opening questions or statements you might use in the first interview.

- Welcome. What brings you here today?
- How can I be of help to you now?
- Tell me what brought you in to the clinic today.
- So, what current concern has led you to my office?

It is possible that none of these opening questions feels right to you either. That is okay. Nonetheless, I encourage you to have in mind an opening question or statement *before* the initial interview gets underway, particularly while you are in training. This is your time to figure out what feels comfortable to you. Knowing in advance how you will proceed in the first interview will facilitate your training as well as your work with patients.

Regardless of the opening question or statement you choose, I urge you to bear in mind: *It not just what you say, it is how you say it.* This aphorism relates to the notion of *process*; namely, how information is exchanged between the clinician and patient. (Process is discussed in further detail in the next section.) I encourage you to be mindful of your intonation, facial expressions, and general self-presentation as the interview unfolds. Consider the verbal and nonverbal cues you are sending as you encourage your patient's self-revelation (review Chapter 4). In so doing, remember your goal: to encourage patients to talk candidly about why they are currently seeking help. It has been most effective, in my experience, to deliver the opening question in a calm, matter-of-fact manner. To this end, I encourage you to practice saying various openings aloud. Go ahead and literally role-play with friends or peers. Moreover, I recommend that you role-play the parts of *both* the patient and the clinician. When you are a patient, consider how you would feel hearing each of these statements or questions. Likewise, when you are clinician, think about what it is like to make such inquiries. Let these experiences inform your work with patients in the middle phase.

There also may be times when you will have information about patients before you meet with them for the first time. This information may come from intake interviews or agency information related to a patient's previous treatment. In addition, you may receive data about patients as a part of a referral procedure. This data is important because of not only what it tells you about the patient but how it influences your assumptions regarding a patient's current need for treatment. Be aware of your assumptions when you meet with the patient and cognizant of how they may inform your behavior as a clinician. Indeed, it may be appropriate to acknowledge what you know and how you know it when you meet with the patient for the first time.

- "I see your primary care physician referred you. She seems to think that your difficulty sleeping may be related to how you've been feeling lately. Tell me what you think."
- "I was told by the medical clinic that you have terrible back pain. They sense that something else may be going on beside a physical problem. What is *your* sense?"
- "I understand that you were at the agency before working with a counselor on parenting issues. At present, how are you with these issues?"

These examples illustrate how you may convey to patients any prior knowledge you have about them. In so doing, you are also checking your assumptions, or hypotheses, about their need for treatment. As a consequence, these examples illustrate another way for you to find out why the patient is sitting before you now without formally issuing any opening question or statement. You may not be able to be as subtle in other instances. An opening question or statement may be necessary. Regardless, you have effectively ushered in the middle phase of the first interview: you have discovered what brought the patient to seek help at this time.

Eliciting the Patient's Understanding of the Presenting Problem

Once the middle phase has begun, your goal is to elicit the patient's understanding of his or her presenting problem. *Your role at this point is to listen and observe.* I recommend that you allow the patient to speak freely, without interruption, as long as the information shared appears relevant and significant. Some patients will be expressive and talk at length. Others may not. Occasionally, a patient will respond with:

- "Where should I begin?"
- "What do you want me to say?"
- "What would you like me to talk about?"

In these instances, patients are asking for more structure and direction. There are several ways you may respond. You may pause, allow for a moment of silence, and observe how well the patient is able to organize his or her own thoughts. Additionally, you might say:

- "Why don't you begin by telling me how things have been going for you today?"
- "Feel free to say whatever is on your mind."
- "Talk about what brought you here today. It may feel awkward to talk at first, but over time it will get easier."

Usually such responses on the part of the clinician are sufficient to get the patient talking. Once the patient has begun to talk, your task of listening and observing is now underway. You are obtaining critical content: the patient's understanding of his or her problem.

Note two general points as you elicit this information. *First,* listen for what the patient expects to get out of treatment—and from you. On the one hand, how much does the patient want to defuse an external situation, such as a spouse's discontent, an employer's concern, or a legal problem? On the other hand, how much is the patient concerned about an internal issue, such as anger management or raising one's self-esteem? *Second,* take notice of the patient's motivation for seeking treatment. This is often revealed by identifying the situation or circumstances that brought the patient in for help today (versus last week or last year). Often, you will discover that patients come in with problems they have had for a long time. In order to be of greater assistance to them, it is helpful to know how their current circumstances have changed. Pay attention to what a patient says is different now at work, at home, or among friends.

Thus far, I have operated under the assumption that the reasons patients tell you they are there for therapy are the *real* reasons they are there. Note that I italicize the word *real.* I do this to highlight that a patient's presenting problem, or stated reason for coming for treatment, may not be why he or she is actually sitting before you. The patient's presenting problem may be masking something else, and the clinician may feel that this something else is the genuine reason for seeking treatment. Consider a client who says:

- "My wife is going to leave me and I'm desperate" (the patient subsequently admits to sexual compulsivity).
- "I am worried about being evicted from my apartment" (the patient later acknowledges having previously received a diagnosis of paranoid schizophrenia).
- "I feel depressed" (the patient meets the criteria for drug dependence).

These examples are intended to illustrate how patients may not be the most reliable reporters of their situation: there may be things they do not yet know about themselves or do not want you to know about them yet. Bear this in mind when you initially ask them what brought them to seek counseling now. You may have a different perspective regarding what they identify as their real reason for seeking treatment. Some patients may be fooling themselves (i.e., may be in denial). Others may be exhibiting sociopathic tendencies (they routinely either evade responsibility or are indifferent to the feelings of others). Regardless, in the first interview I recommend that you respect a patient's understanding of his or her presenting problem. Do not challenge it initially. However, in so doing I urge you to remain curious. Do not to loose sight of alternative explanations for a patient's current struggles.

Many of you may be realizing that what started out as simple "Tell me what brought you here now" has become more complex. And this is true. If you are having this realization, you are right on track in terms of your professional growth. Luckily, there is an approach that will simplify your investigation into the patient's presenting problem; specifically, to inquire further about the specific symptoms of the presenting problem.

Symptoms of the Presenting Problem

In this section, I provide one approach to conceptualizing and inquiring about a patient's symptoms. This approach may vary from what your supervisor or site dictates. For instance, some sites routinely use questionnaires such as Derogatis' Symptom Checklist (Derogatis, 1977) to identify patients' symptoms. As a consequence, I encourage you to ask your supervisor how he or she proceeds in the first interview to gather information about symptoms.

Be aware that there may be specific information about symptoms that are unique to your site. In this instance, it is invaluable to know the nature of the population with whom you will be working. For example, if you will be working with patients who have eating disorders you will need to know how to inquire thoroughly about the physical, cognitive, social, and psychological symptoms specifically associated with eating disorders. In contrast, if you are going to be working in the psychiatric ward of a large hospital you would do well to familiarize yourself with the symptoms associated with the presence of various severe psychopathologies.

There is another issue to bear in mind when inquiring about a patient's symptoms: what information will other staff members who are working with the patient need to know after the first interview? When I worked as a counselor in an inpatient substance abuse treatment program, patients were admitted around the clock, twenty-four hours a day. The first interview was held whether they arrived at midnight or three in the afternoon. I vividly remember hearing the morning report on my first day of work. The nighttime staff was changing to the daytime staff. Everyone gathered around as the patient roster was read aloud. As a patient's name was read, anyone who worked with the patient provided an update regarding the patient's status. If a patient was newly admitted, the counselor who had conducted the first interview was expected to know in detail symptoms of the patient's current and past social functioning. Why? Out-placement counselors worked from the day of admission to find the appropriate aftercare for each patient. Finding the appropriate aftercare was often an arduous and difficult process. There were time deadlines to meet. After all, every patient stayed for only twenty-eight days—no more and no less. Under these circumstances, it was invaluable to know how the patient functioned on a daily basis from the first interview.

At this point, you may be wondering: *What is a symptom?* According to Morrison (1995), "a symptom is any subjective sensation that makes the patient think something is wrong" (p. 38). It is essentially a sign or indicator of what is amiss in a patient's life. A patient's pattern of symptoms provides a snapshot in time of his or her presenting problem. Notably, it is a snapshot you can put into words in order to constructively communicate with others, such as your supervisor and the patient's treatment team.

Information about symptoms comes from three sources: self-report, clinical observation, and historical data. Self-report refers to what the patient *directly tells you* in the interview. Clinical observations are what *you see* in the interview; they are your perceptions of the patient's behavior, affect, and style of interacting with you. Historical data includes information from prior intake interviews, records from a patient's previous treatment, and data from referral sources. It also may include information from friends or relatives who accompany the patient to the first interview. Sometimes no historical information is available. However, self-report and clinical observation are always on hand. Taken together, they form the backbone of the first interview.

Determining the dimensions of a patient's presenting problem requires characterizing symptoms fully. Once you have identified a symptom, such as anxiety, you need to examine it in depth. Bear in mind that typically more than one symptom is present. For each symptom, you will need to inquire about the following domains.

Severity	The gravity of a symptom (e.g., mild, moderate, severe or unknown).
Duration	How long a single episode of a given symptom lasts (e.g., minutes, hours, days, or weeks).
Frequency	How often a single episode occurs (e.g., five times a day, once a week, or once a year).
Antecedents	The cues or precursors to a given symptom.
Consequences	The result, or typical outcome, of a symptom occurrence.
Chronology	Not only what a given symptom is now but how old the patient was when it first began. Note the development of the symptom and how it has changed over time in terms of severity, duration, and frequency.
Attributions	What the patient believes causes the symptom.
Coping	How the patient handles the symptom when it occurs.

This may seem like a long list to remember, but eventually it will become second nature to you. What follows is a flexible list of questions you may use to investigate each symptom domain. In general, I recommend that you begin with open-ended questions. This permits patients to offer any additional information they deem relevant. It also allows you to follow up with a second or third question related to their responses. Over time, you will develop your own style of inquiring about symptoms. In the meantime, the following are sample questions.

Severity	• How intense is it? • Would you consider it mild, moderate, or severe? • Is it always the same or does it vary?
Duration	• How long does it usually last?
Frequency	• How often does this occur? • Is it always present or does it come and go?
Antecedents	• Have you noticed any events that tend to come before the symptom? • What usually leads to it happening? (Explore thoughts and feelings.) • Is there a person or situation you associate with this symptom? • Does it happen only at night or during the day? • Does it only occur when you are alone? (Note: cues or controlling stimuli may include many factors, such as activities, time of day, or social context.)
Consequences	• What usually happens afterward? • How do you feel soon after? • What do you image or what thoughts run through your mind later?
Chronology	• When did the symptom first happen? • Was there ever a time when the symptom was completely absent? • If I were to ask you to rate the symptom on a scale of 1 to 10, with 1 being mild and 10 being intolerable, how would you rate it today? • How would you rate it on your worst day? • When was your worst day? • Has it ever been so distressing you have wanted to die?
Coping	• How do you usually handle this symptom when it occurs? • What helps the most? • Is there any person who helps you get through it?

An additional technique that may be used to inquire about symptoms is to ask the patient to walk through a recent episode in detail. In keeping with the biopsychosocial approach, the following questions can be used to guide this exploration.

Psychological	• What were you doing when it occurred? (behavioral)
	• What thoughts or images entered your mind? (cognitive)
	• What was your mood like at the time? (affective)
Biological	• What did you feel in your body when this symptom occurred?
	• Where do you feel it in your body?
	• What medications, alcohol, or drugs had you recently used?
Social	• Who were you with when the symptom occurred?
	• What does your family think about this symptom?
	• How is this symptom viewed in your culture?

To summarize, a symptom is information: it is a sign or indicator that something is amiss in a patient's life. A patient's pattern of symptoms provides a picture of his or her presenting problem. More importantly, it provides information you can communicate to others who are there to help the patient, such as your supervisor and the patient's treatment team. This section, thus far, has reviewed the content of the middle phase: the opening question or statement, the patient's presenting problem, and symptom characterization. The remainder of this chapter discusses how to gather this content, what is also referred to as the *process* of the session.

Process

The first time you meet with a client, *how* you obtain information is as important, if not more important, than the information you obtain. In the middle phase, you are climbing up the arc of the first session and reaching its center. As you bring the middle phase to a close, you will begin the descent to the end phase of the interview. *Throughout, process is primary*. Nonetheless, it is not uncommon for a clinician-in-training to get led astray in the middle phase. Many trainees worry: "I didn't get all the information I should have." The concern here is misplaced. It is easy to confuse gathering a lot of information with a good session, but the last thing you want is for patients to feel like they are being mined for information, or "interrogated." You want them to feel accepted and understood. And, most of the time, you want them to either return for another session or follow up on your referral.

The middle phase of the first interview is built upon the groundwork you laid in the beginning phase. Introductions have been made, confidentiality has been addressed, consent has been obtained, and expectations have been clarified. Most importantly, you have established rapport. Patients may not know how to make the transition when the time comes to move into the middle phase. This is predictable. In the end, it is not their responsibility to make this transition: it is yours. As Heaton (1998) observes: "If we sit and stare expectantly, our clients can't possibly know what we want" (p. 72). It is your role to clarify what you want in the middle phase; in other words, *to provide structure.*

Clinicians structure a session in many ways; for example, by the questions they ask and the comments to which they respond. Essentially, structure refers to how the clinician—together with the patient—guides the interview. Providing structure has many advantages. One advantage is that it directly communicates your expectations to the patient. And you are more likely to get your expectations met when you communicate them directly. In the middle phase, you expect to clarify in detail why the patient is here now. Providing structure in the middle phase entails establishing this expectation at the outset. It also entails consistently following through with its pursuit and not being led astray into other aspects of the patient's life at this point in the interview. Another advantage of structure is that patients know what to anticipate when structure is in place. In so doing, structure reduces a patient's anxiety. This may be its greatest benefit. Less anxious patients, after all, tend to be more forthcoming with information. Moreover, one could speculate that the information provided is likely to be more accurate and of greater use to the clinician when the patient feels at ease.

Overall, I liken the process of structuring a session to the task of trying to hold as much sand as possible in one's hand. Grip the sand too tightly and you will loose most of it. Grasp it too loosely and much of the sand will slip through. The trick is to hold your hand just so, neither too rigidly nor too loosely, to contain the most sand. Likewise, in the middle phase you want the patient to feel "contained," or safe. You want to provide just enough structure to get the information you need to be of assistance without making the patient anxious and slip away, never to return.

Structure is a multifaceted concept. The most basic notion of structure may be Robert Langs' (1973) concept of "the therapeutic frame," or what Nancy McWilliams (1999) has referred to as "the establishment of the consistent conditions of therapy." Here, structure includes decisions about the time, day, and frequency of treatment, as well as the boundaries of the therapeutic relationship itself, such as "Are we friends?" This concept applies across multiple sessions with the same client. In contrast, within the middle phase of the first interview structure refers to how the clinician guides the interview. The clinician provides structure by *communicating* in a straightforward, clear fashion. The clinician also provides structure by *behaving* consistently rather than erratically or unpredictably. Structuring a session involves three basic elements: (1) pacing, (2) making transitions from one topic to another, and (3) monitoring the depth of a session.

Pacing

The pace of a session is its rhythm. It is the tempo established between the rate of the clinician's inquiry and the rate of the patient's response. The pace may range from fast to slow, and it may vary over the course of the interview. Important issues need to be given sufficient time; they may warrant a slower pace and more time. In contrast, insignificant issues should not be dwelled upon; they may warrant a faster pace and less time. Be aware of the pace of a session, regardless of the pace you establish with the patient. In particular, note the extent to which a patient wishes to move quickly or slowly over a topic; this may indicate a great deal about its meaning to the patient.

A cliché exists in the field of mental health; namely, that of the patient and clinician sitting together in silence. I liken this to the people who hold the sand too loosely in their hands such that much of it ends up slipping through their fingers. In this scenario, the therapist patiently waits for the patient to speak. The session's rhythm is brought to a halt and an ambiguous situation is created. The patient may wonder: "What am I to do now? What does the clinician expect?" In this case, the patient may begin to feel anxious. Some clinicians want to create this anxiety and observe how the patient reacts to it. In the middle phase, however, I do not recommend this approach. I think it is risky. The risk you run is that the client will not return for the help they need. Remember: your goal at this point is to encourage the patient to share his or her story with you. Mind you, there may be some patients for whom silence is reassuring. My sense, though, is that for the majority of new patients silence is not reassuring. Indeed, it may leave the patient feeling quietly judged. This, I believe, it is too great a chance to take. As a result, I encourage you to be judicious in the middle phase regarding your use of silence. Unless you sense it is comforting to your patient, keep the pace of the session going in the middle phase.

In contrast to the stereotype of the silent clinician, there is the clinician as drill sergeant. This is the clinician who sits with a list of questions, firing away. I liken this scenario to the person who grips the sand too tightly and causes much of it to slip away. This approach overlooks the fact that clinicians provide structure not only by asking questions but by selecting the comments to which they respond. Moreover, this approach leaves little room to react to how the patient is feeling. In so doing, it prevents you from truly understanding why the patient has come for treatment now—which is the purpose of the middle phase.

The example of the clinician as drill sergeant highlights another facet of pacing: timing. Timing refers to aptly following up on patient's replies or appropriately introducing new areas of exploration with the patient. At a basic level, effective clinicians follow up a patient's statements with questions that are relevant to the topic under discussion. At an advanced level, effective clinicians follow up a patient's statements with questions that are responsive to the patient's *emotional state*. In other words, a clinician will attend with equal vigor to a patient's words and *feelings*. For example:

- "Ms. Thompkins, you are crying as you talk about Tom's difficulties. I wonder how you are feeling about it all."
- "Mike, it looks like you are frowning. Can you tell me what that is about?"
- "Despite your kind words, Jenna, I sense some anger. I may be mistaken here, but what can you tell me about the anger?"

In each of these examples, the clinician is timing his or her response in reaction to not only the patient's words but to the patient's emotional state. It is important to attend to both when pacing sessions. By listening to what is said as well as how it is said, you will be able to guide the patient through the middle phase with sensitivity and understanding—and at a pace that is comfortable to the client.

Making Transitions

You need to be able to make transitions as well as control the pace of the interview in order to provide adequate structure. There is a lot of information about different topics to be covered in the middle phase. *Transitions are how you move from one topic to another*, such as how you move from exploring patients' relationships to their families to their difficulties at work. They enable you to climb up the arc of the initial interview and move toward closure. Transitions can occur in various ways. Sometimes they are initiated by the clinician and sometimes they are initiated by the patient. They may be smooth or somewhat awkward. Over time, as you become accustomed to making transitions, they will feel more natural. In the meantime, it is useful to be aware of how to make transitions.

There are many ways to think about transitions. Shea (1998) identifies five types of transitions, or "gates," in a clinical interview.

1. *Spontaneous:* Smooth transition. Patient initiated. Patient raises new topic and clinician follows up with relevant response.
   "This is the first time I've heard you mention your mother. Tell me about her."
2. *Natural:* Smooth transition. Clinician initiated. Clinician raises new topic in response to a patient's immediate cues.
   "You just mentioned feeling panicked sometimes. Can you say more about that?"
3. *Referred:* Smooth transition. Clinician initiated. Clinician raises a new topic based on a previous topic raised earlier in the interview by the patient.
   "At one point you described feeling sad. How might it be related to this situation?"
4. *Implied:* Relatively smooth transition. Clinician initiated. Clinician leaves current topic by following up with a closely related new topic.
   "You talked about relationships earlier. Who are some of your close friends?"
5. *Phantom:* Weak transition. Clinician initiated. Clinician abruptly raises a new topic.
   The patient finishes talking about work. The clinician asks: "Do you drink daily?"

Classifying transitions into types is helpful because it makes you aware of the different ways to move from one topic to another in an interview. It is also helpful because it reminds you that therapy is not a conversation. A conversation is a social interaction; this is a professional relationship. Some rules of social etiquette may apply, but others do not. There will be times when you will interrupt and redirect; in other words, make a conscious transition in the interview. Together with the patient, you are guiding the middle phase of the first interview.

For example, sometimes a patient will spontaneously initiate a new topic. In a regular conversation, you might go with the flow. This is not the case as a clinician. You will have to deliberately decide whether or not to pursue it. You may, indeed, decide to follow their lead and continue to explore the new topic. Alternatively, there will be times when this is not the case and you will need to make a transition.

- "I know you care about your son, Mr. Smith, but our time is limited. Let's focus on what brought you here today."
- "I am sorry to interrupt, but it seems likes your constant hand washing is what really bothers you. I want to understand it better before we move on."
- "Before you were talking about why you came in for treatment. I'd like to take a moment and return to that now in order to help you."

In general, it is easy for patients to fall into the trap of talking about other people or other problems aside from the one that brought them there. Knowing how to make transitions and keep the client focused is an important part of structuring the middle phase.

Monitoring the Depth of a Session: Depth Versus Breadth

Attending to how to pace a session and make transitions is invaluable in structuring the middle phase. In addition, it is essential to continually monitor the depth of your interactions with the patient. As a supervisor, I have had more than one clinician-in-training tell me: "You would not believe all the personal information this patient told me!" To me, at best these words signaled a yellow light: caution. At worst, they were a red light. I thought to myself, "It is unlikely the patient will return."

According to Arnold Lazarus (1971), each of us has layers or circles of personal domain. Miller (1996) more recently has suggested that these domains become apparent in conversation with others. In particular, Miller distinguishes between outer, middle, and inner circle talk. The outer circle is surface conversation. Typically, it consists of facts and information. Some feelings and behaviors are acknowledged. Within the outer circle is the middle circle. It moves beyond surface conversation into the deeper territory of conflicting information, feelings, and behaviors. There is some self-reflection, and relationship issues may be revealed. The deepest level is contained with the middle circle. This level is the inner circle. Within it lies the information, thoughts, feelings, and behaviors that may have been previously unknown to the patient—or known by the patient but unshared with others. As a result, inner circle knowledge may be associated with shame, fear, or embarrassment (Murphy & Dillon, 2003, p. 103).

It is the clinician's responsibility to monitor patients' movements among the three layers: outer, middle, and inner circle talk. A part of providing structure is navigating how much breadth and depth you will encourage the client to cover. I recommend that you spend most of your time in the outer circle during the first interview. Focus on the breadth of information the patient may provide: the information, feelings, and behaviors that led the patient to currently seek treatment. Some middle circle concerns will arise (such as conflicting issues); some inner circle topics may surface (such as shame and doubt). If you touch upon these issues, acknowledge them. However, they should not be your focus in the middle phase. In so doing, you are allowing your relationship with the patient to develop slowly, and you are permitting the patient to slowly but surely become comfortable with further levels of exploration.

It is not uncommon for clinicians to confuse depth, getting at that inner circle and engaging in intense self-revelation, with success. Having a cathartic moment with a patient in the first session may seem like an achievement. In reality, it is not. In effect, you are encouraging or allowing a patient to become intimate too quickly. And as Lukas (1993) points out, patients may leave your office feeling exposed and humiliated. After all, you may be a professional, but you are still a stranger. "Remember, she has a right—and you have an obligation—to protect her from a sense of premature intrusion into her private feelings, particularly since you have not assessed what effect such revelations will have on her functioning" (Lukas, 1993, p. 9).

There will be times when you will have to work against your patients' desires to "spill their guts." Note when this occurs with a patient. It is data about the patient's functioning. You may wonder, for example, do they tend to lack personal boundaries in all relationships? Nonetheless, you do not want to encourage excessive self-revelation. In response, you may say:

- "That is deeply personal. I appreciate your honesty. We can talk about it further in future sessions, if you like. For now, I think it would help to stay with the issues that brought you here today."
- "Thank you for telling me about this. But I must admit I am concerned about your sharing too much, too soon. Let's focus on why you are here now."
- "Knowing this helps me understand you. Let's go into detail in future sessions. Right now, I would like to stick to the present and what led you to seek treatment today."

Unlike patients who are eager to share, some patients will be reluctant to reveal themselves—they offer neither a depth nor breadth of information. Sometimes patients will speak in a vague or rambling fashion, and disclose only superficial details. Once again, make note when this occurs. It is data that the patient is having difficulty articulating their reason for being there. Is it a cognitive impairment? Is the patient embarrassed? Has the patient been coerced into seeking treatment (e.g., "My girlfriend really wanted me to come in.")? In these instances, you will need to be ready to provide greater guidance. You might say:

- "I know it is hard to talk about these things, but I am here to help. Maybe you could begin by telling me more about the most recent episode."
- "Sometimes people get here and they don't know what to say or where to begin. We'll figure it out together in time. When was the first time you thought about seeking counseling?"
- "It seems as if you are really struggling with this issue. Maybe it would be helpful if we got more into more detail. How would that feel?"

As you engage with the patient, remember that the purpose of the middle phase is to identify why the patient is seeking treatment now. To this end, you need to elicit the patient's understanding of his or her presenting problem. You want to gather information and clarify the patient's symptoms. You do not want patients to leave the first session thinking that treatment will require them to reveal more than they are prepared to reveal. In other words, I encourage you to explore the breadth, rather than depth, of information your patients may provide.

Summary

This chapter focused on the middle phase of the first session: the center of the arc of the initial contact has been reached. It defined the middle phase by both its content (initiating the opening question, identifying the presenting problem, and clarifying symptoms) as well as its process (pacing, making transitions, and managing the depth of the session). In addition, this chapter advocates the implementation of a nondirective, biopsychosocial approach to the first interview. In my experience, such an approach is effective because it enables patients to feel at ease and it is culturally responsive: it directs you to be curious about the multifaceted reasons a patient is seeking treatment now. In so doing, it allows you to develop a way of working, or theoretical orientation, that feels comfortable to you while you are in training.

Some Questions to Consider

1. How will you respond if a patient tells you that he feels crazy?
2. Why is a nondirective approach the best way for you to work with your client in the initial interview?
3. How does the biopsychosocial approach augment the nondirective approach?
4. How can you be "culturally conscious" in the first interview?
5. When does the middle phase begin?
6. What, exactly, does "providing structure" mean?
7. What is the danger in allowing the patient to experience a cathartic moment during the first interview?

7

The End Phase

The best way out is always through.

—Robert Frost

Chapter Goals

This chapter will help you to:

1. Bring the session to a close.
2. Manage process: facilitate termination, encourage dialogue, and convey hope.
3. Clarify content: wind down, review concerns, get feedback, and take next steps.
4. Handle closing concerns: collect payment, doorknob syndrome, and final statement.

Bringing the Session to a Close

Chapters 5 and 6 addressed the beginning and middle phases of the first session. Now we have reached the end phase: the arc of the initial contact is formally coming to a close. Just as you employed an array of strategies to smoothly shift the session from the beginning to the middle phase, so too will you employ an array of strategies to guide the client through to the conclusion. Then the arc is complete.

Take a moment to consider: How exactly do you end a session? As a clinician, it is your responsibility to actively initiate the end phase of the first interview. Nonetheless, I have seen many clinicians-in-training try to evade this responsibility. They approach the process of ending reluctantly. Quite to the contrary, I believe this process is best approached head on—with equanimity and control. I concur with Robert Frost in the quote that began this chapter. When it comes to endings: "The best way out is always through." This chapter describes how to go through the end phase and experience closure with your client. It begins with a discussion of the termination process itself, and how to help clients understand their feelings about ending the first interview. Succeeding sections deal with the content of the termination process; namely, ways to say good-bye to clients, how to schedule the next session or offer a referral, and how to collect payments if necessary.

Managing the Process of the End Phase

Chapter 6 makes a critical distinction between the content and process of the first interview. "Content" refers to the information clinicians gather during a session; "process" refers to how this information is gathered. The termination process in the first interview specifically involves what transpires between the patient and the clinician as the initial contact comes to a close. According to Shea (1998), this process essentially functions as a mini-loss to the patient. I believe it functions as a mini-loss for the clinician as well. To the extent that most people are uncomfortable with loss, how you manage the termination process matters. Now more than ever, I believe you need to carefully attend to what transpires between you and your client as the first interview ends. Remember, what you say is as important as how you say it.

Creating a Facilitative Environment for Termination

According to Craig (1989b), "Just as a surgeon after completing an operation spends the last few minutes suturing the wound, so too must a clinical interviewer spend the last few minutes of a session ensuring that there is closure. . ." (p. 16). The end phase of the first interview is like the moment you prepare to suture the wound: the injury has been exposed, and treatment (for today) must come to a close. It is time for you to secure the injury so that healing can begin. Paradoxically, it is also your responsibility to close the wound today in such a way that your patient is encouraged to open up again in the future. As you may well imagine, this can be difficult work indeed.

Compounding the difficulties of this work is the fact that clinicians are often tired at this phase of the first interview. Frequently, they also feel pressured to end the interview on time. It can be a real struggle to maintain an empathetic presence when you are not only feeling tired and pressured, but also talking about emotionally charged issues such as loss—yet that is exactly what you must do. How can you maintain an empathetic presence as the interview winds down? For all intents and purposes, you need to sustain the rapport you developed in the beginning phase of the interview. To this end, I advise you to remain attentive to your verbal and nonverbal behaviors and what they communicate to the client. Be attentive and respectful. I also encourage you to review Chapter 5 and to continue to consider how you would like "to be" with your patient.

Encouraging Dialogue: Getting Clients to Talk About Their Thoughts and Feelings

The termination of the first interview in many ways is no different than the termination of any therapy session. It raises issues around separation and loss for clients and clinicians alike. Most people are discomforted by separation and loss. In point of fact, most people find it is difficult to say good-bye at all, whether it is from a job, a vacation, or a relationship. Strong, painful emotions such as anger, resentment, and sadness are often attached to these experiences. Nonetheless, endings are important in our lives, and they are unavoidable. It is important to normalize these feelings for your clients if they express them. But first, I recommend that you take a moment and consider *how you feel* about termination and endings in general. After all, your clients will likely take their cues from you about how to behave as the session comes to a close. Take a moment and consider:

- What losses have you experienced in your life?
- How did you handle these losses? What thoughts and emotions did they arouse?
- When it comes to endings, to what extent do you tend to linger and delay the outcome?
- When are you inclined to hurry through good-byes or avoid them altogether?

Like your clients, you are human. You are going to have reactions to termination. Explore how you feel about endings in general. Consider what it will be like for you to undergo the termination process in the first interview with new patients. Do not evade your personal reactions to loss and separation. To the contrary, face your full range of thoughts and feelings. If you are aware of them, you are less likely to act on them inappropriately in sessions with your clients. I encourage you to use supervision to help you sort out your emotions and decide how you would like to be with clients during the termination process. In addition to supervision, seek out other resources: friends, peers, and colleagues at your site. And yet again, I encourage you to engage in personal therapy. Talk with your therapist about your experiences with loss and separation not only in your personal life but in your professional life in your work with clients.

To the extent you are able to be clear about your own thoughts and feelings regarding termination, you will be better able to pay attention to your clients' responses to the termination process. This will facilitate your ability to encourage your clients to talk about their experiences of the first interview coming to a close. It will also facilitate *your ability to observe* how they are experiencing termination. Do they appear detached or at ease? Has their mood worsened or improved? All of these questions concern how to gauge your clients' feeling states about termination. Just as you will have a variety of responses to termination, so too will your clients. For example, some clients become overwhelmed by their thoughts and feelings as the session comes to a close. In response, they begin to talk incessantly.

If this occurs, intervene gently, explore their concerns about terminating, and help your clients to slow down their process (see Chapter 8).

Other clients may suddenly become eager to leave as the first interview comes to a close. This eagerness may communicate their wish to avoid termination. It also may signify that they find endings or separations anxiety producing. Essentially, their behavior reveals that these experiences are touching on something painful they would like to avoid. At this point, you have a choice. You may want to take a moment to explore why they want to leave early. Alternatively, you may to do nothing and simply make a mental note that the client "hates long good-byes." Tackling that issue may remain a future goal. Regardless of the choice you make, it is clear that your clients are expressing concern and fear by avoiding the termination process. Underneath, they may be wondering if their situation will improve. Above all, they may be in need of direction. The most helpful step to take at this point in the termination process is to convey hope.

Conveying Hope

Many times clients come to therapy as a last resort. Typically, they have been struggling with issues, on their own, for some time. One of a clinician's main responsibilities as the first interview comes to a close is to offer hope. It may be as simple as saying:

- "Oliver, I know things feel hard now but I believe therapy can help."
- "Ms. Jaeckle, we've reached the end of today's session, but I think there is some good work yet to come."
- "Norma, it may take time, but given what you've said to me today I think things will get better."

The end of the interview is when clinicians need to focus on their clients' personal strengths as well as familial and social resources. Use the first interview to reinforce any positive actions your clients have undertaken. Ask your clients to describe the strengths they have used to help them get through the hard times. At the very least, tell your clients that simply by talking to you about their struggles they have revealed to you their strengths. Many view asking for help a weakness. However, it is your job to reframe asking for help as an asset. Indeed, your capacity to reframe their perception of their behavior from an asset to a strength may make all the difference in the world.

In a sense, you want to make a genuine effort to "sell therapy." To this end, Sommers-Flanagan and Sommers-Flanagan (1999) suggest saying:

> You've said very clearly that you want to feel better, and I think therapy can help you move in that direction. . . . most people who use therapy to improve their lives are successful, and I believe that you're the type of person who is very likely to get good results from this process. (p. 181)

Be aware, however, that words alone may not be enough. Be mindful of how you communicate your words of encouragement to your clients. Essentially, process matters from the beginning phase to the end phase. Your words will not have the intended effect if you say them tentatively with a pained expression on your face while looking down at your shoes. Quite to the contrary, you want to appear calm, congenial, and confident. All the while, be aware of expressing yourself in a manner that is culturally sensitive to your client's style.

Your goal is to offer clients reassurance and lessen their fears. Their fears will not be eliminated altogether, and this is not unexpected. Some fear is motivating; too much fear is paralyzing. Your purpose is to "right-size" your clients' fears: to put them into proportion with the rest of the lives and make them seem manageable. In so doing, you may not provide your clients with solutions but you will provide them with relief.

Clarifying Content in the End Phase

The information clinicians gather and provide in the first interview constitutes the content of the interview. Perhaps the most important information you as clinician can give to clients at this point is merely notifying them that the interview is coming to an end.

Winding Down: Notifying Clients That the Session Is Ending

Clinicians need to notify clients that the first interview is going to end about five to ten minutes before termination. In so doing, clinicians keep the framework of the first interview clear, and they maintain therapeutic boundaries. They also provide stability and organization to their clients' lives. For example, you may notify your clients that the session is coming to a close by saying:

- "First interviews are always hard. There's so much to cover and so little time. We have about five or ten minutes left. Let's start to bring things to an end."
- "We've covered a lot today. Unfortunately, we have about five or ten minutes left. Let's start to wind down now."
- "Thanks for being so open today. We have about ten minutes left. Regrettably, we need to start to bring things to a close."

Subsequently, you want to make it clear that there are a few points you need to cover before the session ends. The first is that you are clear about the client's concerns.

Reviewing the Client's Concerns

At the end of the first interview you want to check your understanding of why the client has come for treatment now. You want to tell the client, ideally in their own words, your understanding of what their current problems are, as well as what they believe is causing their problems. In so doing, you show the client you have been listening to them. It also enhances your credibility. Sommers-Flanagan and Sommers-Flanagan (1999) recommend simply stating (p. 181):

- "Based on what you've said today, it seems that you're here because you . . . (cite clients' own words)."

Subsequently, invite your patient's feedback of your analysis.
   After delivering the summary, ask:

- "Does this sound right to you? Tell me what you think."
- "Please tell me if I have understood you correctly."
- "How does this seem to you?"

Sometimes clients will immediately agree with you; sometimes they will not. What is most important here is that you create an atmosphere in which they feel free to share their point of view, clarify, or correct what you have said. According to Lukas (1993), "The goal here is to try and arrive at a mutual definition, in a language that seems right to the client, of what the presenting problem is" (p. 9). More importantly, "It is perfectly alright to suggest that the client return again so you can further explore and clarify what it is she would like your help with" (p. 9).

Eliciting Feedback from the Client

It is always a good idea to leave time at the end of the session to ask clients whether they have any questions for you. Essentially, you are checking in with your clients to see if their outlook is similar to your own. Many clients will not have a question for you. Nonetheless, it is worth asking. At a minimum, they may find it an empowering experience to have a clinician ask them for their feedback. For example, you may inquire:

- "I know I've been doing a lot of the questioning here. I wonder, do you have any questions for me?"
- "How has this interview gone for you? Has it been what you expected?"
- "Have I left anything out? Is there anything else you want to tell me that I may have overlooked?"
- "Now that the session is coming to a close, is there anything you want to ask me?"

Prepare Clients for the Next Step in Treatment

At this point, you may offer one of three steps with regard to treatment to your clients. One, you can schedule a second appointment with you or your agency. Two, you can offer a referral to another agency. Three, you can do nothing. In some ways, the third step is the easiest. You simply end the interview by saying something along the lines of "I need to take this information and talk to my supervisor. I will have to get back to you to discuss what your options may be." And then you arrange to be in contact with your client in the future. The other two steps, reviewed in the following, are somewhat more complicated.

Second Appointment.   There are times when you will end the first interview by offering the client a second appointment with you. In this instance, there are administrative issues and practical arrangements with which to contend. You must set a time, day, and place to meet again weekly. You will also need to clarify how long a session is and how often sessions are held. Moreover, it may be necessary to state your cancellation policy. If I take on a new client, I am likely to close the session by saying:

- "Gina, I am glad we met today. I look forward to seeing you next week on Thursday at five P.M. Please call me twenty-four hours in advance if you need to reschedule. By the way, I want you to know that in the first few sessions I tend to work differently. I tend to be a little more active and ask more questions because I want to get some information about your background, like your family and where you grew up. This will help me understand your current situation better. Over time, I will be less active and listen more. I will always want to know whatever is on your mind now."

This closing serves several purposes.

1. It communicates that I appreciated the client's effort in the interview. ["Gina I am glad we met today."]
2. It reminds the client when we will meet again. [I look forward to seeing you next week on Thursday at five P.M.]
3. It reiterates the cancellation policy. [Please call me twenty-four hours in advance if you need to reschedule.]
4. It tells the client what to expect from me in the first few sessions. [By the way, I want you to know that in the first few sessions I tend to work differently. I tend to be a little more active and ask more questions . . . .]
5. It gets the client thinking *about herself* and how her personal history contributes to her presenting problem. [. . . because I want to get some information about your background, like your family and where you grew up. This will help me understand your current situation better.]
6. It tells the client for what I expect from her in subsequent sessions. [Over time, I will be less active and listen more. However, I will always want to know whatever is on your mind now.]

This closing provides the client with structure. In my experience, this structure reduces uncertainty—which is beneficial to you and your clients. It is but one example of numerous ways to end an interview in which you plan to see the client again. Over time, you will develop your own closing in your own words.

Referral.   There will be times when you will know that you or your facility is not suited to your client's needs. In this instance, be direct with the client.

- "Ms. Kiwali, the kind of concerns that you have are not what we typically see at this center. There are places that would be a better fit for you. Let me tell you how you can find out about them."
- "Marcus, we don't usually work with learning disabilities at this clinic. You are smart to seek the appropriate treatment. Let me give you a list of places to contact."
- "I want to refer you to another program, Jeanette. They specialize in the kinds of issues you are facing now."

There are instances when you will make the call to the other agency or provider. Then again, there are instances when you will expect the client to make the call. Whatever course of action you choose, make it clear to the client that they are welcome to contact you in the future, although you may not be able to work with them in treatment. State: "I want to help you obtain the services you need, although I cannot provide them." This does not mean that you are obligated to accept them into treatment; to the contrary, it simply means that you are willing to help clients obtain care on their own behalf in the future.

Handling Last-minute Concerns

Collecting Payments

Before the first interview begins, you need to know how payments will be handled. In many agencies, new clinicians are not required to collect payments directly from the clients; rather, clients are billed through the agency. Nonetheless, in the event you are expected to collect payment, I find that the direct method is always the best method. For example, ask: "Mr. Terwilliger, the fee for today is seventy-five dollars." Then, you proceed to collect the payment in whatever form, cash or check, is acceptable to you and your agency.

Sometimes clients cannot pay or they wish to negotiate the cost of the session. In this instance, I recommend that you state you are not in a position to negotiate and refer your client to your supervisor. As a clinician-in-training, you need not take on more authority than you are able. It is particularly important to defer to others in matters of money. In the future, your supervisor or agency may grant you the authority to negotiate with clients. In the meantime, I do not recommend that you take it upon yourself. Keep your client work and concluding the first interview your priorities.

Doorknob Syndrome

The most common last-minute concern that arises following the first interview is what is commonly referred to as "the doorknob syndrome." According to the doorknob syndrome, the client stops to tell you something important just as they are just about to leave or are literally walking out the door. Fundamentally, what they are doing is telling you something disturbing at the very end of the session when there is no time either for you to do anything about it or discuss it further. In this instance, I recommend you say:

- "That sounds important. We need to talk about it some more. Next time, let's start there."
- "This is something we need to talk about further. Can we begin there next week?"
- "Next week let's begin there. That is important news you're telling me."

What is critical here is that you are communicating to clients that you have heard what they said and you care enough to address their specific concerns in the future. Moreover, you communicate to your clients that each week you will have only a limited amount of time in which to talk. It is invaluable to maintain the structure of the session. (For more on this issue, see Chapter 6.) In this spirit, do not extend the session unless the client appears to present a harm to himself or others (see Chapter 10).

Preparing Your Concluding Statement

As with the introduction, I recommend that you plan your ending in advance. In general, I am in favor of a thank-you and a handshake at the end of a first interview. I also advocate adopting a manner that is calm, congenial, and confident. My approach is to stand up, walk over to the door, and say:

- "I look forward to seeing you Tuesday at noon. Take care."
- "I hope you follow through with the referral. I wish you well."

Over time, you will develop your own style. In the meantime, I suggest that you ask your supervisor's advice and role-play different concluding statements with your peers.

Summary

In this chapter, I have described how to terminate the first interview, from managing the process of closure to attending to the many details involved in closure. It is a surprisingly complicated process given it that takes five to ten minutes. Nonetheless, it evokes a wide range of thoughts and feelings in both clinicians and clients. If you were to ask me what distinguishes the end phase of the first interview from the preceding phases, I would say it is one thing: instilling hope. According to the Buddhist philosopher Thich Nhat Hanh, "Hope is important because it can make the present moment less difficult to bear. If we believe that tomorrow will be better, we can bear a hardship today." Our clients come to us facing struggles with which they need assistance. It is our job to provide them with hope, if not with immediate assistance.

Some Questions to Consider

1. As a therapist, what strategies can you use to maintain an empathetic presence as the initial interview comes to a close?

2. What have you discovered as you explore your own feelings about separation and loss?

3. Why must you check out how the patient's sense of the session compares with your sense of the session? How will you do this?

4. What is your script for your concluding statement?

Part III

When Special Circumstances Arise

A pessimist sees difficulty in every opportunity, an optimist sees the opportunity in every difficulty.

—Thomas Fuller

It is in fighting your way through the darkness that you will eventually see the light. This is true for clinicians and for patients. Fighting through difficulty is a formidable task for both novice and experienced clinicians. We have found the challenge well worth the effort. Finding your way with patients who are challenging and situations that are difficult helps you develop valuable clinical muscle. Of course, it is in facing the difficult, the frightening, and potentially dangerous that you inevitably, invariably face yourself—your fears and doubts. Our capacity to tolerate and explore these disturbing feelings in ourselves is what ultimately enables us to better help our patients. This is at the core of good clinical work. In this way, we grow both professionally and personally.

The following three chapters address how unexpected, unwanted circumstances need not feel unmanageable, even for the beginning professional. A variety of difficult patients and circumstances may arise in the first interview. The emphasis in this section is on both managing yourself and your patient as you work through the unexpected. We detail useful skills and techniques to help you through the interview. The Chapter 8 outlines ways to work with common types of difficult patients and how to distinguish between universally difficult patients from patients who are specifically difficult for you. Chapter 9 concerns how to approach sensitive clinical material and how to deal with crisis situations during a first session. Chapter 10 deals with emergency situations.

8

Dealing with Difficult Clients

Alyson Nelson and Leah M. DeSole

You don't change relationships by trying to control other people's behavior but by changing yourself in relation to them.

—Michael P. Nichols

Chapter Goals

This chapter will help you to:

1. Distinguish among different types of difficult clients in the first interview.
2. Form a picture of your ideal client.
3. Identify difficult clients: chatty, vague, deceitful, hostile, and potentially violent clients.
4. Recognize clients who may be difficult for you.
5. Use yourself as an instrument.

What Makes a Client Difficult?

Nearly all clinicians look forward to working with friendly, appreciative clients with whom they will get along famously. Indeed, most of us entered the helping professions with two unspoken expectations: (1) we will like our clients and (2) our clients will welcome our assistance with open arms. A number of us had other expectations as well. Maybe we assumed our clients would share our beliefs about right and wrong. Additionally, perhaps we thought our clients would share our assumptions about the way the world works. The good news is that sometimes our clients not only meet our expectations but exceed them. The bad news is that sometimes they do not. *There comes a time in every clinician's training in which they sit across from clients who are difficult.* These clients present themselves in such a way that the first interview becomes a challenge for the therapist both intellectually and emotionally (Basch, 1980).

When talking about these challenges, it is important to distinguish between two types of difficult clients. The first type are those clients with whom you feel uncomfortable for some specific, idiosyncratic reason. For example, they might remind you of a bully who teased you as a child or a boss who demeaned you at work. Possibly they resemble a relative who has irritated you for years. These clients are difficult because they are *particularly challenging for you*. Other clinicians may work with these clients and feel unperturbed. The second type of difficult client is one with whom most people will feel uncomfortable. Their behavior is problematic when they interact with just about everyone. Professionals and nonprofessionals alike have difficulties forming relationships with them. These clients make themselves known to you almost immediately during the initial interview, and almost all clinicians find them demanding.

The purpose of this chapter is to help you learn how to work with *both* types of difficult clients: those with whom everyone struggles and those who present a particular challenge for you. Succeeding sections distinguish among clients who are difficult in specific ways—from the chatty or vague client to the deceitful, hostile, or potentially violent client. Subsequently, each section suggests strategies to employ in the first interview and identifies pitfalls to avoid when meeting with demanding clients for the first time. But before proceeding, I think it may be useful to take a moment to consider what might constitute an ideal client in your mind.

The Ideal Client

The ideal client is a good patient: someone with whom you can easily imagine yourself working and whom you can look forward to helping. Over forty years ago, Schofield (1964) observed that therapists tend to prefer clients who exhibit the "YAVIS syndrome"; namely, clinicians have a preference for clients who are young, attractive, verbal, intelligent, and successful. More recently, Kottler (2003) noted that therapists view their ideal patient as "verbal, thoughtful, insightful, eager, moderately affluent, and attractive" (pp. 115–117). Other variations on this good client theme include:

- *Grateful* A client who is grateful for your services.
- *Prompt* A client who arrives on time for sessions.
- *Fiscally responsible* A client who pays on time for services.
- *Polite* Clients who respect their clinician and the boundaries of treatment.
- *Familiar* Clients who are culturally similar to their clinicians in ways the clinician finds meaningful.

As this list reveals, a multitude of opinions exist regarding what constitutes an "ideal client." And, as you might guess, at times one therapist's good client is another therapist's client from hell.

By identifying the types of clients with whom you will *want* to work, you may be better able to identify those clients with whom it will be difficult for you to work. These are, for example, clients who may trigger an anxiety reaction in you or clients with whom you may fear working. It may be embarrassing to allow yourself to acknowledge these feelings. Nonetheless, I encourage you to move out of your comfort zone. What qualities come to mind when you hear the term *ideal client*? Imagine *your ideal client*—the one you picture yourself working with well. Try not to block or filter your thoughts. Take out a piece of paper. Jot down your responses to the following questions.

- What does this client look like?
- What problems does this client present?
- How does the client behave toward you?
- What is the client's attitude toward counseling?
- What are the client's strengths?
- What are the client's weaknesses?
- How does this client resemble you?
- How does this client resemble other people in your life?

Now give yourself permission to think openly about other aspects of your ideal client. This time I want you to specifically contemplate aspects of your client's cultural identity. Chapter 1 used the RESPECTFUL Cube model (Ivey et al., 2002) to explore the cultural characteristics of clients. According to this model, the word RESPECTFUL is an acronym. Each letter, as follows, stands for one aspect of an individual's sociocultural identity.

- **Religion**
- **Economic class**
- **Sexual identity**
- **Psychological maturity**
- **Ethnic/racial identity**
- **Chronological challenges**
- **Trauma**
- **Family history**
- **Unique physical characteristics**
- **Language/location of origin**

Use this framework to tap into your notions regarding who your ideal client is. Again, jot down answers to the following questions.

- **R** What is your ideal client's religion or absence of organized system of belief?
- **E** What is the client's socioeconomic class?
- **S** What is the client's sexual identity? How comfortable are you with it?
- **P** What is the client's psychological maturity? Is the client insightful?

- **E** What is the client's ethnicity? How does the client identify racially? To what extent does the client's visible appearance match his or her internal ethnic and racial self-identification?
- **C** What chronological challenges does the client face (e.g., entering an intimate relationship, raising children, divorce or separation, launching a new career in retirement)?
- **T** What trauma or traumas has the client experienced?
- **F** How has the client's family history shaped who he or she is today?
- **U** What unique physical characteristics, abilities, or disabilities does the client possess?
- **L** What is the client's first language? Does the client speak with an accent? Is the client an immigrant or native to the country in which you will be conducting therapy?

Now, look over what you have written down. Your responses pertained to your ideal client. Ivey and associates (2002) recomend that you go back and answer each question *for yourself*. Instead of thinking about your ideal client, consider such as the following. If you have a religious background, what is it? How do you identify racially and ethnically? How do you identify your sexual orientation? Once you have completed this exercise, contemplate:

- What was it like, overall, to engage in this exercise?
- What feelings emerged about each of your responses?
- What is your sense of how others, especially clients, identify you culturally?
- What cultural characteristics do you anticipate will enhance your clinical work?
- What cultural characteristics do you consider a potential barrier to counseling?

Bear in mind that the RESPECTFUL Cube is but one framework for conceptualizing the cultural characteristics of oneself and one's clients. There are many others. Undoubtedly, some topics have been omitted that you find personally meaningful. For example, I was once at a conference where a participant vigorously advocated for clinicians to think of themselves in terms of rural versus city dwellers. Until she mentioned this point, I admit, its significance had never occurred to me. In retrospect, I can see how my ignorance was twofold: it stemmed from my clients and from me. At that time, not only were my clients primarily from urban areas but I was a lifelong city dweller myself.

What you may find in looking over your responses to these questions is that many of us enter the field with the assumption that our clients will be like us. I now realize that as I began working with clients, first in a community mental health center and later in an inpatient hospital setting, that I expected my clients to share my assumptions about the world. I also expected them to share my beliefs about right and wrong. I did not realize it at the time, but essentially I thought they would think the way I think. This was not always the case. Indeed, I found my clients to be different from me in more ways than I could have imagined.

As a novice therapist, you will find that your clients will differ from you, too. You will enter the first interview, no doubt, with your own set of expectations about them. And this is okay. What matters is that you are fully aware of your expectations. The more you are aware of them the more you will be able to make choices regarding how you act on them. And these choices will enable you to be a more effective clinician, particularly when you find yourself sitting across from a client with whom it will be difficult for you to work.

The Difficult Client

This section reviews strategies for counseling the clients whom almost all clinicians would find demanding when they meet with them for the first time. They include the chatty client, the vague client, the deceitful client, the hostile client, and the violent client. What these clients have in common is that they tend to push people away—not only friends, family, and coworkers but professionals in the mental health field. It can be difficult to simply like them, let alone begin to form a relationship with them during the first interview. The challenge with difficult clients is how to get close enough to them in order to figure out what brings them to treatment. To this end, the following paragraphs suggest several strategies to pursue in the initial contact.

The Chatty Client

Most clinicians in training welcome a communicative client. If truth be told, they dread the client who sits there and says nothing. Indeed, it may seem like a paradox to suggest that clients could talk *too much*. After all, don't clients come to therapy to talk? Aren't clinicians there to listen? The answer to each of these questions, undeniably, is yes. Nonetheless, it is still possible for clients to talk too much in the first interview. These clients are chatty rather than communicative: much of their speech is unproductive and it impedes the work of therapy.

One way to distinguish between chatty and communicative clients is to think in terms of the content of the counseling session. A chatty client in the first interview says a lot, but the ideas discussed are not substantive. As a clinician, you may notice that their responses to questions feel superficial, and you may sense that they minimize their difficulties. The content of the interview, in essence, feels shallow; it is like casual conversation rather than therapy. For example, you leave the interview wondering why they came in the first place. You realize that you have little to say about these clients when you meet with your supervisor or sit down to write the intake report. In contrast, clients who are truly communicative are productive: they not only answer your questions but provide relevant information. When the session ends, you understand what brought them to seek counseling now, and you can readily recall their concerns.

Another way to distinguish between chatty and communicative clients is to think in terms of the process of the counseling session. Chatty clients take over in the first interview; they assume control. Bear in mind, many novice clinicians have been trained to work in an unstructured manner, allowing for the material to unfold. They have been taught not to interrupt clients. While this might be an effective long-term therapy model, it is inefficient in the first interview. In essence, what chatty clients will do during the first interview is to take this unstructured approach and run with it: they will evade direct questions, go off on tangents about other topics, and dominate the interview. They will keep you, as a clinician, at a distance. As a consequence, it may be difficult to ascertain why they have sought counseling now. The effect on most clinicians-in-training is the same: the first interview is a frustrating experience.

What can be done to improve the initial contact with chatty clients? How can you maintain control of the interview and keep the communication productive? There are several strategies. Most of them depend on how attuned the clients are to interpersonal cues. For clients who are reasonably attuned to interpersonal cues, subtle nonverbal signals will be sufficient to get them on track.

Nonverbal Cues.   Effective nonverbal cues communicate what you do and don't need to hear from your client during the interview. Remember: clients need your guidance. They do not naturally know the information you need in order to be of service to them. Sometimes excessive chatter represents clients' hard work to give you, the clinician, what they think you need to hear. Helpful nonverbal cues include refraining from eye contact, not responding to rhetorical client questions, and smiling softly when something irrelevant is said. These nonverbal cues suggest that it is time for the client to take a breath, stop talking, and *start to listen to you*.

I would suggest that you begin to assume control of the first interview with chatty clients by applying the aforementioned, subtle nonverbal cues. Depending on your clients' responsiveness, become more direct as needed. Some explicit non-verbal techniques are putting a finger over your lips or gesturing in a way that tells clients to stop talking. Pairing these techniques with empathetic verbal responses is especially effective; for example, raising your hand as if to say stop and stating:

- "You've said a lot, Mrs. Maelstrom. I want to make sure I understand you. Let's stop for a moment and focus."
- "Zoran, you've made so many useful points from talking about your boss to your stress at home. I think it would be helpful to slow things down for a moment."

Verbal Cues.   There are also several explicit verbal techniques you can apply when working with chatty clients. These verbal cues enable you to continue your line of questioning while acknowledging the client's desire to discuss other issues. Essentially, what you want to do is use something the client is talking about as a jumping off point to begin to gather the data you need. For example, if your client is rambling about a friend's marriage, you would redirect the client to talk about her own marriage. Your intervention might look as follows.

Client: I never thought they belonged together. Every time I saw them they were fighting. Once, when we were all at dinner, they had a big blow-out fight about the car.

Clinician: I'm interested in hearing about your relationships. How do you get along with your husband?

Here, the clinician has intervened and refocused the session to the client's issues and concerns. Depending on the client, it may take one or several interventions to redirect the client.

Exceptional clients call for you to be more concrete. You may need to say something that communicates to them that they have gone astray in the first interview. The key here is to both convey your interest in the client's experiences and redirect the content of the session. This instance requires you to clearly communicate to clients what you need from them now. For example, you might have to say:

- "What you are saying may be useful, but right now it would be more helpful if we kept the focus on (fill in the blank)."
- "This matters, Cornelius. Unfortunately, we don't have a lot of time today. I want to make sure we stick with (fill in the blank) today."
- "I know you have a lot to say. It all makes a difference. However, today our time is limited. I want to make sure we get through (fill in the blank)."

Another technique to use is to respond to *how the clients are feeling rather than what they have said.* Clients' excessive chatter may be the result of their discomfort. They talk to fill silence, ward off anxiety, and/or prevent embarrassment. They talk to prevent you from asking questions they do not want to, or cannot, answer. In so doing, some chatty clients are communicating their distress. In these cases, sometimes it helps to speak to the feelings they may, consciously or subconsciously, be expressing in their behavior. You may reduce their chatter by speaking to their anxiety.

Client: I never thought they belonged together. Every time I saw them they were fighting. Once, when we were all at dinner, they had a big blow-out fight about the car. It was embarrassing.

Clinician: It sounds like it was really uncomfortable to be there. To what extent are you feeling like that now sitting here with me? Let's talk about that.

In other cases, you also may need to actively intersperse closed-ended (yes or no) questions into the interview. This will help manage your client, slow down the counseling process, and get the information you need in order to be of service to the client. For example:

Client: I could tell when I walked in that Jimmy was talking about me. He is so arrogant. And his boyfriend is, too. Whenever they are together all they do is talk about people. Their friends are the same way. Let me just tell you about what they said about my friend Vincent after his mother died.

Clinician: You are saying so much, it is overwhelming. Is that how you are feeling now?" *or* "You seem to be observant and insightful of how others behave, but I'm interested in knowing more about your own observations and insights.

Alternative Cues.   You may be wondering what cues remain aside from verbal or nonverbal ones. Well, in a class all by itself is what I refer to as the nonresponse. Sometimes, you can curb clients' extraneous chatter by simply not responding to it. This may be easier said than done, because most of us have been raised to be polite. In polite conversation, you typically render some sort of response to what has been said. As a new clinician, you must keep in mind that interviews are not polite conversation. During the first interview, it is your responsibility to manage the counseling process, keep the communication productive, and get the information you need in order to be of service to the client. Sometimes that means not being polite. For example:

Clinician: Tell me more about the incident at dinner on Thursday.

Client: It was terrible. I can't stand thinking about what I did and how much I ate this week. It makes me hate myself. It makes me sick just to think about it. And it brings me right back to when I was thirteen and I felt the same way. Do you remember when I told you about that incident?

Clinician: Yes.

Client: It is just the same. I have always had this problem at meals with my family. My sisters back then would watch everything they ate. They would stare as the food was passed around. When it got to me, they'd look at everything I put on my plate. They did not say a thing, but I felt criticized. It was constant . . . .

Clinician: [interrupting] It seems easier for you to talk about the past than the present. However, I think we'll learn more if we stay in the present. Let's go back to the incident at dinner on Thursday. I need to hear more about you—what *you* did during the meal and *your* accompanying thoughts and feelings.

For clinicians-in-training, this can be a challenge. Many new clinicians worry about being assertive: they are concerned about making their clients feel uncomfortable, and they want to be liked. Indeed, the desire to be liked is particularly pronounced for new clinicians working at a training site where they face evaluation by clients and supervisors. Nonetheless, for a clinician being liked is not enough: your primary purpose is to be effective. Be sure to discuss these feelings as they arise with others, such as your peers, your superiors, and in your personal therapy.

When working with chatty clients, I encourage you to begin with the nonverbal strategies outlined previously. Move on to verbal strategies and integrate more direct interventions as needed. Be willing to try many approaches and do what you need to do to get your clients on track. If worse comes to worse, focus on maintaining rapport. Have faith that there will be time in future sessions to get the information you need when the client is ready to share it with you.

One caveat: there are instances, when out of fear or apprehension, a clinician in training will choose not to intervene when a client is rambling. If you begin to feel this way with a chatty client, make note of it. Excessive talking can be a sign of a serious problem; notably, a manic episode. During a manic episode, the client exhibits period of elevated, expansive, or irritable mood as well as at least three of the following characteristics: a decreased need for sleep, talkativeness, inflated self-esteem, racing thoughts, physical agitation, a tendency toward impulsivity, and excessive involvement in activities that lead to negative consequences. To be considered a manic episode, these characteristics must, taken together, cause significant impairment in the patient's occupational, emotional, or social functioning that lasts at least one week. If you think your client may be experiencing a manic episode, be sure to detail promptly these symptoms and share your experience with your supervisor.

The Vague Client

Most clinicians-in-training approach a vague client with dismay. Like hostile clients, whom I will discuss shortly, they are difficult to get close to and difficult to get to know. They also are tough to characterize. Tolstoy once said: "All happy families resemble one another, but each unhappy family is unhappy in its own way." Vague clients are like unhappy families; each is vague in their own way. The challenge is finding a way in to their specific concerns and learning how to understand their experiences.

Vague clients lack clarity in the first interview. Like the chatty client, the content of their speech tends to be unproductive—they say little that helps you understand their struggles. Although they appear engaged during the interview process, they do not provide you with the basic information you need to be of assistance to them. A telltale sign that you are sitting with a vague client is that you feel like you do not know who they are. When the session ends, it remains unclear why they are seeking counseling at this time. You feel puzzled or bewildered. You wonder why they came for counseling in the first place.

The first step in dealing with a vague client is to make an assessment regarding why the client is being unclear. There are two important distinctions to consider in making this assessment. The first asks if the client's lack of clarity is symptomatic of mental illness, such as mental retardation, a thought disorder, or a personality disorder (e.g., paranoid or avoidant). The second asks if the client is unclear simply because he has a difficult time talking about his reason for seeking assistance now. These distinctions matter because they can be of help in orienting your expectations in working with clients. Essentially, you ought to anticipate less room for change with clients who are mentally retarded, thought disordered, or suffering from a personality disorder. In addition, your interventions with these clients should be simple and direct. In the second instance, you can expect that your clients will be more amenable to change. Your interventions, as a consequence, may become more complex over the course of the first interview.

The second step in dealing with a vague client is to help your client become more clear—regardless of your initial assessment regarding why the client is being vague. First and foremost, this is done by controlling the process of the first interview. To this end, I strongly recommend that you review Chapter 6. Focus specifically on the section regarding how to structure the first interview. Remember, you provide structure by *behaving* consistently throughout the interview and *communicating* in a straightforward fashion. You also provide structure by controlling the pacing of the session, making clear transitions from one topic to another, and constantly monitoring the depth of the session.

When dealing with a vague client, you need to use prompting questions. Start with open-ended questions, as you would with any other client. If they remain vague you will need to use more focused, closed-ended questions. For example:

> *Client:* I have been feeling awful, just awful.
>
> *Clinician:* Everyone has a different idea of what "awful" means. What does it mean to you?
>
> *Client:* I don't know, just crummy.
>
> *Clinician:* Awful and crummy. Tell me more.
>
> *Client:* [silence]
>
> *Clinician:* These feelings can affect a lot of things in your life. For example, what has your sleeping, eating, or energy level been like?
>
> *Client:* I feel like I have no energy. It's hard to get out of bed. I am not hungry.
>
> *Clinician:* Are you getting out of bed and going to work?
>
> *Client:* Yes.
>
> *Clinician:* Are you getting done what you need to get done at work? Are you being productive?
>
> *Client:* Not really, and I am afraid people are starting to notice.

In this example, the transition from open-ended to close-ended questioning helped the client become less vague and more descriptive. In so doing, it also appeared that the client began to feel more open, as indicated by the client's statement that "people are starting to notice" her behavior at work.

Another useful strategy in working with vague clients is summarizing what the client has said. This helps clients regardless of whether they suffer from mental illness or are just uncomfortable talking about themselves. For instance:

> *Clinician:* So, lately you have felt awful. You have had less energy than usual, been less hungry, and felt unproductive. And you are worried that people at work are starting to notice.
>
> *Client:* Yes, that is it.

At this point, you may want to follow up with even further specific questions or a more structured interview/survey (e.g., the Hamilton Depression Scale) based on your findings. With particularly challenging cases, it may be useful take out an emotion and/or a symptom checklist of some sort to help your client gain clarity. By way of introduction you might say: "Some people find it helpful to look over this chart to find the words they need. Here, take a look at it and tell me what you think." Subsequently, you may need to guide your clients to generalize their experiences or describe them in greater detail. Sometimes it helps to prompt clients with key words to steer them toward the information you need. For example:

- "Do you *usually* feel awful when you get up in the morning? Out of the past seven days, how many of them have you felt bad?"
- "Do you *typically* lack energy during the day? How is it different in the morning, afternoon, and evening?"
- "Is it *common* for you to not feel hungry? When did you first feel this way— last year or last week—or have you always felt like this?"

If you find that your client continues to be vague and imprecise despite your efforts to direct him with your questions, you may be dealing with a client who is avoidant or resistant. These clients, much like hostile clients, are challenging. I advise you to explore the nature of their resistance before barreling ahead with the interview. After all, clients who are resistant to talking about themselves are resistant for a reason. I believe it can only facilitate the interview if you understand what is motivating their behavior. Their motivations may be many and varied. For instance, it may be that they lack hope or they are protecting themselves from revealing something shameful. Sometimes a client's resistance may be a symptom of an illness itself, such as depression. When a vague client appears avoidant or resistant, I recommend that you do not challenge them. Rather, try to go with the resistance, or empathizing with it. For example:

- "You have said you feel awful. I assume that you are here because you want to feel better. I believe you can feel better. I am hopeful, but I will need your help. I need you to answer some questions."
- "I know you feel bad about it, but everyone feels awful sometimes. I see it as a sign of real strength that you have come here today. In order for me to help, I need your help. I will need you to give me some clearer answers to my questions."

It is difficult to go wrong by going with a client's resistance or empathizing with their struggle. Working in this way, you leave open the option of challenging them if you sense that will facilitate the first interview.

The Deceitful Client

Most of the time clinicians assume clients are truthful in what they tell us. In fact, many clinicians (e.g., Havens, 1989; Yalom, 2002b) contend that the therapeutic relationship is held together by the premise that both the clinician and the client will be truthful. Implicit to the therapeutic contract, therefore, is the notion of honesty. However, it will not take long for a new clinician to learn that not all clients live up to their end of the therapeutic contract in the first interview (Morrison, 1995).

There are many reasons clients may be deceitful. Some will avoid the truth to avoid uncomfortable emotional states such as shame, humiliation, and fear. Misstating or avoiding the truth is a common way of fending off uncomfortable feelings. Just about all clients in treatment experience these feelings at one time or another, and just about all clients work hard to fend them off. Another reason clients may be deceitful in the therapeutic relationship pertains to the client's relationship to their own status. For example, clients may inflate their status because they wish to impress their clinicians. Alternatively, they may deflate their status in a desperate effort to obtain compassion (or perhaps a lower therapy rate). Still others lie to avoid responsibility or to evade punishment, such as being expelled from a treatment program. Yet another reason a client may lie is for personal gain, such as to obtain disability benefits or preserve their job security. Most clients are not habitually deceitful; like all human beings, they lie for a reason. Often it is either to avoid discomfort or to gain additional comfort. I believe it is important to understand what motivates a given client to lie in the first interview. But before you try to tease out why your client is being deceitful you need to determine whether your client is being untruthful in the first place.

How do you know when your client is being untruthful? Morrison (1995) suggests several clues.

- Your client's history is inconsistent with the typical course of his reported disorder. For example, a client with a documented history of paranoid schizophrenia denies any prior hospitalizations.
- Your client has been previously diagnosed with a character disorder. For instance, an adolescent who presents as conduct disordered and an adult who presents with antisocial personality disorder both have tendencies to disregard the truth.
- Your client provides information that is internally inconsistent. For example, within the context of the first interview she reports both living in a homeless shelter and being the president of large record label.
- Your client provides information that contradicts information from other sources. For instance, you may have read in his chart that he attended a methadone maintenance program for two years, but he denies current or past substance abuse.
- Your client denies negative self-attributions and negative affect despite ample objective reasons for negative self-attribution and negative affect. For example, a fifty-year-old man arrives at the first interview appearing agitated. He reports that he dropped out of college, is unemployed, lives at home with his parents, and has no close, personal relationships. He tells you he is content with his life.

All of the aforementioned provide clues that a client is being deceitful in the first interview. In addition, keep in mind that inquiries about sensitive topics can produce enough discomfort that your client might misstate the truth. Sensitive topics include contacts with the legal system, substance use, sexual experiences, and aggressive or violent behavior. Such "misstatements" may be unconscious, and only later does the client realize (with apparent honesty) that they had not responded truthfully to your initial inquiry. Other times these misstatements are conscious choices; for example, the clients do not trust you and thus withhold the truth. Indeed, I have had more than one client in the first interview deny prior physical abuse and later acknowledge that they had lied—the abuse had occurred, but they were not ready to acknowledge it during the intake process. Deception of this type may be healthy insofar as it represents an attempt on their part to protect themselves from potential psychological stigma or shame.

Be mindful, as well, that deceit can be a symptom of a mental or physical disorder. For example, I vividly remember an occasion on internship when I interviewed a new patient for the first time in the Spinal Cord Unit at a veteran's hospital. He was there for his annual physical. As I sat at his bedside, he struck me as a kindly man. It was awhile into the first interview before I sensed that he was not being truthful. He did not understand why he was at the hospital even though he was pretending that he did.

> *Clinician:* Do you know where you are, Mr. Jenkins?
>
> *Client:* Of course I do. I am sitting right here with you.
>
> *Clinician:* And where is that?
>
> *Client:* [silence]

Was the client being consciously deceitful? Whether he was or not, it is clear that he was not being entirely truthful. And in this instance, his behavior was a symptom of mental illness.

This example underscores why it is important to realize that clients can be deceitful. By being aware that clients may be untruthful you can enable them to get the help they need. For example, during my training at a large city hospital I learned quickly that clients were often motivated to lie during a psychiatric emergency room intake evaluation. How did I learn this? Essentially, I learned it from clients' family members. The family members who came in with the clients were often very worried and afraid. As a result, they were motivated to be truthful. They would provide information and describe behaviors that my clients would vehemently deny—particularly the next day when they were psychiatrically stable and wanted to be discharged from the psychiatric ward. It would have been a disservice to my clients to accept their words at face value. It may seem like a paradox, but being aware that clients can be motivated to be deceitful actually may *help them to get the treatment they need.*

An initial interview with someone who lies can be tricky. On the one hand, as with all clients you need to gather information for diagnosis, treatment, and disposition. On the other hand, if you challenge the client too assertively when gathering information you risk a permanent break in the therapeutic relationship. While it is true that treatment is not the primary goal of an initial interview, you need to be mindful that you may work with the client in the future. That is, you need to balance the goal of being able to work with the client through the interview while you constructively address the difficult behavior in a manner that does not undo your relationship with the client.

A basic strategy in determining whether or not your client is being deceitful in the first interview is to gather the information from sources other than your client before you meet with them. Supplementary sources—such as medical records, mobile crisis intake reports, and psychiatric notes from prior treatment facilities—may prepare you to identify inconsistencies. A number of new clinicians, on principle, do not like to look at other professional's notes prior to meeting with a client for the first interview. Other new clinicians just don't have the time to look through supplementary sources prior to meeting with a client for the first interview. If this is the case, over time you will be able to piece together a truer picture of your client by simply paying close attention to the various parts of the client's life history (work, academic, relationship history) during the first interview itself. Admittedly, this can be difficult to do. And if you do spot inconsistencies during the first interview, you will need to know how to handle them.

Let me say up front: I do not consider confrontation an effective strategy for handling clients whom I have reason to believe are deceitful. In my experience, it does not facilitate either establishing rapport or gathering truthful information. While challenging a client and "catching them in a lie" can be momentarily egogratifying, it is rarely helpful. It may even lead to a disruption in the interview that is irrevocable (this is especially true with adolescent clients who may easily get into power struggles with authority figures). Should you feel strongly that a direct challenge is needed (perhaps in the case of a time-limited drug rehabilitation facility), try to craft your challenges in a way that avoids sounding accusatory. Accusations tend to polarize, and polarizing clients may lead them to take flight from the interview altogether. Instead, whenever possible, couch any challenge in a way that allows the client "an out." In so doing, the client can admit deceit and save face.

One strategy I have found useful in encouraging clients to be truthful is to begin with a supportive statement: immediately acknowledge the client's willingness to participate in the first interview. Next, point out the contradiction you have observed and solicit their assistance in clarifying your confusion. For example:

- "I think it was smart of you to come here today for help. I know you told the teacher that your son has never had a problem until now. However, I remember he had a hard time last year. I want to support you and your son. Please help me make sense of this."
- "It shows that you are responsible that you came in today. But I admit I'm a little confused. You said you've never been arrested, yet the county hospital sent us your rap sheet. What do you make of that?"
- "It shows real perseverance that you came in today. Still, there is something a little puzzling I wanted to talk to you about. You just told me you don't use any drugs, yet your medical record indicates you were in treatment last year. Can you help me understand what you meant?"

Another, more basic, strategy in dealing with a deceitful client is to simply restate what the client has said verbatim. A variation on this strategy is to ask clients themselves to repeat what they have just said. For instance:

- "Sonya, let me make sure I heard correctly: you are not pregnant."
- "Mr. McCurdy, could you repeat what you just said?"
- "I may have misunderstood, Nguyen, but did you go to school last week?"

Restatements and/or asking clients to repeat themselves are both safe techniques because, like the aforementioned supportive strategy, they allow the client an out (admit deceit and save face). Basically, you give the client a chance to rescind a lie by checking what you heard. They are also safe strategies because they offer you, as a clinician-in-training, an out. After all, even new clinicians become jaded or mistaken. You may forget *it is possible* that your clients may have misspoken. Likewise, given the pressures of training, the potential exists that you may have inadvertently misunderstood them.

Interviewing a client who does not tell you the truth is tricky. But with some patience, a careful ear, and a willingness to gather information from a variety of sources you can obtain the data you need in order to be of service to your client.

The Hostile Client

You can easily spot hostile clients by their angry facial expression, body language, and tone of voice. The content of the interview, or what they say to you, also will reveal their anger. To work with them effectively, you need to understand the purpose of their anger. Anger, in general, is a defensive maneuver that keeps others away. One way to think about hostile clients is that they use their anger much like porcupines use their quills. The message they send is "don't come near me" and "leave me alone." Like the porcupine, the hostile client is need of a defense. Their anger serves as a type of protection as they move about in the world. Given that your job in the initial interview is to get close enough to your clients to gather the data you need, their anger can seriously impede the counseling effort. The question is how to proceed with the interview in the face of the client's angry resistance.

The first step in dealing with hostile clients is to empathize with their explicit feelings of anger—although it may be tempting to avoid them. Empathy involves putting yourself in your clients' shoes and allowing yourself to imagine what it might be like to be them. Do not challenge their anger. Instead, acknowledge their anger and be curious about its source. For example:

Clinician: What brings you here today?

Client: (An 18-year-old, female adolescent.) My mother brought me here. She's the one with the problems. I don't have any problems. You are the third therapist I've met with because of her. I'm not talking. I've had it.

> *Clinician:*   I bet you are really sick of this and can't imagine how talking to me could be useful.
>
> *Client:*   Yeh. I don't want to talk to you.
>
> *Clinician:*   I can see you don't want to talk to me, but from the way you look, you are thinking about a lot of things. You have got a lot on your mind.
>
> *Client:*   Maybe I do. So what?
>
> *Clinician:*   So, what is on your mind?
>
> *Client:*   I don't want to be here. My mother made me come. She makes me do a lot.
>
> *Clinician:*   What else does your mom force you to do?
>
> *Client:*   Well, she makes me take piano lessons that I can't concentrate on.
>
> *Clinician:*   How long has it been hard for you to concentrate on your lessons?

Although this client's anger was initially directed toward the clinician, it became clear that she was angry with her mother. The client's anger dissipated after the clinician acknowledged and accepted it. In so doing, the clinician made it safe for her to lower her quills and reveal the underlying issues at hand.

There are some responses clinicians should avoid when working with hostile clients. Namely, it is wise to avoid those responses that tend to increase a client's anger. The most obvious is anger itself. Meeting a client's anger with anger is like throwing gasoline on a fire: it only serves to fan the flames and increase the client's resistance. Although this may seem obvious, you may be surprised how difficult it can be to avoid in the first interview. Clinicians, after all, are human. It is natural to become angry when met with hostility. Likewise, it is natural to become frustrated, anxious, or afraid. However, these responses only serve to create additional tension for both the client and clinician. They are rarely productive.

You may be thinking to yourself, "I can't imagine revealing my anger or frustration with a client." Indeed, maybe this is not your style. You may not be given to overt emotional displays when you sit with others, especially clients. Nonetheless, consider the extent to which you might have a tendency to express your emotions covertly. It might be as small as avoiding eye contact or making a postural shift, such as turning your body away from the client. Alternatively, you may make a casual statement that conveys frustration: "You know, if you don't start talking to me things will never change." Let me be clear: such responses are understandable; they are human. They may even feel good in the moment. However, chances are they will not make your client feel good. Thus, they will not be clinically effective. They will only serve to drive your clients away. And the further away you are from your clients the further away you are from gathering the information you need to move forward in the interview.

So, the question becomes how you can monitor and manage your feelings when sitting with a hostile client. One strategy is to remind yourself throughout the interview that the client's hostility is not about you. Instead, it relates to the client's own struggles in the world. Resist the desire to dispute or judge the reasons the client is behaving in a hostile manner. If need be, engage in supportive self-talk. Tell yourself: *It is unlikely that I could have done anything to elicit such a strong response from this client in the short time we have been together.* If you can keep this in mind, you are less likely to take the client's anger personally and react in kind.

Another strategy I find useful when I interview a hostile client for the first time is to recall the porcupine analogy. In so doing, I am able to put the moment in perspective and feel less reactive toward the client's anger. What I do is think about how an angry porcupine reacts with hostility because it feels vulnerable; it sticks out its quills to protect itself. Remembering the analogy allows me to respond to the thoughts and feelings of vulnerability behind the client's hostility, rather than react to the client's hostility itself. In so doing, I am better able to summon my empathy for the client. In my experience, I am a far more effective clinician in the first interview when I respond with respect out of empathy rather than purely out of professional obligation.

A final strategy I recommend when working with hostile clients is that you harness your curiosity. If the client is angry, the client is angry for a reason. I encourage you to be inquisitive about the nature of the client's hostility. It may be as simple as asking the client, in a truly interested fashion, "Tell me more about what you don't like about being here right now?" Plumb the depths of the client's discontent enough to understand what drives his or her hostility—be it fear, vulnerability, or self-protection. In my experience, most clients respond positively to a clinician who is not put off by their anger and displays a genuine interest in their struggles.

The Potentially Violent Client

Clients are rarely angry to the point of violence. And clients are not typically violent toward their clinicians. In some way, our role as clinician protects us, at least initially, from the rage of others. That said, while violence against clinicians is unlikely it does happen. Just about every experienced clinician I know has one story about a frightening or violent interaction with a client.

The problem is that it can be very difficult to make predictions about which clients will become violent. There are some types of mental illness that may make violent behavior more likely. I do not mean everyone you see with a diagnosis of this sort will become violent, but rather that certain illnesses are characterized by unpredictable and sometimes aggressive behavior. You need to employ extra caution when interviewing clients who are diagnosed with one of the following disorders: paranoid schizophrenia, mania, paranoid personality disorder, antisocial personality disorder, cognitive disorders, and substance abuse disorders. Your intuition is also important. If a client scares you, that is a strong indication that he is scary and potentially dangerous. There is no reason to be heroic when a client scares you. Pay attention to your gut feelings. No one in your institution will care as much about your safety as you. Therefore, you should always take precautions.

There are a number of precautions you can take to ensure your safety during an interview. The first precaution to ensure your safety is to read through the medical record and the psychiatric documentation prior to meeting with a new client.

Pay attention to a history of past violence, indications of poor impulse control, and unpredictability. As well, take note of diagnoses that suggest potential violence, unpredictability, or poor impulse control (e.g., psychoses, antisocial personality disorder, and current intoxication). Be sure to ask your supervisor what type of arrangements you should make before you meet with a potentially violent client. Some institutions have a special safety protocol for their workers. For example, my friend worked in a community service agency where there was a security code word. If a clinician felt unsafe, he or she would call the receptionist and say "Mr. Wilson needs attention." Immediately, someone would come to the clinician's office and offer assistance—without the client becoming aware of the clinician's call for help.

A second precaution you can take to ensure your safety is to arrange to sit in a consulting room where other staff members are nearby. Ideally, other staff members can even see you. Often hospitals and community mental health clinics have rooms with windows facing the nurse station (or some other heavily trafficked location) that are designed with a clinician's safety in mind. The room arrangement matters, as well as the room location. Always arrange the seating so that you are sitting closest to the door. In addition, your client's chair should be positioned in such a way that it does not impede your prompt exit. And finally, remember that you can always leave the consulting room door ajar for an additional sense of security. In this way, you can exit easily and help can enter more easily if necessary.

A third precaution to take to ensure your safety is to tell people (staff members, supervisors, peers, and so on) of your concerns when you are preparing for an interview with a potentially violent or unpredictable client. Some clinics have panic buttons located under the desktop in their consulting rooms. If your facility has panic buttons set up, be sure to familiarize yourself with how they work and what to expect when used. Do not meet the client in a secluded part of the facility, and request a security guard or staff member to stand outside the consulting room door during your interview.

Fourth, and finally, remain alert when conducting a first interview with a potentially violent client. Watch your client for signs of heightened tension or escalating rage: a loud voice, angry words, staring narrowed gaze, sudden bursts of verbal aggression directed toward you or others, and a clenched fist or jaw. Also attend to your own verbal and nonverbal cues when interviewing a potentially violent client. Be mindful of your intuition and feelings. By knowing how you feel (e.g., comfortable versus uncomfortable, safe versus unsafe, and so on), you can assess what makes most sense for both you and your client at any moment in the interview.

Be prepared to end the interview if you are concerned for your safety. While it may feel awkward to end the interview prematurely, rest assured that ending things before they get out of hand (or you feel really uncomfortable) will allow you to meet with the client again when there is less potential for violence. Essentially, it will enable you to end the interview in a way that preserves some foundation for counseling in the future. To this end, you can close the interview by saying something that conveys your desire to offer assistance to the client in the future. For example:

- "We need to stop the interview, John. I'd like you to get the assistance you need, but right now you seem pretty upset. I'll contact you to arrange to meet again."
- "I'm sorry, Julia. I'd like to talk with you, but right now things seem really tense. Let's stop now and meet again when things are calmer."
- "I think that you will benefit from counseling, Fernando, but I can't meet with you when you are this angry. Let's quit for now and try again tomorrow. I'll make the arrangements."

Once you have ended the interview, leave the room immediately and tell staff what has transpired. Keep in mind, you do not (and should not) have to deal with a potentially violent client alone. Tell your supervisor and other staff members of your concerns both before and after meeting the client.

Clients who are potentially violent pose a danger to others as well as themselves. Certainly, they are in need of counseling. Nonetheless, you do not do them a service by putting yourself at risk in the first interview. Good can come, however, in the future if they are put in situation in which their potential for violence can be managed and ultimately alleviated. Your role as a new clinician in the first interview with a potentially violent client is to maintain both your safety and the client's safety. Consider your job well done if safety is maintained; it would be icing on the cake if they returned for a second interview.

Clients Who Are Particularly Difficult for You

Clients who are particularly difficult for you are those clients with whom you feel uncomfortable for some reason specific to you. Unlike the other difficult clients discussed in this chapter (e.g., hostile, chatty, or deceitful clients), clients who are especially challenging for you are bothersome for idiosyncratic reasons, of which only you are likely to be aware. Consequently, you need to be mindful of your feelings, thoughts, and assumptions about these clients. And you will need to do some work on yourself to be able to work with them effectively.

Clients who are particularly difficult for you tend to make you anxious. Your anxiety may mask a variety of other feelings that lie beneath. Indeed, you may find yourself working very hard to avoid these feelings. As a result, you will not take care of yourself, or your client, as well as you should. Anxiety is a signal that lets you know you are afraid. It is important to pay attention to this signal and think about your fear. To this end, it may be useful to refer to Shea's (1998) seven core fears as described in Chapter 2. Try to identify not only your anxiety but your fears. In particular, consider how your fears relate to your clients.

I can recall a session with a client while I was working at a state hospital in New York. I was seeing a client, Mr. Daly (fictitious name), who was diagnosed with schizoaffective disorder. This is a psychotic-level disorder in which the client suffers with both a thought disorder and an affective disorder at different times in his symptom trajectory. When Mr. Daly was psychotic, he had a reputation of smearing his feces on the walls of the hospital ward. Even more upsetting to me, he had a reputation for grabbing people, particularly young female psychology interns (like myself).

As a new psychology intern, I was afraid of him and eager to keep my distance. I felt every muscle in my body tighten as the training director told me that I was assigned to do a psychological testing battery with him. I told myself, how exciting, my first testing battery with such an interesting person. I remember literally closing my eyes, taking a deep breath, and walking to his floor to meet this notorious client, who by reputation alone made my heart race. I was not aware of my feelings at the time. All I knew was that my heart raced, muscles tensed, and teeth clenched every time he was near. Like many clients with a mental illness, Mr. Daly was exquisitely sensitive to the feeling states of others. One day as I approached him on the ward he shouted across the hall, "Psychology, Psychology, come here." I walked toward him, telling myself I knew what I was doing, I need to be in charge. As I approached him, I felt more tentative. I tried to convince myself: "What an exciting opportunity, this will be great." We were about three feet apart and Mr. Daly shouted at me, "You're afraid. You're afraid. Why are you afraid of me?" Mr. Daly saw right through my professional demeanor. He saw through my anxiety and could name the feeling my anxiety signaled. I was terrified.

This story had a relatively happy ending. Once Mr. Daly was properly medicated, he allowed me into his deeply sensitive world, apparent in his poetry and drawings. But the moral of this story is that my anxiety masked my feelings to such an extent that I was completely cut off from my fear. This is dangerous for any clinician. It was my client who sensed the fear oozing out of me and identified it for me. In retrospect, Mr. Daly's question ("Why are you so afraid of me?") was the type of question I wished I had asked myself. In other words, "Why was I afraid of this client?" and "What was it that made me uncomfortable to point of professional paralysis?" I was quite fortunate. Mr. Daly gave me a wonderful object lesson on the importance of paying attention to anxiety and the feelings that lie beneath the anxiety. When I look back on this episode, I can now say that I was afraid of loss of control (both my own loss of control and my client's). I was also afraid of failure. I wanted to do a good job so that others (especially those evaluating me) would think of me as a professional. But the most important lesson I learned from my experience with meeting Mr. Daly for the first time was this: I did not help Mr. Daly or myself by hiding from my fears.

Self as Instrument

The idea of a clinician using oneself as instrument is a long-standing concept in counseling. It connotes the importance of using yourself—especially your thoughts, feelings, and behaviors—in the presence of your client as a means of understanding the counseling relationship. For example, in the previous section Mr. Daly served as a fine-tuned instrument for me, making me keenly aware of the importance of attending to my thoughts, feelings, and behaviors when working with clients.

In the first interview, it is just you and your client in the consulting room. All you have is yourself to help gauge what is going on with your client; all you have is yourself to help the client. As explored in Chapter 2, knowing what you feel may be the most important tool you have in counseling. Knowing what you are feeling, thinking, and doing in the session is the first step in helping others. That is, before you can begin to help another person explore how they are feeling you must be open to how you are feeling about that person. You don't need to be able to fully articulate exactly what you feel or think in a neat and succinct manner, but you do need to be open to your emotional states, willing to acknowledge your judgments, and eager to explore how they are manifest in the first interview with a client.

When you begin training as a new clinician, the idea of knowing and using yourself can seem like an odd and uncomfortable proposition. My students and supervisees have told me they feel unprofessional when I've asked them about their feelings during supervision. Only after you begin to work in the field do you become aware that all of the theory and facts don't provide the grounding that your own feelings can provide. That is not to say that theory and facts are not important. They provide a framework for understanding a client. Nonetheless, your keenly honed awareness of what you are feeling, thinking, and doing in any clinical encounter helps clarify the clinical picture.

Your awareness, however, is only the first step. The critical second step is discerning how much of what you feel has to do with you and how much has to do with something about the client. For example, during the first interview you may find yourself irritated, bored, or frightened by a client. Likewise, you may find yourself increasingly agitated or mildly annoyed as the hour passes. You might also experience these feelings regarding a particular topic. It is important to pay attention to these feelings. It is vital to tease out how much of these feelings have to do with you and how much of the feelings have to do with the client. In part, this is why engaging supervision and personal counseling is so important. (I refer to Chapters 11 and 12 for more information on these topics.) Through supervision and your own personal counseling, you will be better equipped to sort out the extent to which the strength of your reactions have to do with you and the extent to which they have to do with your client. Equipped with this knowledge, you will be better able to make choices regarding how to counsel your clients. And these choices will enable you to become a more effective clinician, particularly when you find yourself sitting across from a difficult client in the first interview.

Summary

According to Kottler (1993), even seasoned clinicians meet with "patients who try our patience" (p. 115). This chapter's objective was to make it easier for you to work with those trying patients—both those clients with whom everyone struggles and those clients who present a particular challenge for you. The first part of the chapter focused on strategies and techniques for dealing with clients who are challenging in specific ways, such as the hostile client, the chatty client, the vague client, the deceitful client, and the potentially violent client. The second part of the chapter examined how to handle interviewing clients you will find particularly difficult for you as a counselor. Throughout this chapter the importance of knowing yourself, being attuned to your internal experience during the interview, and identifying your expectations regarding your ideal client was emphasized. Engaging new clients in the first interview will be quite a challenge. Rest assured it is a challenge you will be able to manage in time.

Some Questions to Consider

1. As you complete your inventory using the RESPECTFUL cube, what are the three most important things you learned?

2. What, if any, concerns do you have about asserting yourself with the chatty patient?

3. How will you provide structure throughout the initial interview?

4. Review the reasons a client may not tell you the truth in your first session? Are such deceptions ever a sign of health?

5. Why is confrontation with a deceitful client a poor strategy?

6. What is the safety protocol for your site?

9

Sensitive Subjects

Alyson Nelson and Leah M. DeSole

> *I came to explore the wreck.*
> *The words are purposes.*
> *The words are maps.*
> *I came to see the damage that was done*
> *and the treasures that prevail.*
>
> —Adrienne Rich, "Diving into the Wreck"

Chapter Goals

This chapter will help you to:

1. Identify and handle subjects you find difficult as a new clinician.
2. Talk to clients about sensitive subjects.
3. Determine how deeply to delve into sensitive subjects in the first interview.
4. Recognize and intervene in crisis situations in the first interview.

Sensitive Subjects

A number of topics may arise in the first interview that will be difficult for you either because of your client's discomfort or your own. Clients may bring up past issues concerning sensitive material, such as sexual abuse or physical trauma, in the first interview that you will at least need to acknowledge and make note of for future treatment. Alternatively, clients may arrive at your office in a current state of crisis concerning sensitive material that requires immediate intervention. This chapter begins by identifying subjects that may make you, as the clinician, uncomfortable. Subsequently, it reviews how to talk to clients about subjects that are sensitive for them. In particular, it will provide guidelines for dealing with sensitive material during the first interview and provide a plan of action for addressing crisis situations.

Identifying and Handling Difficult Subjects

Identifying Sensitive Subjects

It is critical to anticipate the subjects you will find sensitive in counseling—those subjects that it will be difficult for you to inquire about, listen to, or discuss. Before proceeding, you need to stop and ask yourself: "What do I consider a sensitive subject? What are the types of topics that make me feel uncomfortable?" We all have different personal sensitivities. Being aware of your own sensitivities will help you work more effectively with clients. As in our discussion of difficult patients (Chapter 8), exploring why you find a topic uncomfortable will help you prepare to work with clients who raise these issues. *The very process* of exploring your discomfort can be freeing, enabling you to work more effectively with these issues as they arise. As you feel freer, less stuck, and increasingly at ease with working with subjects you find sensitive, it is likely that your client will follow suit. Indeed, a large part of your role in the first interview is to normalize their concerns and model for them how to talk about sensitive subjects. Some useful questions to ask yourself before you begin working at your site include the following.

- What topics do I wish to avoid in an initial interview?
- What thoughts arise when I talk about these topics?
- What specific feelings arise when I talk about these topics?
- What do I imagine will happen if these topics come up in a session?
- How do I imagine I will I react if my client brings up this topic?

The list of potential sensitive subjects that may arise in a first interview is long and varied. It is also idiosyncratic. What is a sensitive subject to one clinician may leave another clinician unmoved. Nonetheless, there are some subjects that tend to leave most new clinicians feeling uncomfortable. The possibilities include, but are not limited to:

Abortion	Adoption
Anger or impulse control	Animal cruelty
Bedwetting	Binge eating/obesity
Eating disorders: anorexia and bulimia	Homicidal ideation
Ethnicity	Infidelity
Homosexuality	Obsessive-compulsive behaviors
Language differences	Promiscuity
Questionable sexual judgment	Questionable childrearing choices
Race	Religion
Sadomasochism	Sexual abuse

Sexual fetishes	Sexual identity
Socioeconomic status	Substance abuse
Suicidal ideation	Trauma
Transgender issues	Transsexual issues

As you look over this list, remember that no inventory will be comprehensive. There is always the distinctive sensitive subject, such as the death of one's beloved pet, which may emerge in a first interview. It may catch you by surprise in its poignancy. Nevertheless, I encourage you to use this list as a benchmark. It may enable you to become aware of the subjects you will find sensitive in your work with new clients in the first interview.

Case Example.   As a new clinician, I worked as a counselor at a college-counseling center. One of my favorite clients was a student named Mia. She was a pleasure to work with; she was charming, bright, and articulate. She had many interests on campus, and she was successful academically. As a child, Mia had overcome several painful difficulties, including sexual abuse. Nevertheless, she viewed herself as a survivor: strong and capable. Thus, it came to her great surprise when she began experiencing a series of anxiety attacks. These attacks started after she escorted an ill friend to an emergency room. For Mia, as for many survivors of childhood sexual abuse, helping her friend brought up a lot of feelings about her own trauma.

Initially, in the first interview Mia focused on her friend's experiences: factual information about what had happened in the emergency room. I worked hard to listen carefully and be responsive. However, once she began to talk about the sexual abuse she had survived as a child I could feel my ability to listen calmly diminish. I found myself struggling to pay attention to Mia; I was having trouble staying present with her. Instead, all sorts of thoughts raced through my head. "How could this have happened?" "Why didn't she get help?" "Why didn't she tell someone?" My own responses surprised me. I felt annoyed with myself for being distracted and distant. I began to doubt my skills as a new clinician. As I became aware of my discomfort and self-doubt, I realized that childhood sexual abuse was a sensitive subject for me. And I knew I needed to be able to deal with my reactions to it in order to be an effective clinician.

Dealing with Your Reactions to Sensitive Subjects

In the preceding example, I dealt with my reactions to Mia's childhood sexual abuse in several ways. Number one, for me, was supervision. By talking in supervision about the process and content of the interview with Mia, I became less anxious. In so doing, I was able in future sessions to allow Mia to talk about her prior past experiences in a fuller, more productive, and more helpful fashion.

Many clinicians find it difficult to work with trauma survivors. The experience of disorganization and helplessness that characterizes a survivor's traumatic past is a feeling state that most of us wish to avoid at all costs. It can be excruciatingly painful to sit with someone who is describing a time when they were out of control, helpless, and at the mercy of another's brutality. Clinicians may act on their own uncomfortable feelings while in session with a client if they are not aware of them. For this reason alone, it is imperative *that you think ahead about what might make you anxious* and make use of supervision to help you sort out your feelings. Childhood sexual abuse is but one example; there are numerous others, as detailed in the previous list.

In this example, supervision was helpful. It enabled me to work effectively with a new client. Keep in mind, though, that there may be times when you will not want to raise sensitive subjects with your supervisor. In this instance, consider other alternatives. These alternatives include friends, other students in your program, trusted peers or colleagues at your site, faculty members, or advisors at your school. And yet again, I encourage you to engage in personal therapy. Talk with your therapist about not only sensitive subjects that are of concern to you but about how to make use of supervision as a way of processing your thoughts and feelings about your deeply held concerns.

How to Talk to Clients about Sensitive Matters

While it is invaluable to know your idiosyncratic fears and discomforts regarding sensitive subjects, it is also useful to have some general guidelines for how to address sensitive subjects in the first interview. One of the most difficult matters clinicians face is the element of surprise. It is the element of surprise that has the capacity to throw you off balance in the first interview with a new client. Sometimes the feeling of surprise comes from the topic itself; other times you may surprised by your reaction to material that is not particularly unusual—you just did not expect it at that moment with that particular client. In those moments the best you can do is to work to regain your composure.

Once you find yourself feeling off balance in a session, it is useful to take a deep breath and slow down. In an anxious moment, you are likely to feel a pull to say something, anything at all. Rest assured, the pull to respond is a natural, human reaction. Yet, it is a mistake to speak out of your anxiety when interviewing a client. It is important to first gain your composure. Then, you need to take a breath and say nothing until you feel more grounded. A good general strategy is to let your client respond to your silence. Although this may initially feel uncomfortable for both of you, it is a way of slowing yourself down, allowing the client to follow up, and permitting the client to complete her thought. Once you are more composed and your client has finished her thought, you can begin to sort out your emotions and address the client's underlying concerns. There are several basic guidelines for dealing with the client's underlying concerns regarding the sensitive subject matter at hand. They include:

1. Be respectful.
2. Focus on emotion.
3. Manage the depth of the session.
4. Use your client's language.

Be Respectful

When clients talk to you about issues that are sensitive, they are entrusting you with complicated and often painful and shameful experiences. It is important to always remember that it is a privilege to be entrusted with this information. When you are uncomfortable with what your client is saying, it can be a real challenge to convey your respect. You may find yourself feeling distant and distracted. You may have a strong personal reaction to the clinical material based on your own experience. You may find it difficult to listen. When it is difficult to listen, it can feel easier to ask questions. Asking questions can help a clinician to feel more in control. The problem with asking a lot of questions is that although it often helps clinicians feel more in control of the session it can have the opposite effect on clients. Excessive questioning can feel frightening, intrusive, judgmental, and fundamentally disrespectful. Similarly, as a new clinician you may feel pulled to provide advice or a solution to the situation. Although your intentions may be good, your efforts are likely to result in a frustrated and confused client who does not feel respected.

There are several concrete actions you can take to show your respect. They include:

- *Listening with empathy to what your client is saying.* As we talked about earlier, listening is one of the most challenging tasks you face when confronted with material that makes you uncomfortable. Through listening you can deepen your empathy, your ability to identify with your client's experience: how she is feeling and how she perceives her situation. Although it is impossible to know exactly what your client is feeling, your capacity to imagine yourself in your client's shoes is a way of freeing yourself to listen more openly.
- *Allowing your client to ventilate her thoughts and feelings.* This can be tricky during the first interview because your ultimate goal is to gather information in order to move treatment forward. Nevertheless, you may need to put your agenda aside for a bit to let your client vent her feelings. Some clients react strongly just by being with a clinician. They become overwhelmed by their feelings, eager for someone to bear witness to their experience. Sometimes clients will talk almost nonstop for a period of time that may feel endless to the clinician. Try not to interrupt. In the long run, allowing your client to speak freely will enable her to focus better. If she continues to talk for more than seems reasonable, make suggestions to help her slow down (see Chapter 8).
- *Expressing your concern.* Listening with empathy and allowing your client to talk freely are both ways of demonstrating concern. Nonetheless, you can be more direct by making statements such as "I am so sorry you had to go through this," or "It sounds like that took a tremendous amount of courage." What is vital when you express these concerns is the authenticity of your statements. You need to truly feel and believe what you say to your client.
- *Supporting your client's strengths.* Use the first interview to reinforce any positive actions your clients have undertaken. Ask your clients to describe the strengths they have used to help them get through the hard times. At the

very least, tell your clients that simply by talking to you about their struggles they have revealed to you their strengths. Many view asking for help as a weakness. However, it is your job to reframe asking for help as an asset. Indeed, your capacity to reframe their perception of their behavior from an asset to a strength may make all the difference in the world.

Pay Attention to Emotion

Although you will have your own feelings and discomfort talking about a sensitive topic, your clients will also have feelings and discomfort raising a sensitive topic that exposes them to your scrutiny and possible rejection. Therefore, it is useful to check in with clients after they have disclosed something that is potentially shameful. Above all, your stance should be supportive. Pay attention to your clients' affect. Do they appear flat and distant? Are they emotional? Has their mood dipped or risen? Each of these questions is an example of how to gauge your clients' feeling states about their disclosures.

For some clients with long chronic histories, disclosures about sensitive topics may be a matter of course. They may present sensitive information without affect. In these situations, it can be difficult to try to gauge your clients' emotional states. I encourage you to ask your clients how they felt about the experiences. For example:

- "I appreciate your honesty. Tell me, how does it feel to tell me about this?"
- "You've been through a lot. How is it to tell me about what has happened to you?"
- "I know you've talked about this before, but what is it like for you to talk about this now with me?"

Sometimes clients appear nonplussed about their self revelation. They may tell you that it is no big deal to have disclosed this information. Indeed, well-defended clients will work hard to keep affect away—especially when talking about sensitive subjects that expose their vulnerability. With these clients, it can be useful to veer away from inquiries about their feelings in the past. Instead, ask about their feelings in the present, for example:

- "How are you doing right now?"
- "I can't tell what you are feeling. Can you help me?"
- "What are you thinking about now? I want to help, but I need to understand."

As you probably know by now, asking about feelings doesn't necessarily result in your client responding with feelings. Even so, as new clinicians you may be frustrated by your clients' unemotional responses. Asking about feelings in the manner described previously telegraphs to your client that talking about them is okay. It sends the message: "I can appreciate your sensitive situation. Talk about it further. You have not scared me away." Perhaps it seems odd to talk about being scared away by something your client has said. Nonetheless, bear in mind that patients do worry about revealing parts of their lives that are just too unacceptable or too shameful to share. As clinicians, our job is to listen. Often, the first step in that direction is letting our clients know we are willing and able to listen.

Manage the Depth of the Discussion

Although it is important to respond to clients who disclose sensitive material, it is also important to balance your exploration with the needs of your clients. This can be tricky. An initial assessment is not the place for deep and probing inquiries into clients' traumas. You simply do not know them well enough to encourage such candor and openness. After all, at the end of the therapeutic hour you leave them vulnerable. Where are they to go with the thoughts and feelings they have just revealed to you, a virtual stranger—albeit a professional one—when the interview comes to a close? The goal in the first interview is to gather the data you need in order to direct them to the help from which they would benefit. Often, this translates into gathering certain facts and details of their history without making them, on the whole, emotionally vulnerable.

When a client discloses a sensitive experience, you need to relay your sincere concern. You also need to take three steps. First, balance your concern with the realization that this disclosure is likely to involve a great deal of emotion. Sometimes it is enough to say, "Thank you for telling me about what happened. No doubt this stirs up a lot of mixed feelings for you." Second, make your clients aware that although this disclosure may offer some relief in the short term in the long term some deeply disturbing and ambivalent feelings may arise. Third, you need to limit and focus the discussion. This can be challenging, especially if your clients seem ready and eager to talk about the topic at length.

It can feel mean and unprofessional to curtail clients' disclosures. Should you find yourself working with very open and eager clients, you may need to let them know in no uncertain terms that although you want to hear everything they have to say it would be useful for their treatment to proceed slowly. You may want to say:

- "I appreciate that you trust me enough to tell me a little about what happened. I am very interested in what you have to say. Nonetheless, I think it would be more helpful to get some more information before talking further about what happened."
- "What you are saying is very important, and I want to get back to it next time. Unfortunately, our time together today is limited. Can I ask you some questions about_____?"
- "I appreciate your telling me about this. I'd like to get more information about this and other parts of your life next time. Right now, I need to get a little more background information in order to make sense of what you need today."

Certainly, another important reason to limit your exploration of sensitive topics is that it may be therapeutically counterproductive to deeply explore sensitive material during the first interview. Be aware: *a deep discussion about a sensitive subject may be traumatic for your client regardless of how comfortable your client seems in the moment about self-disclosure.* Essentially, it may be harmful to the client to disclose too much, too soon, to an unknown therapist. In particular, clients with trauma histories (e.g., rape, sexual abuse, physical abuse) or clients exploring sensitive aspects of themselves (e.g., their sexual orientation or gender identity) may disclose more than they should to a relative stranger. Although they may not realize it at the time, afterward they may feel in some way traumatized by their disclosure.

Some clients are compliant by nature and eager to give you the information they believe you desire. Their desire to please you may outweigh their ability to take care of themselves. Your job is to help your client feel safe enough to come back and talk to you or a colleague again. This may mean you will need to limit their disclosure to you during the first interview.

The Language You Use

When clients bring up sensitive material it can be difficult to know how to respond. You may find yourself unsure of what words to use and how to talk about your clients' concerns. One general piece of advice is to try to use the language your clients have used. If they describe themselves as having been attacked, use the word *attacked*. If they use the word *incest*, it's okay for you to use that word in talking to them. By using their language you are conveying some measure of comfort in learning about their experiences. You also are conveying your efforts to understand. And your job is always to find ways to convey that you are trying to understand. While you may find the language used by your client awkward at first, you will become more at ease the more you use it.

Contain Your Anxiety

Clients who disclose sensitive material are keenly aware of the anxiety of others. Your own anxiety is like kryptonite to your clients. Sensitive, knowledgeable clients will stop talking to you in a heartbeat if they sense that you are anxious about what they have to say. There is no quick cure to eliminate your anxiety. As described earlier here and in Chapter 8, the best strategy for containing anxiety is to better understand what makes you so afraid.

Your awareness and openness to your feelings is vital when working with clinical material to which you are sensitive. We talked earlier about the importance of anxiety as a signal that lets you know that you are afraid of something. It is important to pay attention to this signal and examine your fear. Identify your anxiety, think about the fear that lies beneath it, and work to understand what it is that frightens you. Although it is important to explore your feelings before you begin to work with clients, as we described earlier in this chapter you will also need to work through your anxious feelings *during* the first interview. That is to say, you may need to become your own internal supervisor. You need to monitor and be curious about your thoughts and feelings as you are experiencing them. Question yourself and your thoughts, feelings, and behaviors when you are in the midst of the first interview. You may be asking yourself how it is possible to do this. This is not something that can be done quickly, but it is something that can be accomplished with practice.

Recognizing Crisis Situations

In some general way, when clients make the decision (or in some cases have the decision made for them) to come for treatment, they are in some sort of crisis. Even as a novice clinician, you will clearly recognize the difference between a crisis situation and a garden-variety initial interview. Gladding (2002) describes crisis counseling as a special type of counseling in that it is directive and focused on helping a client function in the midst of a disorienting, chaotic emotional experience. It is the feeling of chaos that characterizes a crisis situation.

Clinicians, beginning and experienced, are likely to feel and in some way absorb their client's sense of fear, danger, and chaos. We feel the need to do something, to take some action. Beginning clinicians are especially likely to respond to their client's danger signals with a strong desire to take responsibility. The client's obvious need to be taken care of is difficult to resist. Part of the goal of crisis counseling is to help the client shore up her strengths and resources so that she can take care of herself.

Again, you need to check with your supervisor to determine the procedure your setting follows when dealing with crisis situations. Your supervisor may want you to refer those clients to other professionals at your institution, or she may deem clients in crisis to be good training cases. The bottom line is that you will need to ask your supervisor, preferably ahead of time, how you should handle crisis situations—and above all else follow her guidelines.

The crisis situation is different from a typical first interview. Regardless of how impaired, needy, and problematic a typical client may be, there is a difference between that problematic client and a client in crisis. A distinct feeling of urgency, potential danger, and a pressing need for immediate action mark a client in crisis. Your client will convey her need for something to be done immediately. And you are likely to feel a pressing need to do something immediately. It is ironic that at the very time it is so important to carefully think through decisions both client and clinician are under tremendous pressure to act quickly.

In this section we discuss crisis situations. These are situations that necessitate some sort of "crisis intervention." It is worth noting that anyone can find themselves in a crisis. Any of us can become so stressed by environmental factors that our coping mechanisms fail us and we find ourselves in an emotional danger zone. No one is immune to these danger zone moments (Moursund & Kenny, 2002). What will follow in this section is how you can work with any client during those times when she is in an emotional danger zone.

What Is a Crisis?

This chapter began with a quote from Adrienne Rich (1973, p. 23): "I came to explore the wreck. - The words are purposes. - The words are maps. - I came to see the damage that was done - and the treasures that prevail." These lines are from her book of poetry titled "Diving into the Wreck." Sometimes, when exploring sensitive subjects with a new client you may feel like you are diving into a wreck—crashing into a shamble you never knew existed. Indeed, a basic marker of a crisis situation is that it seems to happen quickly and unexpectedly. Internal and external pressures seem to rise out of nowhere and the client feels overwhelmed.

The danger in this situation lies in that clinicians, too, feel overwhelmed by their clients' feelings. New clinicians can anchor themselves during this time of turmoil by remaining grounded in theory and being knowledgeable of their institution's protocol. You may find that there is a procedure in place for crisis situations. Once you alert your supervisor that your client has a crisis situation, you will receive assistance meeting your clients' needs. Let's assume that you will continue to work with clients beyond the first interview. You should know how to identify a crisis during the initial interview, how to work with your client in the interview, and how to defuse the danger and shrink the problem to a more manageable size. Essentially, these are the tasks of the first interview.

Crisis situations develop in a predictable pattern. James and Gilliand (2004) described four stages of a crisis situation.

1. A crisis situation occurs where a person's "normal" coping mechanisms are taxed.
2. Increased tension and disorganization around an external event escalate beyond the person's normal coping mechanisms.
3. Additional resources are needed to resolve the event.
4. A referral may be needed for long-term treatment.

Typically, people seek professional help in the third stage. This is the time when the person's coping strategies have failed, internal tension has peaked, and feelings of being overwhelmed and disorganization have set in. During a clinical interview, you will know when clients are in crisis because they will tell you—if not with words then with actions. Clients tend to be direct at this stage. They need help. Their defenses are diminished and their coping skills are exhausted. They will tell you they need your help.

There are a great variety of events that trigger crises. Patterson and Welfel (1994) outline the major triggers.

- Death of a friend or family member
- Physical or mental illness (acute disability, injury, abuse)
- Disruption of intimate relationships (infidelity, separation, divorce)
- Violence (domestic, criminal, civil)
- Disruption of school or work (layoffs, firings, strikes, academic failure)

- Financial emergencies (unexpected expenses, bankruptcy, investment losses, theft or fraud)
- Natural and environmental disasters

But how is it possible to deal with these crises in an initial interview? What can you possibly do to help? Something to keep in mind is that by definition a crisis is time limited. It will not go on indefinitely. A crisis has a trajectory of one to six weeks. There is a relatively short time when the crisis will be acute and the client will be most eager to be helped. As the clinician interviewing the client, you have a unique opportunity to help.

Steps in a Crisis Intervention

James and Gilliand (2004) describe a five-step process of crisis intervention that can be implemented in one to three sessions. The steps are:

1. Define the problem.
2. Provide support.
3. Examine alternatives.
4. Make a plan.
5. Obtain your client's commitment.

We will discuss defining the problem in detail, because that is the work of the first session. Defining the problems is the most important step in the process because by defining the problem you will be able to determine what the client needs and if you are the clinician best suited to meet those needs.

Defining the client's problem involves *gathering information* about the current concern. Unlike a typical interview, where you are interested in the client's past, in a crisis session you are focused on the client's current situation. You are only interested in the past as it is related to the current crisis. Similarly, unlike most first sessions when you face a client in crisis it is not necessary or even advisable to take a complete history. Clients are so anxious to talk about their crisis that any delay may be unbearably frustrating. That said, it is first helpful to get a picture of the types of problems or crises the client has faced in the past and how she dealt with those situations.

Gathering information on the client's past crises and coping mechanisms will help you and your client begin to tease out her typical response patterns, examine what has worked and not worked during very stressful times, and gain a sense of her normal state. Given that your client is likely to become anxious when you inquire about her past history with crises, it may be useful to empathize and then explain why you are asking. You might say:

- "I know you have a lot to say right now, Mr. Mehta, but it will be helpful to you if we spend a little time understanding how you've dealt with problems in the past."

- "It sounds like this is a very difficult time for you. I can help you, but I need to know what strategies you've used when you've faced other difficult times."
- "Wow, Ms. Rociolo, you are really going through a lot right now. I know I can help you get through this. Can you tell me about other times when your life felt this out of control?"

The major goal of any crisis intervention is to get your clients back to their baseline level of functioning. This will give you a sense of what you can expect from them when they are at their best, or when they are at their worst. If they weren't doing very well before the crisis, you may only be able to expect a minimal level of functioning after the crisis. If they typically function well and have rebounded from past crises, you will be able to expect a higher level of functioning after the crisis has passed.

In order to assess your clients' strengths and weaknesses, you will need to assess their resources. Clients are eager to tell you what has happened to them and their perceptions of the problem. As you listen to the content of their story, you should also be listen for the following.

- What is going on now?
- What has gone on in the past?
- How have they tried to handle the problem before?
- Who in the client's life has been involved in the problem?
- What demands are being made on the client?
- Why are they seeking help now?

Think about these questions as your clients share their stories. You also may want to directly ask these questions and work together to sort them out. Kottler (1990, 2003) suggests that clinicians spend some time thinking about the meaning of the crisis in the moment. He poses the questions: "How is the crisis getting the client's attention?" and "What is the meaning of the crisis in the moment?" He proposes that merely by thinking about these questions clinicians will be better able to understand what can be done to redirect their clients to solve their own problems.

The next step in crisis intervention is *assessing resources*. Resources take many forms and include the client's support system, economic situation, skills, and problem-solving skills. The most important resource to assess is the social support clients have to address their problems. To begin assessing clients' resources, listen and ask questions about who is in the client's life. For example: Who do they talk about? Ask directly, "Who is there to help?" Moreover, as clients tell you what has transpired, be alert to the people they have to help them. In addition, ask about their use of counseling and how it has helped or not helped in the past during times of crisis.

A crisis is a time when social support needs to be mobilized and activated. It may be difficult for your clients to take on the task of mobilizing resources for themselves. With their permission, you can help them by talking to the important people in their lives. Depending on your setting (e.g., inpatient hospital, outpatient mental health clinic, college counseling center), the nature of support varies and issues of confidentiality differ. Remember, you must have clients sign a consent form before you talk to significant others in their lives. Likewise, while it may feel awkward to talk about the limits of confidentiality when clients are in crisis it is especially important to clarify these issues. Specifically, you need to make clear that what they tell you in session will not be kept confidential if you deem them to be a danger to self or others (see Chapter 10).

The last step of your crisis intervention session should involve you and your client *creating a contract*. In fact, your session should not end until you are able to agree on a contract. A contract is a written document that outlines short-term goals and how they will be accomplished. Contracting is very important because the contract document itself often serves as an anchor for clients, something to hold on to and provide focus when they are feeling fragmented and overwhelmed. Also, the process of thinking through a plan of action is invaluable to clients who are feeling lost because that helps to provide a clear direction for the client over the short term. Perhaps most importantly, a crisis contract is a hopeful sign that they can do something to alleviate their suffering and that over time life will get better. The process of contracting involves identifying short-term goals and determining what is practical, choosing one or two goals, outlining the clients' responsibilities and the responsibilities of others, and gaining your client's commitment to the goals and her responsibilities. Ottens and Fisher-McCanne (1990) state that crisis contracts need to be specific about:

- The focus of the problem: What exactly needs to be changed or fixed?
- Time limits: How long should it take to initiate change?
- Who are the important others that will be involved?
- What are the responsibilities of the client?
- What are the responsibilities of the therapist?

They suggest that once you have made the content clear (e.g., who, what, when, and how), you have created a workable contract. The process of creating a contract entails developing a working relationship based on honesty and trust. The more honesty and trust the stronger the therapeutic relationship, and the more successful the crisis intervention will be.

The bottom-line goal of any crisis intervention is to restore the client's functioning to her pre-crisis baseline. This sounds simple enough. The problem is that when your client is in the middle of a crisis she is operating in a muddled, confused, and disorganized way. She is too deeply in her problem to get herself out of it. Your task is to help her step back and explore possible alternatives, possible solutions. To do this you will need to create some breathing room for her so that she can begin to think more clearly. By listening to your client's story with empathy and respect you can help her think through her options and resources and take charge of her life.

Summary

This chapter began with an overview of ways to effectively work with clinical material that is likely to heighten your anxiety. Crisis situations also undoubtedly raise anxiety. Anxiety has been described as the gift that keeps on giving: it is an emotional state that is contagious from client to clinician and back again. The key to effective work with sensitive material and crisis situations is to be as present and available as possible. This is often easier said than done. To do so you will have to first contain your own anxiety and then be open to absorbing your client's anxiety and other negative feelings. Your ability to be respectful and real when she is feeling bad (angry, conflicted, overwhelmed, numb, and so on) and ashamed gives you traction into the therapeutic relationship whether that relationship is one session or several years long.

Some Questions to Consider

1. What five subjects from the list at the beginning of the chapter make you feel most uncomfortable?

2. What are your strategies for overcoming your discomfort?

3. State the overriding goal of the initial interview?

4. What steps will you take in the first interview with a patient who is in crisis?

5. What is the challenge in conveying respect for a client who tells you something painful and perhaps shameful?

10

Suicidal and Homicidal Patients

Alyson Nelson and Leah M. DeSole

Death whispers in my ear: "LIVE FOR I AM COMING."

—Oliver Wendell Holmes

Chapter Goals

This chapter will help you to:

1. Review your professional responsibility for suicidal and homicidal patients.
2. Clarify the myths and facts about suicide.
3. Inquire about suicidal ideation in the first interview.
4. Develop strategies for responding to a positive risk assessment.

Suicidal and Homicidal Ideation

Conducting the first interview with a suicidal or homicidal patient constitutes one of the most difficult tasks clinicians-in-training face in their careers. It doesn't require much imagination to figure out why. Picture a scenario with a suicidal patient: you have just been assigned a new patient. During your session, he tells you of his desire to kill himself. You act in a professionally responsible manner and conduct a thorough suicide assessment. You notify your supervisor and coordinate his care with other mental health professionals. Two weeks later, you find out he has killed himself. How would you feel? What would you do? According to a 2004 study by the American Foundation for Suicide Prevention, over one-third of the surveyed clinicians suffered severe grief, sadness, and distress following a patient's suicide. Moreover, new and experienced clinicians alike are likely to feel guilty and wonder: "What did I do wrong? What did I miss? What could I have done differently?" Compounding this guilt is anger and shame: "How could he have done this? Why didn't he listen to me?" And compounding it further is fear. All clinicians are likely to fear the reaction of their peers, the response of the institution for whom they work, and maybe even a lawsuit by the patient's family.

This sequence of events can be devastating both personally and professionally to a clinician. It is one reason clinicians dread the prospect of discovering their patient presents a potential harm to themselves or others. Consequently, it can be tempting to believe that you can avoid working with patients who admit to having suicidal or homicidal impulses. New clinicians do this in a variety of ways. Some plan to work with populations they doubt will want to harm themselves or others, such as gifted preschool children. Others choose a specialty such as vocational counseling, thinking that they will avoid patients at risk for homicidal or suicidal impulses. Though both of these strategies are understandable, they are unlikely to be effective. As the saying goes, "You can run away, but you can't hide." It is impossible to avoid counseling a suicidal or homicidal patient at some point in your career. Indeed, it is not uncommon for a patient to acknowledge having these thoughts in the first interview. After all, sometimes patients do not realize the depth of their impulses until they sit down to talk to a mental health professional for the first time. Thus, I encourage you to be prepared to inquire about suicidal and homicidal ideation in the initial contact with all new patients.

This chapter's primary purpose is to help you prepare for conducting the first interview with a patient who may pose a danger to himself or others. Subsequent sections address some of the myths about suicide and provide guidelines specifically regarding how to conduct a suicide risk assessment. But first, it is vital to clarify your professional responsibility in cases where patients pose a potential harm to themselves or others.

Professional Responsibility

Although professionals in the mental health field have a professional responsibility to do all they can to prevent patients from harming themselves or others, it is impossible to actually prevent a determined patient from doing so. Nevertheless, it is possible to assess the likelihood that a patient may pose a danger to themselves or others. On this account, mental health professionals are subject to both federal laws and state laws. State laws, by and large, are the most relevant to professional liability. In addition, each profession in the field of mental health (e.g., psychology, psychiatry, social workers, certified mental health counselors, and so on) has its own code of ethical conduct. It is your responsibility to know your profession's code of ethics; the code establishes the acceptable standards of conduct within your specialty. More importantly, it establishes the standards of practice adopted by the majority of state licensing boards. Consequently, although they are not federal or state laws they may be thought of as "the laws of the profession." Moreover, to the extent that these codes govern state licensing and practice it is incumbent upon you to know your profession's code of ethical conduct as it pertains to working with suicidal and homicidal patients. Indeed, it behooves you to think of your profession's code of ethical conduct as if it were law.

Many clinicians have heard of the *Tarasoff* case, a malpractice lawsuit in California that dealt with a clinician's duty to protect the general public from patients who express homicidal intent (Behnke, Perlin, & Bernstein, 2003). To this day, the *Tarasoff* case evokes anxiety and apprehension in the hearts of many clinicians. Nevertheless, the case's ruling and its implications for mental health practitioners around the country are often misunderstood and misinterpreted. The fact is that no single case, statute, or regulation will ever directly and completely address what your professional liability is when a patient sits before you in the first interview and talks about harming themselves or others. What will address your professional liability are the complex of federal laws, state laws, and your particular mental health specialty's standards of practice. Above all, what matters most is your documentation of the process you undertake when you work with a patient who presents a danger to themselves or others.

Understanding Your Liability

All patients must be asked about suicidal and homicidal thoughts in the first interview, although some patients may need to be questioned more fully than others. The responsibility of all mental health professionals is *to assess the probability that a patient presents a danger to themselves or others*. It is not a clinician's responsibility *to predict* whether or not a patient will commit suicide or harm someone else. Prediction is impossible; no behavior can be predicted with complete confidence. What a clinician can do, however, is evaluate the circumstances in which a patient's life that may place him at a risk for harming himself or others. Some circumstances, such as current or chronic substance abuse, are associated with a greater risk. Other circumstances, such as living with other people, are associated with a lesser risk. This evaluation of a patient's life circumstances and estimation of risk are referred to in the field of mental health as *a risk assessment*.

When the time comes to conduct a risk assessment, you are professionally liable to document the process you have undertaken. According to Behenke, Perlin, and Bernstein (2003), your documentation should address three fundamental questions:

1. What did you do?
2. Why did you do it?
3. On what basis did you reject other ways of responding?

Whenever possible, report a patient's statements regarding suicidal or homicidal ideation verbatim in your documentation. It is also advisable that you document any consultation with others professionals involved in the patient's care, such as the psychiatrist who is prescribing medication to the patient.

Informing Patients

Knowing about federal and state laws as well as your profession's code of ethical conduct regarding patients who pose a danger to themselves or others is only one piece of the puzzle. The other important piece of the puzzle is informing your patients about your responsibilities as a professional. Essentially, this entails explaining *the limits of patient confidentiality* in the first interview with a new patient. (For an extensive discussion of confidentiality, see Chapter 5.) Consequently, you will need to know the nature and limits of confidentiality particular to the profession and site in which you are working. State professional organizations can often provide you with this information.

As a new clinician, the sites in which you are working should have a standard confidentiality agreement. It is best if it is in a written form that can be presented to your patients for their signature. Check with your supervisor to see if this is the case. Typically, a confidentiality agreement specifically addresses the limits of confidentiality as they pertain to a patient's suicidal and homicidal ideation. In situations where you have a real reason to believe the patient is at risk, I also advise you to emphasize aloud:

- "Lydia, there are some limits to confidentiality. If I think that you present a danger to yourself or another person, I am professionally obligated to share this information with others."
- "Jorge, there are some limits to confidentiality. For example, if you tell me that you are a danger to yourself or another person, I am obligated to share this information with others."

In addition, it is often reassuring to your patient to acknowledge:

- "If safety concerns arise, and I have to break confidentiality, I would like to remain available to you in any professional capacity I can."
- "If I have to break confidentiality for this reason, it is out of my concern for you. If possible, I still want to be here for you as your counselor."

Of course, only make these statements if they are true. In my experience, offering such reassurances to patients can go a long way toward engaging them—particularly those patients who are experiencing suicidal or homicidal ideation.

Suicide: Myths and Facts

According to Susan Lukas, in her assessment handbook *Where to Start and What to Ask* (1993), there are two important myths surrounding suicide that need to be dispelled at the outset. These myths are commonly held beliefs, not founded on facts that may discourage new clinicians from talking about suicide with patients in the first interview. Consequently, they need to be debunked at the outset.

Myth 1: A person who is thinking about killing himself won't tell anyone.

Most people who attempt or succeed at taking their own lives *do tell others* within the weeks before their attempt. They may make a passing remark that goes unnoticed by others, such as "I really wouldn't care if I fell asleep and did not wake up in the morning." They may teasingly ask "What do you think is the chance that I could get hit by a bus tomorrow?" In addition, they may make other comments that communicate they are thinking about suicide—even if they don't say outright "I want to kill myself." What these remarks have in common is the feelings of despondency or hopelessness they convey. When patients talk to you in this way, even if what they are saying is spoken in a passing manner or teasing way, you need to take their statements seriously.

Although a person may not say that she is thinking about killing herself, she may communicate it nonverbally. For example, she might stop eating or begin giving away her possessions, she may not show up for appointments or for work, or she may complain about vague physical symptoms. She also may display intense apathy or a serious lack of interest in typically pleasurable activities. Sometimes this behavior is accompanied by statements of "Nothing interests me anymore," or "What difference does it make whether or not I pass the exam?" A more dramatic way a person can show she is thinking about suicide is by making an attempt on her life that is harmful but not lethal. Such incidents are referred to as suicidal gestures rather than attempts at suicide. Nonetheless, they should be taken very seriously: these gestures signal to others that the person is in terrible pain. Often they are thought of as cries for help—ways that people let others know the pain they are feeling.

The bottom line is that a person who is thinking about killing himself will often tell others. This makes it all the more important to directly inquire about suicidal ideation in the first interview.

Myth 2: Talking about suicide makes it so.

The second myth surrounding suicidality is that *talking about suicide makes it so.* According to this myth, you will put the idea of suicide in your patient's head if you attempt to bring up the subject, let alone explore it in depth, in the first interview. The concern, essentially, is that merely talking about suicide will lead to dire consequences. In reality, the opposite is true: allowing patients to discuss their thoughts about harming themselves decreases the risk they will commit suicide. Indeed, patients who are thinking about hurting themselves are often grateful to others who bring up the topic. Why? It relieves them of the burden of having to raise the topic themselves, and it alleviates the shame many patients carry with them of keeping these painful thoughts to themselves.

People across all cultures have thought about or talked about committing suicide since the beginning of recorded history. The majority of people contemplate killing themselves at some point over the course of their lifetime as a way out of a crisis or to alleviate suffering. However, the vast majority of these people do not act on these impulses. There is a considerable difference between thinking about suicide and acting it out. This may be an important distinction to share with your patients. It may also be an important point to bear in mind during the first interview with a new patient: "Asking about suicide does not increase the risk" (Kaplan & Sadock, 2003, p. 249).

The bottom line is that encouraging someone to talk about their suicidal thoughts and feelings will not cause them to commit suicide. That being said, it requires real skill and forethought to talk to patients about suicide in the first interview.

How to Talk about Suicide and Homicide in the First Interview

Given that most patients are willing to talk about suicide and talking about it does not make it so, one of the dilemmas new clinicians face is how to raise the topic with their patients. I recommend being direct and asking:

- "Have you ever thought of hurting yourself or someone else?"
- "Have you had thoughts of death or suicide?"
- "Do you have thoughts of harming yourself? What about harming someone else?"

As you proceed to inquire about either suicidal or homicidal ideation, your method should be simple and straightforward. Your manner should be calm and deliberate. You need to feel comfortable asking these questions. You can be certain your patient will sense it if you do not. As a result, it will be difficult to get the information you need to make an adequate risk assessment. If the patient acknowledges suicidal or homicidal ideation, you will need to inquire further in order to assess:

- Risk
- Depression
- Ideation
- Planning
- Impulse control
- Intent

When possible, take detailed notes describing the patient's behavior and the content of his thoughts. Be aware that a suicidal or homicidal patient may express intense feelings. How you talk about and tolerate these feelings while you are with the patient in the first interview matters. It is critical that you resist the tendency to react in kind and echo the intense feelings of the patient. Rather, your goal is to acknowledge the feelings while maintaining a calm atmosphere of comfort and support.

Above all, you want to balance the patient's feelings of fear, anger, anxiety, sadness, and so on with a sense of hope. I find it helpful to bear in mind (and perhaps share with the patient) that although things may feel terrible now they can get better. Indeed, they may feel worse before they get better—but eventually they will improve.

Assessing Risk

The first step in conducting a risk assessment is to evaluate the circumstances in a patient's life that may place him at a risk for harming himself or others. These may be further separated into to two categories: sociodemographic factors and health factors.

Sociodemographic Factors. Noteworthy sociodemographic risk factors include age, employment status, family history, gender, immigration status, marital status, occupation, race, religion, sexual orientation, and social relations. See Table 10.1 for concise risk assessment summary.

Some of these factors are apparent or easily obtained (e.g., gender and occupation). Other factors require a careful inquiry (e.g., family history and social relations), beginning with general questions and progressing further as needed. To start, you might simply ask:

- "How are things going in your marriage?"
- "What has been happening in your family recently?"
- "How are your relationships with your friends these days?"
- "What is work like lately?"

Depending on the patient's response and the level of risk it reveals, these questions may be followed up with a more detailed inquiry. Moreover, be aware that each patient's risk assessment must be ascertained in the context of his or her culture. Some cultures strongly oppose suicide or homicide; others sanction such actions under certain conditions. When in doubt, ask the patient how suicide or homicide is viewed within the context of their cultural and/or familial environment.

- "Latisha, how would your family view your desire to harm yourself?"
- "Mario, how might your Italian Catholic upbringing influence your wish to hurt yourself?"
- Ms. Porte, how would your desire to commit suicide be regarded within your Phillipino community?"

Overall, keep in mind that a patient's risk may be strongly mediated by the extent to which his or her culture sanctions suicide. Interacting with these cultural considerations are the reactions of immediate family members and the degree to which the patient identifies with his or her racial/cultural background.

TABLE 10.1   *Suicide Risk Assessment: Sociodemographic Factors*

Risk Factor	Low Risk	High Risk
Age	Under 45 years old	Over 45 years old
Employment status	Employed	Unemployed
Family history	Stable	Unstable; chaotic
		Early parental loss/separation
		Family history of suicide
		Recent childbirth
		Recent death in family
		Severe family pathology
Gender	Female	Male
Immigration status	Native born	Immigrant
Marital status	Married	Divorced
	Married with children	Widowed
	Never married	
Occupation	High social status occupations (see next column for exceptions)	Musicians, dentists, subgroups of physicians, law enforcement officers, lawyers, insurance agents
Race	People of color (excluding American Indians)	Whites
Religion	More orthodox groups	Less orthodox groups
	More socially integrated	Less socially integrated
	Catholic	Protestant
		Nonreligious
Sexual orientation	Heterosexual	Homosexual
		Bisexual
		Transgender
		Transsexual
Social relations	Socially integrated; stable	Socially isolated; unstable

Health Factors.   In conducting a risk assessment, factors pertaining to both physical and mental health should be evaluated in addition to sociodemographic factors. See Table 10.2 for concise risk assessment summary.

Overall, the relationship between mental and physical illness to increased suicide risk is significant. According to Kaplan and Sadock (2003), postmortem studies reveal that serious or significant physical illness is present in 25 to 75 percent of all completed suicides. Specific physical illnesses that correlate with increased suicide risk include syndromes associated with chronic pain, epilepsy, multiple sclerosis, head injury, AIDS, heart disease, Cushing's disease, Klinefelter's syndrome, porphyria, gastrointestinal disorders, and urogenital problems. Moreover, as patients age the risk of suicide associated with physical illness increases. The risk also increases given the extent to which physical illness creates a disruption in patients' recreational or occupational activities.

TABLE 10.2 *Suicide Risk Assessment: Health Factors*

Risk Factor	Low Risk	High Risk
Mental	Mild depression	Severe depression
	Neurosis	Psychosis
	Normal personality	Severe personality disorder
	Social drinker	Alcohol abuse or dependence
		Other substance dependence
		Schizophrenia
		Multiple psychiatric hospitalizations
		Recent release from psychiatric hospital
Physical	Good physical health	Medical attention within past six months
		Diseases of the central nervous system
		Cancer
		Certain endocrine conditions
		Illness or disease causing mobility loss

At face value, the connection between mental health and increased suicide risk is more obvious than the connection between physical health and increased suicide risk. In particular, a diagnosis of depression in the first interview merits special attention when conducting a suicide risk assessment. Patients with severe depression have a markedly increased suicide risk. According to Kaplan and Sadock (2003), "Depression is associated not only with completed suicide but also with serious attempts at suicide" (p. 916). The next section directly addresses how to assess depression, particularly with a patient you have never met before.

Assessing Depression

The depth of a patient's depression may vary from mild to major. Major depression is associated with increased suicide risk; minor depression is associated with decreased suicide risk. Depression may be characterized by variety of symptoms: a low mood, diminished interest or pleasure (anhedonia), appetite and weight changes, problems sleeping, fatigue or agitation, self-esteem issues, and diminished ability to think or make decisions. In addition, clinicians often categorize depressive symptoms into either "vegetative signs" (e.g., psychomotor retardation and hypersomnia, loss of appetite, and diminished sexual interest) or "agitated/anxious signs" (e.g., restlessness, insomnia, excessive appetite, and irritability). When conducting a risk assessment, it is essential that the clinician get a clear picture of the type and depth of depression the patient is experiencing. To do this you will need to ask questions. For example:

- Mood: Have you been feeling sad or down lately?
  If yes: For how long have you felt like this?
  Would you say you feel this way every day?

How much of the day does the feeling last?

Does the feeling change over the course of the day (e.g., is it worse at night)?

On a scale of one to ten, one being the worst, how bad is the feeling now?

- Interest: Have you noticed that you get less pleasure out of things you used to enjoy?

  If yes: What are the kinds of things you used to enjoy (e.g., reading, sex, watching television, socializing)?

  Which of these no longer interests you?

  How long have you felt this disinterest?

  Is it like that nearly every day or are some days better than others?

  What do you still like to do?

- Appetite: Have you noticed any change in your appetite?

  If yes: How much more or less have you been eating?

  Is your appetite like that almost every day or are some days better than others?

  For how long has your appetite been like this?

  Have you gained or lost any weight? If so, how much?

- Sleeping: Have you noticed any change in your sleeping habits?

  If yes: How many hours a night do you normally sleep?

  How does this compare to how much you have been sleeping lately?

  Is there a problem nearly every night, or are some nights better than others?

  Do you have trouble falling asleep (initial insomnia)?

  Do you have trouble staying asleep (middle insomnia)?

  Do you have trouble waking up too early?

  How often do you sleep later or more than you intended?

- Fatigue or agitation: How is your energy level?

  If low: Have you felt worn out or like you were moving in slow motion lately?

  Have others noticed that you have slowed down?

  For how long have you felt like this?

  Would you say you feel this way every day?

  How much of the day does the feeling last?

  Does the feeling change over the course of the day (e.g., is it worse at night)?

  If high: Have you been feeling more fidgety?

  Have others noticed your restlessness?

  For how long have you felt like this?

  Would you say you feel this way every day?

  How much of the day does the feeling last?

Does the feeling change over the course of the day (e.g., is it worse at night)?

- Self-esteem: How have you been feeling about yourself lately?
  If yes: Tell me about the kinds of thoughts you've had about yourself these days?
                  Do you ever blame yourself for things that go wrong? Like what?
                  Have you been feeling guilty lately? About what?
                  Do you find yourself feeling worthless or hopeless sometimes?
- Thought process: Do you ever have a hard time thinking or concentrating?
  If yes: When does this occur (e.g., reading, watching television)?
                  Do you ever have trouble following a casual conversation?
                  Do you find it harder to make everyday decisions than it used to be?
                  For how long have you felt like this?
                  Would you say you feel this way every day?
                  How much of the day does the feeling last?
                  Does the feeling change over the course of the day (e.g., is it worse at night)?

As you assess the depth and nature of your patient's depression, you need to pay close attention to his or her behavior in the consulting room. Be alert to vegetative signs of depression, such as slowed speech, long pauses, silence or limited verbal response, difficulty concentrating, and slowed body movement. Likewise, be alert to anxious or agitated manifestations of depression, such as speaking quickly, tangential thought processes, inability to sit still, and difficulty focusing in response to direct questions.

Overall, you may observe that the patient has a difficult time responding to your questions. This may lead patients to feel frustrated. The danger with frustrations is that it leaves patients feeling like they have no choices and therefore no ability to ease their depression. Under these conditions, it is easy for hopelessness to set in. Suicide, therefore, may seem like their only possibility for relief. This leads to the next section, on exploring suicidal ideation.

Assessing Ideation

Exploring suicidal ideation entails asking your patients directly if they are having thoughts about harming themselves. It may be useful to have a standard question you can use with all patients. For example:

- "You seem to be very depressed. Have you found yourself thinking of suicide?"
- "From what you've told me, you seem to feel pretty miserable. When you are feeling miserable, do you think about hurting yourself?"
- "You sound very depressed. How often do you think about ending your life?"

If you are interviewing a patient you believe has suicidal thoughts but may be inclined to deny them, it may be helpful to normalize the patient's feelings. To this end, Wollersheim (1974) proposes saying:

- "Well, I ask this question because almost all people at one time or another during their lives have thought about suicide."
- "There is nothing abnormal about thinking about hurting yourself. In fact, it is very normal when one feels down in the dumps."
- "The thought of suicide, itself, is not harmful. Yet, if you find yourself thinking about it a lot, it may be a cue that all is not well and you'd benefit from making some efforts to make life more satisfying again."

Once a patient has disclosed having suicidal thoughts, the content of these thoughts needs to be explored. You must ask about the duration, frequency, and intensity of these thoughts. Standard inquiries include:

- "Can you recall when you first had thoughts about hurting yourself?"
- "Would you say you have these thoughts daily?"
- "Do your thoughts of suicide vary over the course of the day; for example, are they worse at night or when you first wake up in the morning?"
- "On a scale of one to ten, one being the worst, how strong are your thoughts of committing suicide at present?"

Taken together, your patient's responses to these questions will go a long way toward clarifying the nature of your patient's suicidal ideation. It will also help you assess the severity of your patient's risk for suicide. Overall, patients who express infrequent, short-lived, and low-intensity suicidal ideation are at low risk for committing suicide. In contrast, it is patients who express frequent, prolonged, and intense suicidal ideation who are at high risk for harming themselves.

Assessing Planning

The next step in the risk assessment is determining whether the patient has made any plans to commit suicide and what those plans may be. Once your patient has acknowledged thinking about suicide, it is likely they will give you information regarding their suicide plans. I recommend that you preface this discussion by echoing the patient's words. For example:

- "Mr. Gordon, you said you think about suicide. Have you thought about how you might do it?"
- "Devon, you said you want to die and you think about hurting yourself. How might you hurt yourself if you could?"
- "Marcus, you said you want to kill yourself. Have you ever rehearsed or practiced how you might do it?"

Sometimes, in response to such direct questioning, patients will backpedal. They will try to reassure you that they did not really mean what they said when they talked about hurting themselves or committing suicide. They may talk about family, religious convictions, responsibilities, or some other reason they have to stay alive. If what they say truly feels plausible, the evaluation may end here. You may not feel the need to assess a patient's plans further. Sometimes, however, lingering doubts remain. You may not be sure that the patient is telling the truth when he says he did not really mean what he said when he discussed his thoughts of suicide. If this is the case, normalize your questions to make it easier for your patient to answer affirmatively. For example, you might say:

- "In my experience, most people who've thought about suicide have at least had a passing thought about how they would kill themselves. Tell me one thought you may have had."
- "It's perfectly normal if you think about hurting yourself to also think about how you'd do it. Have you ever thought of a way?"

Asking a follow-up question in this manner does a couple of important things. First, it is reassures the patient that their thoughts are normal: it's common to not only think about suicide but to fantasize about how to do it. Second, it reassures you, if you have any qualms about your patient, that you have been thorough in your assessment.

If your patient acknowledges having a suicide plan, you will need to explore several details further. In particular, the specificity of the plan needs to be assessed. *The more specific the plan the higher the risk.* In other words, has the patient thought through the details necessary to complete a suicide? Another important area to inquire about is lethality. Lethality refers to how likely the patient's plan could result in death. *The greater the lethality the higher the suicide risk.* You also need to ask about the method they plan to use and how they will employ the method. For example, if they say they will use a razor blade, ask what will you do with the razor blade? If they plan on overdosing on medication, what medication will they use? *The bottom line: some methods have a higher risk than others.*

Another area to explore regarding the plan is availability: how fast your patient could implement his suicide plan and does your patient have the means to immediately implement his plan? *A plan that can be implemented quickly with the available means at hand carries a higher suicide risk.* Finally, the last piece of the plan to consider is proximity of help. That is, are there individuals who could intervene and help the patient if the patient actually made an attempt? Questions to bear in mind are: does the patient live with roommates or family or does the patient live alone? Is your patient's day spent at work surrounded by people or does your patient tend to spend the day alone? *As a general rule, the more isolated and distant from helping resources the greater the risk of suicide.*

Assessing Impulse Control

Often overlooked in a suicide risk assessment is an evaluation of the patient's capacity for self-control. Impulsivity presents a high risk for committing suicide. Patients who state they feel out of control and may commit suicide are at a higher risk than those who claim they can control their suicidal impulses (Wollersheim, 1974). You can check for impulsivity by first asking more general questions and then becoming more specific with regard to suicide risk.

- Do you tend to be impulsive?
  If yes: In what situations?
               How often does this occur?
               What helps you resist your impulses when they arise?

- Some people have intermittent thoughts or impulses to hurt themselves or others. Has that ever been an issue for you?
  If yes: What is it like?
               How many times a day do you have these thoughts?
               How does it feel to have these thoughts?
               How do you deal with them when they arise?
               How often have you acted on these thoughts or impulses?

- Some people are bothered by recurrent images that involve hurting themselves or others. Has anything like this occurred to you?
  If yes: What are the images like?
               How many times a day do these images come to mind?
               How does it feel to experience these images?
               How do you deal with them when they arise?
               How many times have you acted on these images?

Another means of assessing a patient's capacity for impulse control is to inquire into his or her history of suicide attempts. Patients who have acted on their suicidal impulses in the past are a greater suicide risk in the present. This is especially true for patients who have harmed themselves and acted impulsively on multiple prior occasions. Indeed, it has been suggested that prior suicide attempts by the patient (as well as previous suicide attempts by other family members) is one of the best indicators that a patient is likely to attempt suicide again.

Assessing Intent

Another part of suicide assessment is identifying patients' intentions to kill themselves. Intent is most easily established through self-report. You may want to directly ask:

- "How strong is your intent to harm yourself?"

Some contend that it isn't helpful to ask patients about their intentions. They claim it is unlikely patients will disclose their true intent given that such a disclosure would lead a clinician to take action to prevent the patient from following through on their intentions. Nonetheless, I am of the point of view that it does not hurt to ask, even if the patient's self-report may be inaccurate. After all, you never know when you will get a patient who will tell the truth.

Another means of assessing intent is by talking to family members and friends. Medical records may also be source of information. In addition, do not forget that your own observation of the patient can also be crucial. Use your observations, combined with what a patient reveals about their thoughts and feelings, to assess a patient's intentions. Resnik (1980) provides a useful scale for assessing severity of suicidal intent. Keep this scale in mind as you evaluate a patient's potential risk for suicide. It ranges from least at risk (nonexistent) to most at risk (extreme).

1. *Nonexistent* No suicidal ideation or plan exist.
2. *Mild* Suicidal ideation and a general plan exists. Self-control is intact. Patient knows several reasons to live and patient does not intend to kill himself.
3. *Moderate* Ideation and a general plan exist. Patient is in control and has reasons to live.
4. *Severe* Suicidal ideation occurs often and is felt intensely. Patient has a specific plan that is lethal and patient has the means to act on the plan. Patient seems to not really want to kill himself.
5. *Extreme* Patient expresses a clear intent to kill himself as soon as the chance arises. The stronger a patient verbalizes his or her intent, the greater the risk of suicide.

There is one fact about suicide and homicide that is difficult, but vital, to address. Patients who are truly intent on hurting themselves or anyone else will find a way to do so regardless of our efforts. Perhaps this is what makes the discussion of this topic so difficult. Despite your best intentions, you have to accept that you cannot control the behavior of others. Another way to think about this conflict is that although the pressure to be helpful is great the fear of being helpless may be even greater. Having accepted this conflict, it is important to be aware of how to respond to a positive risk assessment.

Risk Assessment: Responding to a Positive Assessment

It is extremely challenging to work with patients who present as potentially harmful to themselves or others. Before you begin to see patients, talk to your supervisor about the procedures in place in your agency or hospital for managing potentially suicidal patients. For example, some sites may require that a psychiatrist do the formal assessment, whereas other sites encourage new clinicians to conduct risk assessments themselves. Some sites may ask that a quantitative assessment be administered; others rely on a mental status exam. Specific information about what telephone number you call or where to ask the patient to sit and wait for further assessment are all questions to sort out with your supervisor *before* you begin seeing patients. It may feel awkward raising the specter of suicide with a new supervisor. Yet, by not raising the issue you put both yourself and your patient at risk.

Much of this chapter has focused on patients who primarily pose a danger to themselves. Bear in mind that there may be special procedures for you to follow at your site if you sense that a patient may be a danger to yourself or others. Again, I urge you check out these procedures *prior* to conducting the first interview. Many agencies have policy and procedure manuals regarding safety issues. I also recommend that you talk to peers and co-workers. Although there may be a standard operating procedure for dealing with dangerous patients, you will want to know informally what has happened in the past and how your peers keep themselves safe. An important step in keeping yourself safe is to follow the guidelines for safety outlined in Chapter 8 concerning potentially violent patients. Once you have a good handle on the procedures and policies for protecting yourself in your setting, you can breathe a sigh of relief and proceed with the first interview.

During the first interview itself, *I advise clinicians-in-training to immediately consult with their supervisors if they have a sense that the patient with whom they are meeting is suicidal or homicidal.* If your supervisor is not available, consult with other senior treatment team members (e.g., the head nurse, psychiatrist, and so on). Remember, different sites may have different policies for dealing with patients who pose a danger to themselves or others. There are two specific circumstances you must be prepared to handle in the first interview. The first is when patients present an imminent risk to themselves or others. The second is when patients present a risk to themselves or others but this risk appears more remote and less urgent. If the patient presents an imminent risk of suicide:

- Do not leave the patient alone.
- Arrange for an immediate psychiatric consultation.

You may be looking over these two points and thinking that they are obvious. Well, there was a time when they were not obvious to me. When I was on internship, I met with a patient for a first interview and during the interview I observed that she presented a high risk for suicide potential. Indeed, she directly stated that she was feeling particularly impulsive, and she asked to be hospitalized on the inpatient psychiatric unit. In order to have her admitted to the unit, I needed the assistance of the hospital's attending psychiatrist. As she sat in my office, I paged the attending psychiatrist, who responded that she would be there shortly. The patient's mood immediately brightened considerably. I began the paperwork, brought the patient to the waiting room, and waited for the psychiatrist to arrive.

When the psychiatrist arrived, the patient was nowhere to be found. Frantically, the hospital paged all units for the patient. I felt distraught, embarrassed, and anxious. Finally, the patient appeared. Apparently, she had gone off to the cafeteria to locate a candy machine and buy some supplies in preparation for her stay on the unit. In this case, I got lucky. All that was injured was my pride. Moreover, I learned a great lesson: never leave a suicidal patient alone. It was shear luck that she did not wander off and hurt herself.

Now consider a different case. Suppose you conduct a first interview with a new patient but it appears that the patient presents a less urgent risk to themselves or others.

- Refer the patient for appropriate treatment.
- When possible, assist the patient in obtaining treatment.
- Encourage the patient to inform a supportive person of his or her condition.
- Offer hope.

The goal is to connect the patient to the help they need. One method of connecting the patient to the help they need is called "contracting for safety." Contracting for safety is an oral *or* written agreement whereby the patient stipulates that he will not hurt himself for a period of time. If your patient has had suicidal thoughts in the past, explore what kept him from acting on those thoughts at that time. Include these actions in the contract whenever possible.

Summary

This chapter began with a quote from Oliver Wendell Holmes: "Death whispers in my ear: "LIVE FOR I AM COMING." Death, itself, is inevitable. Death by suicide and homicide, however, are preventable. Unfortunately, new and experienced clinicians alike cannot predict them. What all clinicians can do is to evaluate the circumstances in a patient's life that may place him at a greater or lesser risk for harming himself or others. This chapter described how to make this assessment. First, it reviewed the concept of professional responsibility. Second, it clarified two myths regarding suicide. Third, it detailed how to inquire about suicidal and homicidal ideation in the first interview, with an emphasis on suicide risk assessment. Fourth, it discussed the issue of how to respond to a positive risk assessment. Overall, this chapter emphasized that how you talk to your patients about their suicidal and homicidal ideation matters. It is invaluable that you remain calm and supportive. Above all, strive to balance patients' feelings of despair with a sense of hope.

Some Questions to Consider

1. What is your professional specialty's code of ethics in regard to suicidal and homicidal patients?

2. What are some of the fundamental questions to include in a risk assessment in the first interview?

3. What are three ways in which a suicidal person may manifest their intent?

4. How will you manage your feelings as a therapist if your client admits suicidal or homicidal ideation?

Part IV

After Making Contact with Your Client

Give what you have. To someone, it may be better than you dare to think.

—Henry Wadsworth Longfellow

Congratulations! It is quite an accomplishment to have completed the first interview with a client. As clinicians at the early stage of your professional development, some of you may have come to expect great things from yourselves. Others of you may have developed more modest expectations. Regardless, in Longfellow's words, I encourage you to "Give what you have." In the end, that is all that each of us has to give, and it may indeed be more than you realized. If you have followed the guidelines in this book thus far, you can rest assured that you have been successful in accomplishing what was required of you in this initial contact.

Just as it typically takes time to prepare to see clients, so too does it take time to process what transpired in the room once the first session has ended. What tools or methods can you use to gain understanding and clarity about the experience you have just had with your client? Consider supervision: In what manner can supervision be most helpful? How can you make the most of supervision? Consider where you are working: What do you need in order to get your educational needs met at your placement site? How do you manage the paperwork expected from you in your agency?

The following three chapters tackle these and other questions. Essentially, this section addresses what to do once the client contact is over. Chapter 11 focuses on how to reflect productively on the session and make the most of what you have learned. It describes the tools of journaling and the importance of developing a support network of friends, peers, and colleagues. Chapter 12 revisits the topic of supervision that was briefly discussed in Part One. And finally, Chapter 13 addresses the notorious topic of paperwork: why it is required, what it entails, and ways to handle this seemingly overwhelming, nonnegotiable task. Overall, this section will help you move from the minute your client has walked out the door to the moment you become accountable for completing what is required of you—for yourself as a clinician, for your supervisor, and for the agency itself.

11

Reflections on What Has Transpired

Laura L. Young and Leah M. DeSole

He who knows others is wise; he who knows himself is enlightened.

—Lao-tzu

Chapter Goals

This chapter will help you to:

1. Begin to process what has transpired in the first interview.
2. Develop your confidence as a clinician.
3. Identify writing tools that will help you become a more competent clinician.
4. Encourage you to develop your own clinical support team.

Processing First Reactions

First, I offer the suggestion to allow yourself simply to be and feel: *relax. Let yourself breath, smile, cry, and laugh.* Accept your full range of thoughts and feelings. More importantly, take a moment to congratulate yourself on passing through a major professional hurdle! The initial contact, sitting face-to-face with your client, is over. Note that I have chosen the word *over* and not *complete*. The session itself ends when your client walks out the door, but it is not complete. There is more work to be done.

Immediately after the session, take a few moments to consider what transpired in the last fifty minutes (or however long the session ran). Allow your thoughts and feelings about the session to arise, and give yourself time to experience what just happened. I encourage you to immediately reflect on:

- *Your performance as a clinician.* How do you feel about the way you handled the session?
- *Your reactions to the client.* How did you feel sitting with the client? What thoughts came to mind during the session?

In Chapter 3, there is an emotions words checklist you may want to give your clients to help them identify how they are feeling. From time to time, you may want to use it as well. Now might be one of those times.

You may even want to get into the habit of keeping a journal of the experiences that emerge after the first interview. After all, there may be times when you finish the first contact with your client and don't know how you feel. Perhaps you feel no empathy for your client. In this instance, it may be useful to refer to Chapter 1 and review your initial thoughts and feelings about your placement site. Remind yourself that there may be things you have in common as well as ways that you differ from your clients that can impede your ability to establish an empathetic presence.

A few years ago, I was working in a mental health clinic and one of my first clients was from the Liberty Project, a project for people needing mental health services after the 9/11 attack on the World Trade Center. Unbeknownst to me, the client had waited a long time from his initial assessment to being assigned a therapist. He was angry, and his anger scared me. I was uncomfortable with not only his feelings but their intensity. In addition, I was startled by his disoriented and tangential recollection of 9/11 and the extent to which it continued to affect him 16 months later. Immediately after the session, I was aware of feeling fearful and thinking I did not want to see him again. I kept a journal about this client after the first session, and doing so enabled me to access my feelings. Journaling was invaluable to the extent that it allowed me to be aware of my thoughts and emotions. Armed with this self-awareness, I was able to make better use of my supervision session about the client. I was also able to prevent my thoughts and feelings from subconsciously influencing my experience with the client in a negative manner. Working with this client ultimately became a significant educational experience. Had I acted out of my initial fear, I might have rejected the client. In so doing, I would have harmed the client as well as started off my tenure at the agency in a bad light.

Remember the saying from Lao-tzu that began this chapter: "He who knows others is wise; he who knows himself is enlightened." Before I saw this client, I was familiar with textbook descriptions of post traumatic stress. I was knowledgeable ("He who knows others is wise . . . "), but my knowledge was incomplete. After all, I was unaware of what my own thoughts and feelings would be about the client until the first interview. Meeting him, allowing my fears and expectations to surface, and processing this information in supervision proved invaluable to the client's treatment. To me it reinforced the second half of the adage ("he who knows himself is enlightened"). It also underscores the value of the exercises mentioned in Chapter 4; namely, developing a "watching attitude," developing self-awareness, and maintaining congruence with your verbal and nonverbal cues during the first interview.

Gaining Confidence

I've often heard beginning clinicians talk about their frustrations at not accomplishing their goals in the initial session. They worried that they did not get a clear picture of the presenting problem, did not offer enough hope to the client, or generally felt incompetent. Presumably, you have entered a helping profession to be helpful, so it can be painful to perceive that you have not accomplished this goal. Likewise, it can be difficult to maintain your confidence while in training. There are those who would argue that self-doubt is okay: a little humility can go a long way toward inspiring the beginning clinician to be open to the guidance of others. Too little confidence and too much humility, however, can undermine your effectiveness as a clinician. The best stance to take may be somewhere between these extremes: acknowledge your strengths, admit your weakness, and above all remain teachable.

It is invaluable to remember that just being an empathic listener who cares about what a client is saying can lead to an incredibly healing experience for the client. Sometimes it helps to have a mantra or maxim to bear in mind, particularly when you are in training and feel unsure of yourself. I once had a supervisor say to me, "It is not what you do, it is what you do next that matters." I found this statement very powerful. Periodically, I would worry about whether I did "the wrong thing" in a session. Having this mantra in mind helped me to remain calm. It communicated to me that it is okay to make mistakes and that mistakes need not be irreparable. Indeed, learning can come for both the clinician and the client from the process of reparation. Much like Winnicott's (1958, 1965) famous phrase "the good-enough mother," I encourage you to strive to be a "good-enough therapist." The reality is, after all, that none of us will ever be perfect. Fortunately, you do not need to be—you need only to be enough. And you will be enough if you apply your basic counseling skills and provide a growth-inducing environment for clients.

It is critical to remember, particularly while you are in training, that perfection cannot be achieved. You will make mistakes. You will learn from them. In the meantime, continue to breathe and relax. Applaud yourself for finishing the initial session with a new client. Remember, as a clinician you are a work in progress. As often as necessary, remind yourself that simply by being an effective interviewer you can make a tremendous difference in the life of another human being (Evans et al., 2004). Rest assured, you will continue to gain confidence as long as you are willing to reflect on what happened in the room with the client with an open heart and mind.

Writing Tools

Having an open heart and mind certainly is an enviable goal, but how is it to be achieved? One way is through the development of self-awareness, and writing is one means to this end. In this chapter, I suggest two simple, specific writing tools: keeping an inventory and maintaining morning pages.

The Inventory

Businesses periodically stop and take stock of their inventory; they identify areas of credit and deficit. Essentially, they determine where their assets lie and what their shortfalls are. The goal is to examine their performance at a given moment. This concept of taking stock is also one way to reflect upon your performance in the first interview. It is called taking your inventory, and it entails reviewing what transpired in the session (see Figure 11.1). Rather than keeping account of your credits and deficits, you are making note of your clinical strengths and weaknesses.

To start your inventory, put pen to paper and create three columns. In the first column, list your strengths as they relate specifically to the first interview. Recall what went well in the session, such as your ability to focus the client, express empathy, or ask an effective question. In the second column, consider your deficits. Where do you think you fell short in the session? Recall where you found yourself challenged, less comfortable, or perhaps even fumbling and make note of it. Finally, use the third column for exploration. Bear in mind:

- What made each asset a strength?
- What made each liability a weakness?
- What were your intentions?

Assets	Liabilities	Exploration
I stayed present, in silence, with the client while she was crying.	I may have stayed quiet for *too long* with the client while she was crying.	Did I stay quiet for too long? Initially, I was glad that I was able to sit silently while the client cried. I thought I was listening empathically. My sense was the client felt understood and this strengthened our rapport. But then my feelings shifted from being glad to getting uncomfortable. I started to feel inept, and I did not know what to do. What else could I have done? When did my silence become unhelpful? I wonder if the client was feeling inept by making herself vulnerable in front of me? In general, this example makes me think that I need to examine when silence is helpful and when it is problematic in my work with clients.

FIGURE 11.1   *The Inventory.*

If possible, review your inventory with your supervisor or a peer. Otherwise, put it down and review it yourself later. You may want to let some time pass in order to gain perspective on what transpired. Reflect on the choices you made. Consider what you liked about your performance.

With an inventory of yourself as a clinician in the first interview, you may feel drawn to notice the deficits—what you would have liked to have done differently. Indeed, for the next interview it is important to identify the areas you plan to pursue another way. Perhaps you allowed the session to go on a tangential ride into areas you did not know how to negotiate. Maybe the client took more control of the session than you liked. There probably were periods of silence with which you felt ill at ease. The possibilities are endless. Nonetheless, I urge you to resist the impulse to dwell on your deficits. I strongly encourage your list of clinical strengths to be as long, if not longer, than the list of areas in which you would like to see improvement. In conclusion, for deficits and strengths alike identify two behavioral alternatives you could have made during the first interview. Armed with your knowledge of these alternatives, you will be better prepared for the next first interview.

I once had a supervisor who was able to readily admit that it was not her personal therapeutic style to be directive or in the least bit confrontational. I, on the other hand, possess a more straightforward style. I tend to be direct in sharing my perceptions regarding what clients reveal and identify as challenging in their lives. Not surprisingly, my supervisor had been trained psychoanalytically, whereas I had been trained eclectically. I knew that neither style had inherently more validity than the other. However, working with this new supervisor helped me to learn the value of diverse perspectives, and it taught me to be more clinically flexible. I discovered that what may be an asset with some clients may be a liability with others. Ultimately, I learned that contrary to my assumptions it is more effective with some clients to be less directive.

Morning Pages

Morning pages provide another way of developing your clinical self-awareness. They are particularly useful during the training process as a means of processing your experiences in a personal, private manner. Initially, Julia Cameron (2002) developed morning pages as a tool for artists to develop their understanding of themselves. I believe that being a clinician is not so dissimilar from being an artist. Both clinicians and artists require the utilization of instinct, creativity, and inventiveness to perform effectively. Both professions use "the self" as their main tool. Although an actor is not the character he portrays, he may use parts of himself to create a role. Likewise, as clinicians we may use parts of ourselves to inform our clinical work. Moreover, the most successful artists are those individuals who, within appropriate boundaries, allow themselves to be authentic and vulnerable in the never-ending process of learning about their craft. So, too, do successful clinicians continue to assess, alter, and use their professional skills in their work according to their increasing experience and the needs of their clients.

With this dotted line connecting artists and clinicians, I have found morning pages to be a very helpful tool over the years, both professionally and personally. They consist of three pages of stream-of-consciousness writing; that is, writing without thought or judgment. Preferably, they are written in the morning (hence the name), when you are relaxed and before your day is underway. The goal is to clear your mind of chatter or negative ruminations about the session or your personal life that are distracting and creatively stifling. In reality, I can attest to the fact that I have found a regular routine of writing in the morning to be very helpful. Perhaps most important is what I do *after* writing my morning pages: I refrain from looking at or reading what I have written. Instead, I let it go and go on with my day.

I would argue that another way in which artists and clinicians are similar is their tendency toward self-criticism. According to Cameron (2002), artists possess an 'internalized perfectionist', who is an eternal critic. In my experience, clinicians also possess a predilection for perfection. For example, I am well aware that sometimes I set high standards for myself and may become myopic in my negative self-judgment. Therefore, if (or more accurately, when) I have negative thoughts or perceptions after a client session I allow myself to be critical on paper for a limited amount of time. I don't carry it with me the rest of the day, night, or week. I trust that I'll remember what I need to remember for supervision, and I jot down notes for needed areas of specific supervision. Indeed, some of my criticism may be justified.

Some of you may be reading about these writing tools (the inventory and morning pages) and feeling overwhelmed by the work they entail. Let me say up front: my intention is not to needlessly add to your already tight schedule by suggesting more "work" for you to do. Rather, my goal is to ease your transition to becoming a competent clinician by offering ways for you to process your initial experiences as a clinician-in-training. After all, seeing clients face-to-face for the first time can be not only an exciting experience but an anxiety-provoking experience. For me, having options regarding how to gently, productively, and positively evaluate my clinical experience lessens my self-criticism and increases my confidence as a professional.

Our Field, Ourselves, and Our Team

Our Field

The field of mental health encompasses a wide range of vocations, ranging from psychiatrists to paraprofessionals. Regardless of your formal title, currently you are in the midst of a significant transition: you are moving from being a trainee to becoming a full-fledged professional. Although you may not feel like it, in all probability you already *are* a professional in the eyes of your clients. Your work at this time matters. It influences how your clients think and feel about themselves. However, mental health is not an exact science; it lends itself to interpretation. I believe your interpretation depends on who you are: your cultural background and individual belief system. I encourage you to begin considering these factors now. Writing tools are one means of examining these factors. Personal therapy and peer support are others.

Ourselves

Other highly skilled professionals constantly work on themselves to be the finest in their fields. Likewise, so must practitioners in the field of mental health. And so must you. Much of our work is internal; it entails what we demand of ourselves. I contend that we owe it to ourselves, our respective professions, and our clients to be self-reflective.

Recently, I heard of a disturbing trend: several highly esteemed schools of social work have become reluctant to recommend that students engage in their own personal therapy. This reluctance does not reflect a change in view about the value of therapy; rather, it reflects concerns about litigation. Apparently, some students hesitate to engage in their own personal therapy and some schools fear that they will be sued if they strongly recommend it. I find this circumstance troubling.

I believe it is imperative for clinicians in training to engage in their own personal therapy. Although I would only recommend counseling to a friend who is going through difficult times, I consider it crucial for students who are experiencing the pressures of clinical training. It is an invaluable source of support, both personally and professionally. On a personal level, you will benefit from going on the journey of self-exploration that therapy entails. On a professional level, you will be working with someone who truly understands what you do and the pressures of training: your own therapist. Your own therapist is in the unique position of being able to serve many purposes—teacher, supporter, confidante, and ultimately role model. Engaging in personal therapy offers you another benefit as well. It enables you to learn empathy for your clients. Once you have the experience of knowing what it is like to share your intimate thoughts and feelings with a stranger, you will be in a better position to understand what it is like for your clients to do the same with you.

For those of you who still question the necessity of personal therapy, I ask you to explore the nature of your reluctance. Do you fear the stigma of being a client? Are you uncomfortable with the prospect of being in the position of vulnerability that being a client entails? Do you worry about appearing unable to help yourself? Rest assured that you are not alone if you answered "yes" to any of these questions. Just like our clients, we are bound to feel reluctant to engage in the process of counseling from time to time. It is not easy. I encourage you, nonetheless, to face your fears. At the very least, I entreat you to work on developing your willingness to engage in personal therapy while in training. Otherwise, you may want to reconsider your career choice. In this regard, I think Jeffrey Kottler (1990) said it best when he said,

> This resistance to examining ourselves with the same critical, diagnostic eye that we would direct toward a client amounts to utter hypocrisy. If we do not genuinely believe that the therapeutic tools of our profession can work on us, we have no business practicing them on anyone else. (p. 127)

Our Team

As the poet John Donne said, "No man is an island." Likewise, I believe that no clinician is an island; that is, we do not function at our best alone. The same may be said for clinicians in training: your learning improves when you have the support of others. In this spirit, I encourage you to create your own support team. I encourage you to sit down and write a list of people in your life you may call upon for support or advice during your training. Your goal is to create a helpful network of helpful friends and colleagues with whom you may consult, on an as-needed basis, as you strive to become a competent clinician. They may be peers, family friends, former professors, or current professionals in the mental health field. Regardless of how you know them, what matters most is that they are familiar with the challenges you are facing. They know what it is like to sit down for the first time with a client. Their knowledge may be an invaluable source of support during your clinical training.

I, myself, have put together a mock "Board of Directors" for my career path. This is a group of friends, former supervisors, fellow clinicians, and some esteemed mentors I periodically call upon for encouragement and assistance. Some individuals on my board don't even know they have been selected! Nonetheless, I view them as important to my being better able to productively process my work as a clinician (and as a former student). I enlist their aid, on an as-needed basis, in a variety of areas ranging from my choice of therapeutic interventions to the writing of my cover notes and resume. You never know when they can be useful. For example, I once had trouble working with a supervisor at one of my field placements. I was able to handle this situation constructively after I contacted several members of my board and asked for their advice. Their assistance was invaluable not only for my sanity but for the sanity of my clients.

Summary

In this chapter, I offer kudos and congratulations for all of you who have successfully completed the initial contact with your client. Subsequently, I describe how to begin processing what transpired in the first session. You need to be aware at the outset of maintaining balance—not giving too much credence either to self-criticism or satisfaction. What I do encourage is the development of your self-confidence as a clinician. To this end, the chapter presents two specific simple writing tools for self-exploration that will enable you to accurately take stock of your first session with a client (i.e., the strengths you brought to the session and what therapeutic skills you may need to hone). I underline the importance of balance in your evaluation of the session and your professional responsibility to develop deeper self-knowledge in order to be of greater service to your clients. A master therapist, Irving Yalom 2002a, (p. 1), reportedly received a consoling thought early in his training from a teacher: "Remember, you can't do all the work. Be content to help a patient realize what must be done and then trust his or her own desire for growth and change." Like Yalom's wise teacher, I too urge you to remember that you cannot do all the work yourself. To be the best clinician you can be, I encourage you to form a support team for yourself and to continue learning about yourself in your own personal therapy.

Some Questions to Consider

1. Recall one experience that taught you wisdom beyond knowledge.

2. Consider an instance from your past when a person whose cultural background or style is very unlike your own surprised you with her effectiveness.

3. Write morning pages for five successive days. On the sixth day reread what you have written and see what you discover.

4. List your mock "Board of Directors" you will call on for guidance and support.

5. Take a deep breath and congratulate yourself for reaching this point in your training.

12

Supervision

Laura L. Young and Leah M. DeSole

The important thing is to not stop questioning.

—Albert Einstein

Chapter Goals

This chapter will help you to:

1. Define supervision.
2. Clarify expectations for supervision: your own, your school's, and your site's.
3. Identify inadequate supervision and develop appropriate avenues to address it.
4. Cultivate tools to get the most out of supervision.

Defining Supervision

Supervision entails observing and managing the work of others. In general, it involves more senior and experienced clinicians overseeing, educating, and supporting more inexperienced clinicians in their work with clients. According to Itzhaky and Itzhaky (1996), the purpose of supervision is threefold: (1) to advance supervisees in the cognitive, emotional, ethical, and behavioral fields, (2) to help supervisees working on their own make professional decisions, and, (3) to help develop a personal style of work. Supervisors aid their supervisees by continually juggling many roles. Sometimes these roles appear to conflict: your supervisor will be your teacher as well as your judge. Other times these roles seem to converge: your supervisors will be your mentors as well as your guardians at the site in which you are in training. Specifically in the first interview, supervisors are there to help you reflect on and process what transpired during your initial contact with

174

the new patient. They are also there to help you gain clarity and to offer a seasoned perspective about the experience you have just had with your new patient. In this regard, supervisors wear two hats: they serve as patient advocates and they model for you how to be of service to your patients.

The purpose of this chapter is to help you learn how you can you make the most out of supervision. Succeeding sections clarify the role of a supervisor and help you identify your expectations regarding the supervisory experience. In conclusion, the final sections address how to learn the most from supervision—including those times when you may not get the supervision you need (or deserve).

Clarifying Expectations

Your Expectations of Supervision

In your mind's eye, imagine your ideal supervisor. What are your expectations? Do you want someone who holds your hand, meets with you daily, and gently guides you through the ropes of the site to which you have been assigned? Would you prefer someone who is hands-off, pushes you to work independently, and meets with you only once a week? I encourage you to tap into your assumptions about supervision. Talk to your peers about their outlook and expectations. Make a list of assumptions in the margins of this book if need be—do whatever will help you become conscious of your own expectations. Why make this effort? Because the expectations you have about supervision matter. They influence how you conduct yourself in supervision, and they affect what transpires between you and your supervisor.

The word *supervision* itself comes from the Latin root *supervidare*, meaning to look over or see above. One implication of this derivation is that a supervisor in some way is superior: he or she can see beyond what you can observe as a new clinician. Ideally, your supervisor will perceive what you cannot yet see in your work with patients. To go a step further, and break down the word *supervision* literally, new clinicians are sometimes apt to believe that supervisors have "supervision"; that is, that they are able to see things others cannot (and that maybe you have missed).

Good supervisors will, indeed, have good vision. They will use this vision to guide you during your training in your work with clients. Moreover, exceptionally effective supervisors will help you to develop *your own insight*. Exceptional supervisors will even go a step further: they will not only share their vision but value your vision. They acknowledge how everyone, supervisors and new clinicians alike, comes to the table with a different vision: diverse lenses and different prescriptions. Hence, each has his own type of clarity. For example, some clinicians have a talent for working with adolescents. Their insight into adolescents' experiences is inexplicably superior to other clinicians. In this way, they have supervision. Likewise, I once had a supervisor who had an uncanny ability to hone in on the diagnosis of patients. She developed supervision in identifying and accurately utilizing diagnostic criteria.

Nonetheless, therapy and supervision in the field of mental health are not exact sciences. The notion of supervision may exist in theory, but it seldom exists in reality. In fact, I advise you to be wary of setting unrealistic expectations for your supervisor. Resist the urge to put them on a pedestal. Although they will have more experience than you do, it also is likely that they will make mistakes (as we all do sometimes). As an illustration, the following case study demonstrates how I, as a trainee in the field of mental health, allowed myself to learn not only from my supervisor's vision but from my supervisor's blind spots.

Case Study.   One of my first supervisors was a tall, beautiful, articulate woman. In addition to her employment at the site in which I was training, she had a private practice that consisted primarily of upwardly mobile patients—even some celebrities. I aspired to be like her as a therapist, and I considered her a mentor. In addition, I felt passionate about the organization for which we worked and proud to be part of her team. As a result, I readily took on her vision and designated it as superior to my own. Looking back, I realize I was wearing rose-colored glasses; my vision was obscured by optimism, inexperience, and personal need.

I learned a great deal under her guidance. She gave me duties that were beyond the scope as a newcomer in the field, and I enthusiastically took them on. Indeed, I felt honored; my ego was stroked. As I became more skilled over time, I developed my own vision—thoughts and ideas independent of my supervisor's that I shared with others at the organization. During my training, these ideas and my work were supported by those around me. My supervisor, in contrast, became increasingly critical of me (perhaps she was not pleased by my increasing independence). One day, when we were alone, she screamed at me about an issue. I was devastated and unable to respond to her reaction. Afterward, I felt ashamed of my lack of response.

I subsequently consulted a colleague for counseling. He asked me: "What would you do if you were walking down the street and a crazed, hysterical person started screaming at you? Would you respond?" I rapidly replied "No, I would not respond." He then asked me to consider why I expected myself to promptly respond to my supervisor when she was similarly crazed and hysterical. I realized that I had no reason to be ashamed. Furthermore, I realized that although I had learned from my supervisor she was not perfect. More importantly, I did need to denigrate her or all of my experiences at the organization just because she had fallen off the pedestal on which I had placed her. My site experience may have broken into some pieces, but I did not need to make matters worse by punishing myself and shattering it entirely.

As a result of that early experience, I reconsidered my goals. I wondered if all successful clinicians behaved like that in the workplace. I wondered, "Would I have to be like her to be successful?" With more experience, I realized that I did not have to be like her to be an accomplished clinician. It helped that before long I had more than one supervisor who could both give and receive in their work with patients and clinical trainees alike.

Now, in my experience as a supervisor, I am wary of any trainees or patients who intimate that they believe my vision is "super" or superior to their own. I work not to put others on a pedestal, and I don't let people put me on one either.

I also learned from that experience that clinicians need to know themselves in order to learn from their supervisors, just as clinicians need to know themselves in order to be of service to their patients (see Chapter 11 for more on this topic). Over time, I learned more about myself in various ways, from personal therapy to utilizing the inventory described in Chapter 11. In particular, I learned that I tend to seek out strong women to emulate and yearn to be taken under their wing. My own mother was divorced and worked full-time. The guidance I was not able to get from her I have sought out in other women. Sometimes the results have been good; sometimes they have not. But before this opportunity, I was unaware of how my expectations influenced the way my supervision had unfolded at this site.

To summarize, supervisors may serve many roles: teachers, mentors, and agency representatives. Above all, they are also human beings who come to the supervisory relationship with their own personal and professional challenges. Chances are they have their own clear vision of what the supervisor and supervisee relationship entails. In the best circumstances, they will be interested in what your vision is as well. But sometimes, they may not be particularly interested. What matters most, and what is within your control, is being aware of your own expectations. I encourage you to be aware of your own vision. I also encourage you to remain open to changing your prescription—without necessarily altering your entire field of vision.

Your School's Expectations of Supervision

You have just examined at length your own expectations regarding supervision. It is critical to realize that your school also may have expectations regarding the type and amount of supervision you will receive as a clinician-in-training. You would do well to be aware of your school's perspective before you begin supervision. Some questions to think about include:

- Is there a general orientation at your school about training sites and the supervision they provide?
- Have students from your school previously been placed at your site? If so, try to contact them to learn more about not only the site but the supervision provided.
- Is there an office, or do you have a specific advisor, at your school where you can take your questions and concerns about supervision?
- Is there a course at your school where you can discuss cases and address supervision issues while in training?
- Is there a liaison between your school and the supervisor at your site?
- Will your supervisor be evaluating your training on your school's behalf?
- Will your school give your supervisor specific forms to complete? If so, ask to see them before you start supervision at your site.
- What are your school's criteria for the evaluation of your training by your supervisor? If there are any, find out about them before supervision starts.
- Will you receive a copy of any evaluation your supervisor forwards to your school?

You need to know the answers to these questions; they affect your career. Think of it as a test: Would you prepare for a test without asking what topics are being covered on the exam? You probably would not. Likewise, you need to know your school's criteria for your training. You need to know who will be providing this information to your school. Mostly likely, it will be your on-site supervisor. Some of you may find this all distasteful. Having a good training experience and learning are more important than reviewing your evaluation. However, it is likely that future employers will ask someone at your school, such as your school's training coordinator, about you. It will help if your program is able to say something about you that is positive. It is wonderful to have your opportunities be wide open. Good evaluations widen your opportunities.

Your Site's Expectations of Supervision

You have already thought about your own expectations of supervision as well as your school's expectations. Rest assured, supervisors have their own idea of what constitutes supervision as well. In order to fulfill their expectations, it is essential that you know your supervisor's expectations for you as a clinician-in-training.

In particular, you need to know what your supervisor wants you to accomplish in the first interview. What does your supervisor consider the objective of your initial contact with a new patient? After all, a variety of outcomes are possible. Will you be expected to provide a referral? Will you be expected to continue seeing the patient for therapy? Or, is your sole responsibility to provide information to your supervisor so that together you can determine what the next steps will be? To clarify your supervisor's expectations in the first interview, I recommend you directly ask:

- "What are my objectives when I meet with a new patient for the first time?"
- "What information, in particular, would you like me to obtain in the first interview with a new patient?"

I encourage you to see Chapter 1 for additional basic questions you may wish to ask your supervisor before you start seeing patients. This chapter also provides prompts, or examples, of how to communicate with your supervisor about issues that may arise with patients. Be aware that your supervisor may not be able to readily respond to all of your questions. Nonetheless, the questions are worth asking. Your inquiries may serve as a valuable point of reference for further discussion regarding your supervisor's expectations of the first interview. It may surprise you, but sometimes supervisors are as unaware as clinicians-in-training of their expectations regarding supervision. To this end, supervisors may welcome questions asked in a cooperative spirit.

Your supervisor will have expectations about your work not only with patients but in regard to other areas. Chapter 1 explored three specific areas: time, paperwork, and the fulfillment of general role obligations. Your supervisor's time expectations include what days and hours your supervisor requires you to work each day. Time expectations also include your supervisor's requirements regarding the time of day, duration, and frequency of supervision. Paperwork expectations essentially entail the report writing that is expected of you following a first interview. And finally, role obligations concern your supervisor's expectations of you as a professional-in-training. It is important to clarify what your supervisor considers your role obligations to be, as well as how your supervisor will evaluate your completion of these obligations. To this end, you may need to ask:

- Is your supervisor the liaison between your school and your training site?
- How does your supervisor expect you to record what transpires in the first interview (e.g., progress notes, process recordings, tape recordings, written or oral reports)?
- What criteria will your supervisor use to evaluate your training? If there are specific criteria, ask to see them.
- Will your supervisor complete a written evaluation of your performance? If so, find out who will receive the evaluation and whether you will have the opportunity to review it.

Many of these questions you will want to ask directly the first time you meet with your supervisor. Some of them you may want to ask later, or you may want to ask them of someone other than your supervisor. Whatever you choose, I encourage you to be judicious; do not deluge your supervisor with a long litany of questions the first time you meet. Ask those questions that are the most salient for you at this juncture. In addition, I encourage you to take detailed sessions notes during supervision. When I was a new clinician in training, I often thought that I would remember my supervisor's feedback, especially about anything that was important. Usually, I did remember my supervisor's comments. However, on those occasions when my memory failed it was embarrassing to have to contact my supervisor again about something specific when all I needed to do in the first place was write it down.

Handling Inadequate Supervision

It is inevitable: you will experience poor supervision over the course of your clinical training. Knowing this, it will probably still come as a surprise to you when it occurs. I remember my first experience with inadequate supervision. I was one of two interns working in a palliative care unit. Basically it was a hospice, and I was working with patients who were terminally ill and their families. I was assigned a supervisor when I arrived. We met once for supervision and then we scheduled a regular weekly meeting time. The next week I arrived at his office, but he was not there. Unsure of what to do, I waited in the hallway for an hour. Afterward, I called him. He apologized, said he could not make up the session that week, and we planned to meet the following week at our regular time and day. The next week the same thing happened. I was shocked. Afterward, I called him. Again he was apologetic, again he could not make up the missed session, and again we agreed to meet the following week at our regular time and day. Sure enough, the same thing happened. I was surprised, but not shocked. This time, I came prepared. I waited only ten minutes, left a note with a telephone number where I could be reached, and asked him to contact me if he wanted to reschedule.

Eventually, the time came for our monthly staff meeting on the unit. Afterward, I approached the other intern on the unit and asked her how supervision was going. Unbeknownst to me, the entire time the other intern on the unit was having the same experience! Well, misery loves company. We commiserated. We talked about our work with our patients and our experiences on the ward. We shared our feelings of abandonment by not only our supervisor but our dying patients. In essence, we held a terrific peer supervision session. Until the end of our rotation, we mollified ourselves by joking about the situation, sharing real and imagined sightings of the "ghost" supervisor on the terminal ward.

We eventually learned that this supervisor was renowned for his absentee style of supervision. We knew that we could not change it. We did, however, change our response to his behavior. Each of us stopped going to the appointment or even attempting to reschedule it. Although we continued our peer supervision, we both sought outside help. We learned to get our needs (essentially our patients' needs) met elsewhere. As trainees, how would we know if we were doing adequate work? He consulted with a supervisor on another unit. I sought supervision from my private therapist. Together, we struggled with whom to tell or even whether to tell anyone about our supervisor's behavior. Neither of us wanted a reluctant supervisor, a person who really did not want to be there. We were concerned about criticizing a superior, especially one who had a good reputation in the field and would be writing our evaluations. With some trepidation, we notified our respective school programs of the situation. After much agonizing, we decided not to tell our supervisor's boss about the situation. To our surprise, one day it did come out at a staff meeting. For a week or two, our supervisor began to meet with us again. But the change was short-lived. He quickly resumed his old patterns.

This example may seem extreme, but you would be surprised how common "absentee supervision" actually is. In this case, it was obvious that the supervision was inadequate. In many cases, it is not. What is inadequate supervision? Essentially, I define it is as supervision that does not meet your reasonable needs as a trainee. The outcome is insufficient training, often accompanied by a lot of unpleasant feelings. There are two keys to handling inadequate supervision. In that there are two people involved in the process, you and your supervisor, each of you has a part in its failure. The first key, therefore, lies in recognizing your part, if any, in its failure. The second key to handling inadequate supervision may be more difficult to accept. You need to realize that you are not going to be able to change your supervisor's behavior. You can only change your behavior in relation to your supervisor.

As human beings, we all have blind spots regarding our own behavior; there are things we do of which we are unaware. Likewise, as a new clinician you will have blind spots when it comes to perceiving your own behavior in supervision. After all, the experience of supervision is novel to you. Chances are it will be difficult for you to recognize your part when sessions with your supervisor are not going well. However, it is critical for you to understand your part so that you can change your behavior appropriately. Essentially, you want to stop contributing to whatever failure is occurring and instead find ways to contribute to the solution. Those ways, inevitably, entail changing your own behavior. Again, you will not be able to change your supervisor's behavior—you will only be able to change yourself in relation to your supervisor.

Identify the resources you have to help you understand where and how your supervision is not working. Resources include friends, other students in your program, and faculty members or advisors at your school. In addition, I encourage you to engage in personal therapy to explore your experience in supervision, examine how you contribute to any failures that are occurring, and understand your reactions to what is transpiring between you and your supervisor. Now is also the ideal time to contact the mock "Board of Directors" suggested in Chapter 11 (your group of friends, former supervisors, fellow clinicians, and some esteemed mentors you can call upon for assistance). Last, but not least, you may want to consult with a trusted peer or colleague at your site with your supervision concerns. Share with them your concerns about supervision. *Check to see if they consider your concerns valid.* Ask what changes you might make on the topic of how you react to your supervisor. Solicit advice regarding how to talk to your supervisor about your anxiety and the problems you are encountering. And finally, develop tools to improve your supervisory experience.

Tools to Improve Your Supervisory Experience

Your goal as a new clinician is to learn and become skilled. In order meet this goal, you need to remain teachable. This is not as easy as it sounds. Ideally, some of the tools discussed in the following will help you in this process. Some of them will help you when your supervisors are not meeting your needs.

- *Writing* Each internship or job that I begin, I make a list of all of the positive things about the environment, the patients, my co-workers, my supervisor, and the work. This helps me when or if I start to feel discouraged or burned out. It also serves as a barometer as to whether things have significantly changed, and how.
- *Education* I respect the knowledge that my supervisor has to offer, I honor the tenants of the agency with which I work, and I strive to find my own clinical voice from varied sources. Do not put all of your supervisory eggs in one basket—gain knowledge from all that you read and all whom you meet. To this end, there are two books I would recommend regarding supervision: Neufeldt's (1999) *Supervision Strategies for the First Practicum* and Fall and Sutton's (2004) *Clinical Supervision: A Handbook for Practitioners.* They may be helpful in alerting trainees to not only their own perspective in supervision but to the perspective of their supervisors.
- *Feelings* In recording, in detail, my supervision sessions I pay particular attention to my feelings during the session. Although feelings are not facts,

they can serve as an important source of information regarding what has transpired in the session.

- *Ego* I strive to let go of my ego in supervision. If I am having problems with my supervisor, I do not handle those problems on my own. I embrace knowing when and where to ask for assistance. I believe in humility; there is always room to grow. I believe humility is the firm bedrock from which to grow as a clinician.
- *Support* Surround yourself with friends and colleagues with whom you can candidly discuss your problems in supervision. Sometimes you need someone to validate that the supervision you have been receiving is inadequate. The validation alone can be a healing experience when you are in training.
- *Goals* Set goals for yourself in supervision. When possible, share them with your supervisor. Enlist your supervisor's assistance in helping you to change your behavior to meet your goals.
- *Paper trail* Document any inadequacies you experience in supervision. You can use this list to generate solutions to improve your supervision. You can also use it to protect yourself. For example, if something goes wrong on a case you are assigned you may need to prevent being scapegoated by an inadequate supervisor. Alternatively, if your supervisor writes a scathing evaluation of you this list may keep you from being branded a failure.
- *Optimism* Maintain optimism. I never know what new training adventure lies around the next corner. When supervision isn't going well, I often fall back on the belief that when one door closes another door opens. The challenge comes when you find yourself in the hallway between the doors. When will the next door open? I encourage you, if you have to wait for the other door to open, to take the time to decorate the hallway.

Despite my final call for optimism, I recognize that each new experience in supervision can be intimidating. Sometimes the most important tool in handling inadequate supervision is to do nothing. Give yourself permission to rest and assess. Then, when you are ready, take action.

Summary

As Einstein once said: *"The important thing is to not stop questioning."* I believe this statement holds true for both yourself and for the supervision you are being given. The key is to continually ask important, sometimes tough, questions so that you can develop appropriate expectations of your supervision sessions, of your supervisor, of yourself and of your education. I encourage you to use supervision to discover your own vision, clinical perspective, and understanding. I underline the importance of returning to Part One of this book for other important questions about supervision. And finally, although no one wants to experience inadequate supervision it is imperative that you are able to handle it when it occurs.

Some Questions to Consider

1. Describe your ideal supervisor. What expectations do you have regarding his or her control background?

2. Recall an experience in which you overestimated a person you looked up to as a role model.

3. How did you handle your disappointment when your expectations were not met?

4. List the questions you think are most important for your first meeting with your supervisor?

5. What causes you to feel anxiety about supervision? Can you discern the cause for this anxiety?

13

Paperwork

Laura L. Young and Leah M. DeSole

"Discipline is . . .
1. Do what has to be done;
2. When it has to be done;
3. As well as it can be done; and,
4. Do it that way every time."

—Bobby Knight

*Chapter Goals*_____

This chapter will help you to:

1. Understand the purpose of paperwork.
2. Distinguish among categories of paperwork at your site.
3. Increase your productive work habits.
4. Access support at your site.

The Function of Paperwork

Paperwork is necessary, important, and nonnegotiable. As clinicians, we often view ourselves as people oriented; we tend to be averse to paperwork and agencies that are paperwork driven. Be that as it may, clinicians cannot avoid paperwork. In actual fact, *we should not avoid it*. Complete records are necessary to provide quality services to our clients. Paperwork provides a written record of your client's past and present concerns. Any responsible business maintains files on its clients, ranging from a client's name and contact information to details regarding a client's needs. Health care agencies and private practitioners must keep files on their clients. Indeed, there are critical legal requirements governing all mental health care providers—in compliance with both HIPAA regulations and malpractice regulations—specifying the forms that must be completed, signed, and maintained in each client file.

As a clinician-in-training, you will be responsible for opening new client files and maintaining current ones. Be sure to ask your supervisor about your site's paperwork requirements. Sites may vary a great deal in their requirements. Some are quite lenient; others are notably stringent. This chapter begins with a general overview of the types of paperwork you may encounter at your site. Next, it describes how to develop productive work habits. In conclusion, it reviews ways for you to enlist assistance, as needed, in your work environment to help you get your paperwork completed thoroughly and on time.

Categories of Paperwork

It has become a cliché in the field of mental health that the paperwork is endless. In truth, it does end. However, in the midst of its completion it often feels endless. Depending on your site, you may be responsible for many types of paperwork. The type of report you will have to prepare depends on the audience for whom you are preparing it. Examples of possible audiences include:

- Future case workers
- Supervisors
- Court officers and judges
- Schools
- Nursing home workers
- Physicians

This chapter will not review reports designed for specific audiences. Instead, it will address reports typically required of clinicians-in-training. These include, but are not limited to:

- Intake reports
- Progress notes
- Quarterly reports
- Termination reports
- Transfer summaries
- Consent forms
- Case summaries
- Referral forms

There are many books and online resources that provide novice practitioners with sample formats for each of these reports. Depending on your discipline, there are numerous resources that may serve as templates for your own report writing. Two useful general resources are Phil Traver's (2002) *The Counselor's Helpdesk* and Edward Zuckerman's (2002) *The Paper Office: Forms, Guidelines, and Resources to Make Your Practice Work Ethically, Legally, and Profitably*. Both of these present forms applicable to trainees working in various helping professions and settings.

Be aware, however, that work samples provided outside your site may not fully satisfy the requirements of the supervisor to whom you have been assigned. I encourage you to ask your supervisors or peers to provide you with sample reports at your agency. Use these records as models for your own report writing. I strongly recommend that you ask your supervisor directly for a few models of *well-written* reports. It can be as simple as asking, "Dr. Smith, can you direct me to an intake report that is written in the style you prefer." Often, supervisors welcome such inquiries. After all, given their own voluminous workload they often are not eager to revise poorly written reports.

One final note: remember that any form you complete about a client becomes a part of the client's file. In other words, it becomes a *permanent part* of his or her record. Be judicious in what you write. It is recorded for posterity, and it will remain long after you have moved on from training at a given site. It is essential to show any forms to your supervisor (and have them approved as necessary) *before* your documentation enters a client's permanent record. Legal issues may be involved. You need to act in accordance with not only your client's but your site and supervisor's best interests at heart.

Productive Work Habits

Productive work habits are work habits that satisfy the requirements of your site and your supervisor. The following are some suggested means of fulfilling these requirements.

- *Know the expectations of your site and supervisor.* As detailed in Chapter 12, you need to know both your site and your supervisor's expectations. In this instance, you need to inquire specifically about paperwork requirements. If you don't fully understand what they are, then ask—ask and ask again if need be. If you are concerned about badgering your supervisor, consult with a trusted peer or someone you believe can advise you appropriately on the paperwork requirements.
- *Keeping a comprehensive "to do" list.* For me, keeping track of all that I need to do is imperative. There are many options to choose from in organizing your tasks. Many computers have software such as Microsoft Outlook with a daily calendar. You might use a handheld organizer such as a palm pilot or visor. Sometimes, an ordinary piece of paper with a list prioritizing your demands for the day will suffice. One word of caution: do not to get bogged down in creating the perfect "to do" list. If it exceeds 10 items, move on to accomplishing the tasks. As you complete the items, revise the list.
- *Create and maintain a comfortable workspace.* Part One emphasized the importance of creating a pleasant and functional work environment. The ideal

environment is not only for your clients but for you. To the extent you create a pleasant place for you to work, you may enhance both your skills in report writing and your productivity.

- *Procrastination—dangerous or incentive-producing?* Some clinicians-in-training believe they work better under a tight deadline. They think that their procrastination helps them to be productive. Others decompensate as deadlines come close. What is your style? Has procrastination been effective or ineffective for you in the past? Now is the time to ask yourself these questions: you are a new clinician, starting at a new site, and you are facing new demands. You will be evaluated at your site based in part on your ability to complete well-written reports on time. If procrastination has worked for you in the past, use it now. If it has not, now is the time to consider changing your behavior. The avenues for change are many, from personal therapy to professional consultation. We owe our clients no less than we expect from them: we must challenge our own self-destructive behaviors as they arise before they become a burden for our supervisors and a danger to our patients.

I urge you to not let paperwork pile up and overwhelm you. Use the aforementioned strategies and work habits to facilitate your ability to write reports. I also encourage you to develop strategies of your own to handle the paperwork obligations at your site. To this end, ask colleagues you admire about their methods of organization. Remember coach Bobby Knight's strategies as cited at the beginning of this chapter and be disciplined: "1. Do what has to be done; 2. When it has to be done; 3. As well as it can be done; and, 4. Do it that way every time." With this effort, you will succeed. Develop a "do it" mind-set and tame the paperwork beast.

Access Support at Your Site

Supervisor Support

As an intern, I found it extremely challenging to balance client time and paperwork demands. They often felt at odds. Initially, my session notes for my clients' files took a lot of time. At it turned out, my session notes were much longer than they needed to be. With my supervisor's help, I learned to condense the session notes so that each note took less than five minutes rather than the twenty-plus minutes I had been spending on it. Clearly, I was going into too much detail.

What helped me change? My supervisor gave me examples of her session notes. I learned through these examples what was important to include and what was superfluous. Also, she suggested abbreviations that can be used as a time-saving measure in client charts and for writing client notes, such as "hx" for history, "tx" for treatment, and "dx" for diagnosis. These aids may seem small, but they were real time savers for me.

I also perused old client files in order to understand the forms that were expected of me. I made sure to go over with my supervisor any forms I did not understand. If you are lucky enough to be reading this book before you begin your internship, there are books and guides with sample forms that may give you an idea of some of the paperwork you may be expected to complete. I recommend *The Therapist's Guide to Clinical Intervention: The 1-2-3s of Treatment Planning* by Sharon L. Johnson (1997). Also, review Part One regarding the Mental Status Exam and try out the relevant exercises (i.e., to practice doing a mental status exam with someone from your class at school).

Paperwork Balance and Time Management

While I was an intern, at the end of the day I might have had five to eight client session notes to complete. In addition, I may have had the rest of the ten-page intake form to fill out from a first interview I had done earlier that day. Eventually, I learned to designate thirty minutes for the session notes, and I recorded as many details as possible for the assessment so that I might complete it for the following morning when my client load was not as great.

I made a real effort not to be at work late every night, feeling shackled to my desk in order to complete every last bit of paperwork. However, there were those days when I needed to stay late to finish all I needed to get done for the next day. I am not counseling you to stay locked at your desk every night until all paperwork is completed. I am encouraging you to form good time management habits so that you don't neglect your paperwork to the point at which your peers, your supervisor, and maybe even the director of the agency are asking you for work you have yet to complete.

I appreciate what M. Scott Peck (1978) states: "Delaying gratification is a process of scheduling the pain and pleasure of life in such way as to enhance the pleasure by meeting and experiencing the pain first and getting it over with. It is the only decent way to live" (p. 19). Paperwork does not have to be painful, but it can be arduous. I recommend that you schedule it first and get it over with, in that it is inescapable. It has to be done. For me, getting it done early and efficiently provided my life with greater balance and a peace of mind when I went home at night from my placement.

Your Agency

Every agency will have different paperwork requirements as well as information they need to have in their files. Most agencies will have a packet of forms that new clients will be expected to fill out prior to their first interview. Make sure you understand the forms your clients are being given and your agency's expectations about what must be completed by the end of the first session. Often, the client will not arrive early enough to complete the forms before the interview, so you will need to either use some of the session time to aid your client in the completion of the forms or ask them to complete the forms after the session has ended.

Be aware that the administrative staff at your agency can be extremely helpful in guiding you through your agency's requirements regarding the paperwork that is due following the first interview. Probably the most important suggestion

I have for new clinicians is to make it a priority to always be patient, gracious, and sincerely appreciative of the administrative staff. New clinicians come and go, but the administrative staff is a constant. Frequently, they know things about clients and how things work in the agency that you will never be privy to without their assistance. Moreover, they work hard and they deserve your respect.

I was once transferred to an agency mid-semester. At the agency there was an inordinate amount of paperwork, including forms of which I had to keep track. As both a newcomer in the field and a new clinician at the agency, I consistently made errors in protocol. The administrative staff, who had to put up with my mistakes, were incredibly nice to me. I believe they treated me kindly because I always treated them with respect and with concern for their well-being. The golden rule— *Do unto others as you would have them do unto you*—is a salient point to remember when working in your agency.

Summary

In the field of mental health, paperwork is here to stay. This chapter reviewed the rationale and functions of paperwork. It also discussed how to manage paperwork by developing productive work habits. In addition, I underlined the importance of accessing the support available at your site: your supervisor and agency resources. Finally, I emphasized being respectful to the agency staff. Above all, I encourage training yourself early in your tenure as a clinician to be disciplined and to form productive work habits. Remember Benjamin Franklin's wise saying: "You may delay, but time will not."

Some Questions to Consider

1. Consider your history of doing the "paperwork" in other areas of your life. What are your habits?

2. What are three ways you can reinforce your good habits?

3. Have you developed a strong relationship with several peer colleagues with whom you can review what you are learning and what you are doing?

4. What resources do you have to consult when cultural considerations arise?

5. Have you practiced doing the mental status exam with one of them?

6. What specific changes will improve your time management habits?

References

Basch, M. F. (1980). *Doing psychotherapy*. New York: Basic Books.

Behnke, S. H., Perlin, M. L., & Bernstein, M. (2003). *The essentials of New York mental health law*. New York: W. W. Norton & Company.

Cameron, J. (2002). *The artist's way*. New York: Penguin.

Clemmens, C. (2004). A synthesis of dialectical behavioral therapy and treatment for addiction/mental health troubled clients. *Gestalt Review, 8*(3), 369–371.

Craig, R. J. (Ed.). (1989a). *Clinical and diagnostic interviewing*. New York: Jason Aronson.

Craig, R. J. (1989b). The clinical process of interviewing. In *Clinical and diagnostic interviewing*, R. J. Craig (Ed.), pp. 3–19. New York: Jason Aronson.

Derogatis, L. R. (1977). *SCL-90: Administration, scoring and procedures manual I for the (revised) version*. Baltimore, MD: Johns Hopkins School of Medicine.

Donne, J. (1986). *John Donne: The complete English poems*. London: Penguin.

Egan, G. (2002). *The skilled helper* (7th ed.). New York: Jason Aronson.

Evans, D. R., Hearn M. T., Uhleman M. R., & Ivey, A. E. (2004). *Essential interviewing* (6th ed.). Thousand Oaks, CA: Brooks/Cole.

Fall, M., & Sutton, J. M. (2004). *Clinical supervision: A handbook for practitioners*. Boston, MA: Pierson. (AU: Pearson meant?)

Frost, R. (1979). *The poetry of Robert Frost: The collected poems, complete and unabridged*. New York: Holt, Rinehart and Winston.

Gerson, B. (Ed.). (1996). Introduction. In *The therapist as a person*. p. xxi. Hillsdale, NJ: The Analytic Press.

Gladding, S. T. (2002). *Becoming a counselor: The light, bright and the serious*. Alexandria, VA: American Counseling Association.

Goleman, D. (1997). *Emotional intelligence*. New York: Bantam.

Greenson, R. R. (1967). *The technique and practice of psychoanalysis* (Vol. 1). New York: International Universities Press.

Gruba-McCallister, F. (1989). Phenomenological orientation to the interview. In *Clinical and diagnostic interviewing*, R. J. Craig (Ed.), pp. 19–31. New York: Jason Aronson.

Guthrie, R. V. (1998). *Even the rat was white* (2nd ed.). Boston: Allyn & Bacon.

Havens, L. (1989). *A safe place: Laying the groundwork of psychotherapy*. Cambridge, MA: Harvard University Press.

Heaton, J. A. (1998). *Building basic therapeutic skills: A practical guide for current mental health practice*. San Francisco, CA: Jossey-Bass.

Hill, C., & O'Brien, K. M. (1999). *Helping skills: Facilitating exploration, insight, and action*. Washington, DC: American Psychological Association.

Itzhaky, H., & Itzhaky, T. (1996) The therapy–supervision dialectic. *Clinical Social Work Journal 24*(1).

Ivey, A., D'Andrea, M. E., Ivey, M. B., & Simek-Morgan, L. (2002). *Theories of counseling and psychotherapy: A multicultural perspective* (5th ed.). New York: Allyn & Bacon.

James, R. K., and Gilliand, B. E. (2004). *Crisis intervention strategies* (4th ed.). Belmont, CA: Wadsworth.

Johnson, S. L. (1997). *The therapist's guide to clinical intervention*. San Diego, CA: Academic Press.

Kaplan, H. I., & Sadock, B. J. (2003). *Synopsis of psychiatry* (9th ed.). Philadelphia: Lippincott Williams & Wilkins.

Knight, R. (2004). Turning procrastination into productivity. Accessed November 20, 2004 at *www.atlantaparent.com*, pp. 4–11.

Kottler, J. A. (1990). *On being a therapist.* San Francisco, CA: Jossey-Bass.

Kottler, J. A. (2003). *On being a therapist* (3rd ed.). San Francisco, CA: John Wiley and Sons.

Langs, R. L. (1973). *The technique of psychoanalytic psychotherapy: The initial contact, theoretical framework, understanding the patient's communication, the therapist's interventions* (Vol. 1). New York: Jason Aronson.

Lazarus, A. (1971). *The practice of multimodal therapy.* New York: McGraw-Hill.

Lukas, S. (1993). *Where to start and what to ask.* New York: W. W. Norton & Company.

McWilliams, N. (1999). *Psychoanalytic case formulation.* New York: Guilford.

Merriam-Webster online dictionary. (2005). New York: Merriam-Webster Inc.

Miller, D. (1996). Challenging self-harm through transformation of the trauma story. *Journal of Sexual Addiction and Compulsivity, 3,* 213–227.

Miller, W. R., & Rollnick, S. (1991). *Motivational interviewing: Preparing people to change addictive behavior.* New York: Guilford.

Morrison, J. (1995). *The first interview.* New York: Guilford.

Moursund, J., & Kenny, M. (2002). *The process of counseling and therapy* (4th ed.). Englewood Cliffs, NJ: Prentice-Hall.

Murphy, B. C., & Dillon, C. (2003). *Interviewing in action* (2nd ed.). New York: Wadsworth.

Neufeldt, S. (1999). *Supervision strategies for the first practicum* (2nd ed.). Alexandria, VA: The American Counseling Association.

Nichols, M. P. (1995). *The lost art of listening.* New York: Guilford.

Othmer, E., & Othmer, S. C. (1994). *The clinical interview using DSM-IV* (Vol. 1: fundamentals). Washington DC: American Psychiatric Press.

Ottens, A. J., & Fisher-McCanne, L. (1990). Crisis intervention at the college campus counseling center. In A. R. Roberts (Ed.), *Crisis intervention handbook: Assessment treatment and research,* pp. 78–100. Belmont, CA: Wadsworth.

Patterson, L. E., and Welfel, E. R. (1994). *The counseling process* (5th ed.), pp. 169–171. Pacific Grove, CA: Brooks/Cole.

Peck, M. S. (1978). *The road less traveled.* New York: Simon and Schuster.

Resnik, H. L. P. (1980). Suicide. In R. Sommers-Flanagan & J. Sommers-Flanagan, *Clinical interviewing* (2nd ed.). New York: John Wiley and Sons.

Rich, A. (1973). *Diving into the wreck: Poems 1971–1972.* New York: W. W. Norton and Company.

Schofield, W. (1964). *Psychotherapy: The purchase of friendship.* Englewood Cliffs, NJ: Prentice-Hall.

Shea, S. C. (1998). *Psychiatric interviewing: The art of understanding* (2nd ed.). Philadelphia: W. B. Saunders.

Sommers-Flanagan, R., & Sommers-Flanagan, J. (1999). *Clinical interviewing* (2nd ed.). New York: John Wiley & Sons, Inc.

Sue, D. W., & Sue, D. (2003). *Counseling the culturally diverse: Theory and practice* (4th ed.). New York: John Wiley and Sons.

Sullivan, P. M. (2003). *Work with meaning, work with joy.* New York: Sheed & Ward.

Tolstoy, L. (1978). *Anna Karenina.* Garnett, C. (trans.), Indianapolis/New York: Bobbs-Merrill.

Travers, P. (2002). *The counselor's helpdesk.* New York: Wadsworth.

Winnicott, D. W. (1958). *Collected papers: Through pediatrics to psychoanalysis.* New York: Basic Books.

Winnicott, D. W. (1965). *The maturational processes and the facilitating environment.* New York: International Universities Press.

Wollersheim, J. P. (1974). The assessment of suicide potential via interview methods. *Psychotherapy, 11,* 222–225.

Yalom, I. D. (2002a). *The gift of therapy.* New York: HarperCollins.

Yalom, I. D. (2002b). *Existential psychotherapy.* New York: Basic Books.

Zuckerman, E. L. (2002). *The paper office: Forms, guidelines, and resources to make your practice work ethically, legally and profitably.* New York: Guilford.

Index

DATE DUE

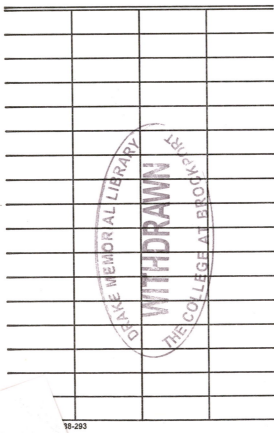